A PRACTICAL GUIDE TO CRITICAL THINKING

D1288069

A PRACTICAL GUIDE TO CRITICAL THINKING

Deciding What to Do and Believe

Second Edition

DAVID A. HUNTER
Department of Philosophy
Ryerson University
Toronto, ON, Canada

Published by John Wiley & Sons, Inc., Hoboken, New Jersey.
Published simultaneously in Canada.

For general information on our other products and services or for technical support, please contact our Customer Care Department within the United States at (800) 762-2974, outside the United States at (317) 572-3993 or fax (317) 572-4002.

Wiley also publishes its books in a variety of electronic formats. Some content that appears in print may not be available in electronic formats. For more information about Wiley products, visit our web site at www.wiley.com.

Library of Congress Cataloging-in-Publication Data:

Hunter, David A., 1965– author.
  A practical guide to critical thinking : deciding what to do and believe / David A. Hunter, Department of Philosophy, Ryerson University. – Second edition.
      pages cm
  Includes bibliographical references and index.
  ISBN 978-1-118-58308-1 (cloth)
 1. Critical thinking.   I. Title.
  BF441.H86 2014
  121–dc23

                                                                                            2014012671

Printed in the United States of America

10 9 8 7 6 5 4 3 2

For Jane,
my beloved and my friend.

CONTENTS

PREFACE

In preparing this Second Edition, I have benefited from many people's advice. First, I would like to thank all of the students at Ryerson University who have taken my critical thinking courses, and all of the graduate students who have worked for me as a TA. I have learned a lot from you all about how to organize, simplify, and present this material. I have also benefited from detailed and constructive comments on every chapter from my colleague, Klaas Kraay.

PREFACE TO FIRST EDITION

This book has been a long time in the making, and has benefited from the influence of a huge number of colleagues, friends, and family. Here is an inevitably incomplete accounting of some of these debts.

I first began to think systematically about the nature, value, and pedagogy of critical thinking as an assistant professor of philosophy at Buffalo State College and it would be difficult to overstate the influence of my colleague George Hole on my thinking. He is one of the most gifted philosophy teachers I have ever known and I learned a good deal from him on how to teach philosophy. But even more than this, I am indebted to him for the way he so easily mixes philosophy, wit, and good humor in equal parts. I learned more from him than from anyone about how to teach critical thinking, and about the central role it ought to play in education and in a full life. I also owe a great deal to Gerry Nosich, whose work on critical thinking is without equal. Gerry joined us at Buffalo State College as we were designing and implementing a required first-year critical thinking course, and his gentle and wise advice proved invaluable. While with SUNY, I worked on a statewide committee to design a rubric for the assessment of critical thinking. I learned a lot in this time about the importance of teaching critical thinking across the curriculum, and I am especially indebted to Shir Filler.

Since beginning the writing of this book, I have learned a good deal from my new colleagues at Ryerson University, where the philosophy department teaches several sections of a critical thinking course that is required by students in several programs. I owe special debts to Andrew Hunter, Klaas Kraay, David Ciavatta, Jim Dianda, and Paul Raymont.

I am indebted to Steve Quigley, my editor at Wiley, for gently persuading me to write the book; to Jackie Palmieri, an editorial assistant at Wiley, for gently persuading me to complete it on time; and to several anonymous referees who provided useful feedback on my initial proposal.

I am enormously indebted to my family. I learned as much about how to think critically from my parents as from anyone. They showed me that critical thinking begins at home, and that is a lesson that Miranda and Emily, my wonderful daughters, now champion with exhausting ingenuity.

My greatest and deepest debts, however, are to Jane, whose love and support have never been conditional on sufficient and acceptable reasons or on anything else.

NOTE TO INSTRUCTORS

Teaching students to think critically is more about imparting a set of skills and habits than about teaching bits of theory. In developing this textbook, I tried to incorporate several features that I thought would make teaching critical thinking both easier and more effective.

Most significantly, I steered clear of any formal notation aside from the very simplest. It is not that I doubt the value of learning formal logic. In fact, I think that many students thrive while studying it. But in my experience there is so much that most students need to learn before they can see the value of mastering a formal system, and so much more benefit they can derive from a non-formal approach to critical thinking. Instead, I tried to think of this text as like an introduction to practical or applied epistemology: offering systematic advice, and lots of practice, on the best way to go about deciding what to believe and what to do.

It is worth noting here that I treat what is sometimes called enumerative induction as a form of reasoning by analogy. It seems to me that using samples to draw a conclusion about an entire group or population just is reasoning by analogy, and that it can be usefully taught as such. I also say, and this perhaps is more controversial, that reasoning by analogy can be valid. Of course, I do not mean that it is formally valid in the way that modus ponens is formally valid. Reasoning is valid when it is not possible for the premises to be true and the conclusion to be false. The fact that some reasoning can be known to be valid just from its form alone is, of course, important, and I discuss some of these forms in chapters 5 and 6. But it is important to keep in mind that not all valid arguments are formally valid, (e.g., The table is blue, therefore it is colored), and not all arguments that are formally invalid are really invalid (e.g., If Jones is a male, then he is a bachelor; Jones is a bachelor; so, Jones is a male.) Judgment is always needed, it seems to me, in assessing the strength of a piece of reasoning, and this judgment is better taught by focusing on the idea of validity itself. I also think that what I say in Chapter 6 makes a reasonable and pedagogically responsible case for my view that reasoning by analogy can be valid.

I had originally planned to dedicate a chapter to thinking critically about what to do. But I worried that much of it would simply repeat points that had been made earlier and, in so doing, would make deciding what to do seem like a lesser cousin to deciding what to believe. As I worked (and then re-worked) the first 6 chapters, it seemed to me that I could elegantly discuss deciding what to do as we went along, when the topic at hand seemed relevant. I have thus included several "boxes" discussing various aspects of deciding what to do.

The book includes several other kinds of boxes as well. Some identify important mistakes that a good critical thinker ought to avoid. Some provide summaries of the discussion in the body of the text. Some offer examples of critical thinking across the curriculum. Some offer practical tips and rules of thumb. All are intended to make the text more readable and the concepts and skills more accessible.

I also decided that rather than dedicate a chapter to informal fallacies, I would discuss them in what struck me as their proper context. It seems to me that there is no easy way to organize the different kinds of mistakes into a small number of categories without distorting their differences or exaggerating their similarities. Some of the mistakes have to do with clarifying meaning; others with ascribing views to others; some with assessing evidence; others with assessing validity. Several mistakes can occur at several otherwise quite distinct stages in deciding what to do or to believe. Rather than try to force the various mistakes into artificial categories, it seemed to me better to discuss them as we went along. For easy reference, though, I have collected them all in an appendix at the end of the book.

Careful training and repeated practice are crucial to learning any skill, and critical thinking is no exception. I have tried to include a large and varied collection of exercises. But I strongly encourage you to bring your own exercises to class and to encourage your students to seek out arguments and reasoning to share during the class time. In my experience, students learn far more when they are required during class time to participate in the construction, analysis, and assessment of examples of reasoning about what to do or believe. I have included, at the end of most of the chapters, exercises that are specially designed to help students transfer the concepts and skills they are learning to other corners of their lives. My thought is simply that there is little point in teaching someone to think critically if they see no place for it at home, in their own discipline, or at work. Over the years I have experimented with all of these exercises, making adjustments as I went along. The exercises are in a form that I find to be both effective and not overly intrusive. But I encourage you to adjust, alter, add, subtract, and modify as you see fit. The important thing is to find ways to help students see that they are learning skills and concepts that have application and value after the final exam.

1

THE NATURE AND VALUE
OF CRITICAL THINKING

This book is a practical guide to critical thinking. It might seem unnecessary to be reading a guide to something you do all the time and are probably already pretty good at. When I tell people that I am writing a book on critical thinking they sometimes tell me that they consider themselves to be very good critical thinkers. At the very least, they say that they consider critical thinking to be very important. I am sure that they are right on both counts. We think critically a good bit of the time, and on the whole we do it pretty well. Still, I think there is always something to learn from thinking hard about what one is already good at.

In this chapter, we will explore the nature and value of critical thinking. We will ask what critical thinking is and how it differs from other kinds of thinking. We will explore what it *means* to think critically; what makes that kind of thinking *critical*. As part of this, we will consider whether critical thinking varies from one discipline to the next. Is critical thinking in geology different from critical thinking in design or in humanities? We will see that while the concepts, methods, and standards may differ from one discipline to the next, there is a basic essence or core of critical thinking that remains the same across all disciplines. Whether one is doing chemistry, design, astrology, or philosophy, there are common standards that you should strive to maintain, and practical strategies to help you make sure that you do. This book is designed to introduce you to this essential core of critical thinking while at the same time providing you with the tools you need to identify the concepts, methods, and standards distinctive of different disciplines.

A Practical Guide to Critical Thinking: Deciding What to Do and Believe, Second Edition. David A. Hunter.
© 2014 John Wiley & Sons, Inc. Published 2014 by John Wiley & Sons, Inc.

Once we have said what we mean by critical thinking, we can then ask what place this kind of thinking does or should occupy in our daily lives, both in and out of the classroom. When is it appropriate to think critically, and are there some parts of our lives where critical thinking tends to dominate or where it tends to be ignored? We will see that critical thinking is appropriate whenever we are trying to decide what we ought to believe about some matter of fact or whenever we are trying to decide what to do or what course of action to adopt. In short, critical thinking is needed whenever we reason about what to believe or what to do.

Finally, and perhaps most importantly, we will ask why being a critical thinker **matters**. What makes critical thinking valuable? Why should we engage in it? We will see that being a critical thinker is valuable for several reasons. Perhaps most obviously, thinking critically about a question or problem can help one get the right answer or solution. By thinking critically about what to believe or what to do, we increase our chances that our beliefs will be true and our actions effective. Thinking critically may not guarantee that you get the right answer; but a good case can be made that unless you think critically you will get the right answer only by luck, and relying on luck is not a wise policy. But critical thinking has a deeper value than just its ties to truth. Critical thinking is also closely tied to one variety of freedom. By thinking critically, one can make up one's own mind and making up one's own mind is essential if we are to be the master of our own lives. Critical thinking, we will see, is essential to personal autonomy.

1.1   THE NATURE OF CRITICAL THINKING

There are many definitions for critical thinking, but Robert Ennis, one of the leading researchers on critical thinking, offered the following definition many years ago and it remains, to my mind, the best of the bunch.

> Critical thinking is reasonable, reflective thinking that is aimed at deciding what to believe or what to do.

We can see that there are several elements to this definition, so let us look at them one at a time, starting with the last one.

Critical thinking is the thinking that is *aimed at deciding what to believe or what to do*. Deciding *what to believe* is a matter of deciding what the facts are, figuring out what the world is like, or at least what some little corner of it is like. We make these kinds of decisions when we decide whether it is raining out or sunny, whether the Blue Jays stand a chance this year, whether the kids will put up with another meal of macaroni and cheese, whether the movie was as good as its billing, whether the restaurant has gotten better over the years, or whether we should trust what our teachers tell us. In deciding what to believe on some matter we take a stand on it. If it is a decision on a factual matter, like the decision about the weather or about the Blue jays, then we take a stand on what the facts are. If it is a decision on an evaluative matter, like the one about the movie or the restaurant, then in deciding what to believe we are taking a stand on what is good or better. In either kind of case, critical thinking is aimed at helping us to make those kinds of decisions about what to believe.

> Critical thinking is reasonable, reflective thinking that is aimed at deciding what to believe or what to do.

> Deciding **what to believe** involves reasoning about what the facts are. This is *theoretical reasoning*.

Critical thinking is also **aimed at decisions about what to do**. Deciding what to do really has two parts. First, one has to decide what to value or to strive for. This is a matter of deciding on one's goal or end. Then, one has to decide how best to achieve that end. This is a matter of deciding on the best **means** to that end. Should I go for a run now or keep working on my book? Should I spend my savings on a new car or continue using my beat up one? Should the city spend its limited resources on building a new bridge? Should the country move toward a universal health care plan? Should I tell the truth when my friend asks me about her boyfriend? Should I give to charities? Usually we decide what to do on the basis of what we already value or on what we already think makes for a good life. I decide to go for a run instead of continuing to work on this book because I feel that running and staying in shape is an important part of my life. I decide to tell the truth to my friend about her new car because I value honesty in my friends and want them to consider me trustworthy. But sometimes, deciding what to strive for or what goals to pursue requires first deciding what one will value, what kind of person one wants to be, and what kind of life one wants to lead. In deciding whether to pursue graduate school in philosophy, I had to make a decision about to value, about what kind of shape I wanted my life to take. Decisions about what to value are among the most difficult and profound decisions we can make. Critical thinking can help us to make these kinds of decisions. But once we make them, once we decide what we want out life to be like, we still need to decide what the best way is to make our life that way. Once we choose the ends, we still need to decide on the means. Here too, critical thinking can help.

> Deciding **what to do** involves reasoning about what to do and how to do it. This is *practical reasoning*.

According to Robert Ennis' definition, critical thinking is **reasonable** thinking. This is so in several respects. First, critical thinking is reasonable thinking because it is sensitive to methods and standards. If we are trying to decide what to make for dinner or whether the Blue Jays stand a chance this year, there are various methods we should use and standards we should keep in mind. If we try to make up our minds on these topics without relying on those methods or respecting these standards, then we will fail to be thinking critically about the topic. Part of what makes critical thinking *critical* is that it is governed by rules and methods. This does not mean that there is no room in critical thinking for reasonable judgment and flexibility. In fact, as we will see in a moment, part of what makes critical thinking different from other kinds of thinking, such as arithmetical calculation, is that there is usually plenty of room for judgment and a case-by-case flexibility. Still, it is essential to critical thinking that in thinking critically about what to believe or do we rely on methods and are subject to standards. We will spend lots of time in the following chapters learning what these methods and standards are.

> Critical thinking is reasonable thinking because it is governed by general methods and standards and because it demands that we have good reasons for our decisions.

Critical thinking is **reasonable** in another and deeper sense. Critical thinking about what to believe or what to do is reasonable, in that it demands that we have reasons, and good ones, for the decisions we make. The aim of critical thinking is not simply to make a decision on what the facts are or what to strive for. In a way, it is easy to make such decisions. What is hard is having **good** reasons for the decisions we make. It is not enough to decide to believe that it is sunny out; one has to have a good reason to decide this. Likewise, it is not enough just to decide to value honesty or justice; one has to have good reason for this decision. So critical thinking is reasonable in that it demands that we have reasons, and good ones, for making the decisions we do. We will be spending a lot of time in what follows exploring what makes something a *good reason* to believe or to do something.

> Critical thinking is **reflective** because it involves thinking about a problem at several different levels or from several different angles all at once, and because it sometimes requires thinking about what the right method is to answer or solve some problem.

Finally, Ennis says that critical thinking is **reflective**. We can see what he has in mind if we contrast critical thinking with arithmetical calculation. There is no doubt that calculating the square root of a large number is a kind of thinking and no doubt that it is a thinking that is sensitive to methods and standards. In this respect, arithmetical calculation is like critical thinking. But when one calculates a number's square root, one does not need to think about the methods one is using. One simply uses the formula to get the right answer. In this kind of case, the problem at hand (finding the number's square root) is pretty straightforward: it is perfectly clear from the beginning what is to count as the right answer and what the best means is of finding it. The same is true for many kinds of decisions we make in our daily lives. But some problems are **open-ended**. A problem is open-ended when it is not clear from the outset what would count as a solution to it. In such cases, progress may require thinking hard about the problem itself, and not just calculating an answer to it.

To solve it, we may need to analyze the problem into parts, and we may need to think about the best method to use to find a solution, and while we employ that method we may need to be thinking about whether we are employing it correctly. We may even need to adjust the method or even develop one from scratch. I will have more to say later about open-ended problems and no doubt the line between straightforward ones and open-ended ones is not hard and sharp. Calculating a square root the first few times requires a good deal of reflection even when one does have the formula; and deciding whether it is raining or sunny is usually as straightforward as looking out the window. Still, the contrast should be clear. Critical thinking is **reflective** in the sense that it involves thinking about a problem at several different levels or from several different angles all at once, including thinking about what the right method is for answering or solving the problem.

One of the chief virtues of this definition is that it does not restrict critical thinking to the study of **arguments**. An argument is a series of statements, some of which (the premises) are meant to provide logical support for another (the conclusion). Because we can and often do formulate our reasons for believing or doing something in the form of an argument, critical thinking is surely concerned with arguments. In later chapters we will discuss some strategies and standards for analyzing and evaluating arguments. But the notion of an argument does not always fit naturally across the curriculum. It is hard to see how reasoning about experimental design or about statistical sampling fits the paradigm of an argument. What is more, evaluating reasons for believing something involves assessing their acceptability and their meaning, and neither of these tasks is ordinarily considered argumentation. It is, of course, possible, to stretch the ordinary concept of an argument or of argument analysis to include all these different aspects of critical thinking. But this definition captures them all without artificially extending our ordinary words.

EXERCISE 1

A. Comprehension questions. (When you answer these questions, pretend that you are explaining or teaching the answer to a friend who is not in the class. Doing that will force you to put in LOTS more background information that you would if you were trying to explain the material to your teacher.)

   a. In what sense is critical thinking reflective?

   b. What makes critical thinking a reasonable thinking?

   c. Why is simple arithmetical calculation not a kind of critical thinking?

   d. Does critical thinking have to be "critical" in the sense of being negative or skeptical? Explain, using an example.

B. Which of the following activities involves critical thinking? If an activity does not involve critical thinking, identify which element in critical thinking is missing.

   a. Riding a bike

   b. Watching the news on TV

   c. Doing laundry

   d. Ordering coffee at a local coffee shop

   e. Planning a vacation

C. Identify five activities you do on a daily basis that do not involve critical thinking. Identify two or three activities that you do on a daily basis that would be improved by thinking critically about them, and explain how thinking critically would improve it.

D. Now that you know what critical thinking is, list five reasons why it is good to think critically.

E. List five possible obstacles to thinking critically. Describe one strategy for overcoming each obstacle.

1.2 CRITICAL THINKING AND KNOWLEDGE

We have been discussing what critical thinking is. But why is it important? Why does it matter whether or not we think critically when we decide what to believe or what to do? The answer is that critical thinking is valuable for two main reasons. First, thinking critically increases our chances of gaining **knowledge**, and knowledge is valuable. Second, thinking critically is essential to making up one's own mind about what to believe or what to do, which is essential to being **autonomous**, and being autonomous is valuable. We will start by discussing knowledge and then turn to autonomy.

> Critical thinking aims at knowledge. We don't just want to have opinions about what is true or about what to do. We want to **know** what's true and what to do.

We have seen that critical thinking is thinking that is aimed at deciding what to believe or to do. But ideally we want more than just to have an opinion about the facts; we want to **know** what they are. When we check the weather, our goal is not just to reach a decision about whether it is sunny or not; we want to come to **know** whether it is sunny or not. We want to *know* whether the city ought to spend its scarce resources on building a new bridge. We want to *know* whether HIV causes AIDS all by itself or only in conjunction with other factors. So critical thinking is really aimed at knowledge. But what is knowledge? What is it to know something? By answering these questions we can get quite a bit clearer on what critical thinking is and why it is valuable.

EXERCISE 2

We can start with an exercise. Make a chart with three columns, as follows:

- In the first column, list things that we, either individually or as humans in general, know for a fact. These can be particular facts or kinds of things.

- In the second column, list things that we can know, but currently do not know.
- In the third column, list things that we do not and probably cannot ever know about.

The more variety you can provide in each list the better. (Include something in one of the columns only if you are fairly sure that everyone else in your class would also include in that column. This will avoid controversy from the start.) When you have the Knowledge Chart completed, compare the items in the first and second column and try to identify the relevant differences? What is lacking in the items in the second column that prevents their being in the first column?

The traditional definition of knowledge developed by philosophers says that knowledge is justified, true belief. According to this definition there are three elements to knowledge. We can look at each in turn. Then we will ask how the three elements are related to one another. Let us start with truth.

Knowledge is justified, true belief.

1.3 KNOWLEDGE AND TRUTH

It would be ideal at this point in our discussion to provide a clear and precise definition of truth. I do not mean just a listing of all the truths that there are, though such a list would be valuable. We already know some of what such a list would include. It would have to include the truths that George Bush was the 42nd President of the United States, that a virus causes the flu, and that the Earth orbits the Sun. And we know what things we should leave off that list: that fish are birds, that $2 + 2 = 27$, and that George Washington was the President of France. It would probably be impossible, or at least really hard, to make a complete list of all the truths.

But even if we could, making such a list would not be the same as giving a definition of truth. Think of an analogy. Suppose we made a list of all the people there are, or even of all of the humans that have ever existed. That list would not be a **definition** of human nature. It would not tell us anything about what it is to be a human. To know what it is to be human, we would have to say what all humans have in common and what makes humans different from every other species. Likewise, a list of all the truths would not tell us what it **is** for something to be true. It would not reveal the **nature** of truth. To give a definition of truth we would have to say what it is for something to be true. We would need to say, in a general sort of way that would apply to every case, what *makes* something true.

I do not have any idea how to do this. Nor, I think, does anyone else. Or rather, the only plausible definition that I know of is not very helpful: a statement is true just in case it corresponds with the facts. This is not that helpful because the notion of **corresponding with the facts** is not much clearer than the notion of truth itself. Thankfully, though, we do not really need a definition of truth. For our purposes it will be enough to contrast three attitudes we might take to some subject matter: **Realism, Relativism, and Nihilism.**

1.3.1 Realism, Relativism, and Nihilism

Imagine that there is a large jar of jelly beans on a table in front of you and that you and your friends have to guess the number of jelly beans it contains. Suppose that Ezra guesses that there are 13,451 beans in the jar, and that Ahmed guesses that there are 11,587 beans in it. Neither one really knows for sure how many beans are in the jar. They are just guessing. But now here is a philosophical question: is there a **fact** about the number of beans in the jar? We know that Ezra and Ahmed have different opinions about the number of beans in the jar. But is there a right answer? Is there a fact of the matter? We can ask this same question for any subject matter, not just the number of jelly beans in a jar. In this section we will consider three answers one might give to it.

Suppose that Rachel looks at the jar of beans and says this: "Well, I am not sure how many beans there are in that jar, but I know that there is a right answer. Maybe Ezra is right, maybe Ahmed is right. Maybe neither one is right. But there is a single right answer." If Rachel really believes this, then she is a realist about the number of beans in the jar. A **realist** about a certain subject matter thinks (i) that there are truths about that subject matter and (ii) that what those truths are is independent of what anybody thinks they are. For the realist, truth is simply "out there."

> A realist about a subject matter thinks that (i) there are **truths** about that subject matter and (ii) that what those truths are is **independent** of what anybody thinks they are.

Because a realist thinks that truth is independent of our beliefs, she also thinks that it is possible (even if it is highly unlikely) that we could all be totally mistaken about or ignorant of the facts in that subject area. She might even think that some facts are just beyond our understanding, that no matter how hard we tried or for how long, we simply could not come to know them. Of course, being a realist does not mean that we have to be skeptical or doubtful about whether we do know anything about that subject matter. One can be a realist about a subject matter and still be quite confident that we know a lot about it. Being a realist simply requires thinking that the facts in that subject area are not determined by or dependent on our beliefs about them. They are what they are, regardless of what we might think that they are.

Suppose, now, that Rebecca looks at the jar of jellybeans and says this: "There is no **single** right answer about how many beans there are in that jar. It all depends. It is true for Ezra that there are 13,451 beans in the jar, and it is true for Ahmed that there are 11,587 beans in it. But there is no such thing as the single, unique truth." If Rebecca really believed this, then she would be a relativist about the number of beans in the jar. A **relativist** about some subject matter holds that (i) there are truths about that area but (ii) that what they are depends (in some way or other) on what we (or someone) take those truths to be. The relativist and the realist agree that there are truths or facts of the matter in that area, but they differ over how those truths or facts are related to our beliefs about them. The relativist insists that those facts are what they are because of our beliefs about them, whereas the realist insists that our beliefs have no bearing at all on the facts themselves. The relativist maintains that had our beliefs or our natures been different, then the facts might have been different too. The facts somehow depend on us. This means that on a relativist's view of some subject matter, it is in a certain way impossible for us to be wrong or ignorant of the facts in that area, since our beliefs about what the facts are is at least part of what makes them the facts. We cannot go too far wrong in trying to know that subject matter because we play an essential role in making the subject what it is.

> A **relativist** about a subject matter thinks that (i) there are truths about that subject but (ii) that what they are depends on what we (or someone) believe that they are.

There are different versions of Relativism, differing in terms of whose beliefs play the role of determining what the facts are. A **subjective relativist** about some topic thinks that the truth in that subject matter is whatever any one individual takes it to be. She might express this idea by saying things like: "Well, that might be true for you, but it is not true for me." A **social relativist**, by contrast, holds that the truth in that subject matter is whatever the majority of the society or culture takes it to be. "It is true for us, even if it is not true for you or for them." What is common to all versions of Relativism is the idea that the facts are in some way dependent on our beliefs about them; that, in one way or another, the facts are what they are because we are the way we are.

We need to be a little careful about what the realist and the relativist disagree about. We all know that there are lots of different ways to say how many beans the jar contains. Suppose that the jar contains 13,879 beans. There are lots of different ways to state this. Instead of using Arabic numerals, we could use Roman numerals, and say that there are XIIIDCCCLXXIX beans in the jar. Or instead of using numerals, we can say that there are thirteen thousand, eight hundred and seventy nine beans in it. Or we can say the number of beans is the square root of 192626641. These are just different ways of saying the same thing, different ways of putting that single truth into words. A realist can agree on this. She can agree that there are many different ways to say what the truth is about the number of beans in the jar. So, when the realist says that there is just one truth about the number of beans in the jar, she does not mean that there is only one way to say what that truth is. And when the relativist says that there are many truths, she does not just mean that there are many ways to say how many beans there are in the jar. She means something more radical: she means that how many beans there are in the jar depends on us in such a way that the number there are for you might be different than the number there are for me. It is not just that there are different ways to state the truth—there are different truths!

Suppose, now, that Nigel looks at the jar of beans and says this: "There is no single, right answer to the question how many beans it contains. Every opinion is just as good as any other opinion. There is no right answer!" If Nigel really believes this, then he is a **nihilist** about the number of jellybeans in the jar. A **nihilist** about some subject matter holds that there are no truths at all about that subject matter. There are, on the nihilist's view, no facts to be right or wrong about. It is not that the facts depend on us in some way; there are no facts at all (aside from the fact that there are no facts). There is no such thing as truth, according to Nigel, about how many beans are in the jar. Since there is no such thing as truth in that area, there is also no such thing as knowing the truth, and not because we are incapable of coming to know it, but because there is nothing there to be known at all. The nihilist thus disagrees with both the realist and the relativist, though as we just saw, the realist and the relativist also disagree with each other.

> A **nihilist** about some subject matter thinks that there are no truths at all about that subject matter.

I have been illustrating the differences between Realism, Relativism, and Nihilism using the story of the jellybean jar. Now maybe this was not really fair. Maybe everyone already thinks that Realism is the right attitude to take to the matter of how many beans there are in the jar. It would, after all, be pretty odd if Rebecca really did believe that the number of beans might be different for Ezra than for Ahmed. And it would be really odd if Nigel really did believe that there is no right answer! So maybe it is most reasonable to be a realist about the number of beans in the jar. Still, there may be other subject matters where Relativism makes most sense, or where Nihilism makes most sense.

One final point. One could be a realist about one subject matter and a relativist about another and a nihilist about a third. One might think, for instance, that Realism is the proper attitude to take to particle physics or to human history, but think that Nihilism is the right attitude to take toward the nature of Santa Claus. Or one might be a realist about human biology but a relativist about humor, thinking that while the facts about our biological natures are independent of our beliefs about them, whether something is funny or humorous does depend on whether we find it or believe it to be funny. Indeed, it is hard to see how we could possibly all be wrong about whether some joke is amusing. Maybe what makes something funny is simply that we all (in normal conditions) believe it to be funny. If so, then perhaps Relativism is right about humor.

But one cannot take two or all three of those attitudes to one and the same subject. One could not be both a realist and a nihilist about, say, particle physics. For this would mean holding (as a realist) that there are facts about particle physics while also (as a nihilist) denying that there are facts about particle physics. But this is incoherent. Realism and Nihilism about some subject matter are contraries of one another: they both cannot be true, though they could both be false. Likewise, one could not be a relativist and a realist, or a relativist and a nihilist about one and the same subject matter. But in principle one could, and I think we in fact sometimes do, take different attitudes to different subject matters or topics.

One has to have good reasons for being a realist, relativist, or nihilist about some subject matter. It is not enough simply to decide or declare that one will be a relativist about, say, particle physics or geometry, or a nihilist about morality and geography, or a realist about humor and beauty. One has to be able to provide good reasons for thinking that one is taking the appropriate attitude to that subject. If one is a realist about particle physics but a relativist about humor, then one has to be able to explain what the difference is between those subject matters or about our relations to them that warrants taking those different attitudes to them. The explanation cannot simply be that the facts about particle physics are independent of us whereas those about humor are not. To say this is simply to express your attitudes, not to justify or explain them.

1.3.2   Relativism and the Argument from Disagreement

Relativists about a subject matter sometimes try to justify their attitude by pointing to the fact that there is little or no agreement among otherwise well-intentioned and sincere people about what the facts are in that subject matter. Relativists about morality, for instance, point out that there is considerable disagreement among sincere people about just what our moral duties are, or about how to balance competing moral demands. Different people who are sincere and well-meaning disagree about the moral evaluation of such things as abortion, euthanasia, the recreational use of drugs, capital punishment, etc. The list could go on a long time. Relativists about morality suggest that the existence of this kind of disagreement lends support to their Relativism. We can formulate this reasoning for Relativism about morality as an argument.

(i) There is considerable sincere disagreement over morality.
(ii) If there is considerable sincere disagreement over the facts in some area, then Relativism is true of that subject area.
(iii) So, Relativism is true of morality.

Let us call this argument for Moral Relativism, the **Argument from Disagreement**. It would be easy to transform it into an argument for any kind of Relativism. We could get an argument for Relativism about humor by replacing the words "moral" with the word "humor." But let us focus on this argument, since the main lessons will apply across the board.

The Argument from Disagreement for Moral Relativism

(i) There is considerable sincere disagreement about morality.
(ii) If there is considerable sincere disagreement over the facts in some area, then Relativism is true of that subject area.
(iii) So, Relativism is true of morality.

VALIDITY

An argument is valid when it is not possible for its premises to be true and its conclusion to be false. If its premises were true, then its conclusion would have to be true too.

This is the most important logical virtue in an argument, and of central importance to critical thinking. We will discuss it more in Chapter 3.

The *Argument from Disagreement* has an important logical property. It is **valid**. This means that if the premises (i.e., claims (i) and (ii)) are true, then the conclusion (i.e., claim (iii)) would have to be true too. In other words, it is not possible for those premises to be true and yet for the conclusion to be false. If the premises are true, then they constitute a *conclusive proof* that Moral Relativism is true. We will have much more to say about validity in Chapter 3. But for now, it is enough to note that when an argument is valid, the only question that needs to be considered in evaluating it is whether the premises are true. So let us consider each premise.

The first step in deciding whether a premise is true is to make sure that we know exactly what it means. This is a bit difficult in the case of **The Argument from Disagreement's** premise (i) because it is not very clear what "considerable" means. How much disagreement counts as "considerable?" Does everyone's opinion count equally in deciding when moral disagreement is considerable, or are there moral experts whose opinions matter more? We know that philosophy departments usually have several professors who specialize in moral theory. Are they experts? What would it take to be an expert at moral theory? But suppose they were the experts, and suppose that the moral theorists all agreed on the moral evaluation of some practice (say, euthanasia) but that most everyone else held different opinions? Would premise (i) be true in that case? These are difficult questions about just what claim premise (i) is making, and it is not clear how best to answer them.

Let us set aside the question of what exactly the premise (i) means. Let us ask whether we have good reason to accept it. Is it **true** that there is considerable sincere disagreement over moral facts? It is certainly true that there is disagreement over moral facts. Different societies have held different views about what morality requires or permits. There are sometimes disagreements among people in our own country or even within our own family about morality. People who are sincere and well-meaning can disagree about the moral evaluation of such things as abortion, euthanasia, capital punishment, the recreational use of alcohol and drugs, and the list can go on. So it is hard to deny that there is disagreement over morality.

But even though different societies disagree about some moral claims, there is also often quite broad and deep agreement about others. For instance, even though different societies have different views about which marital and sexual practices are morally acceptable, every society thinks that sexually assaulting one's own children for pleasure is morally wrong. And even though we might disagree with our friends over whether it is morally wrong to be drunk, we probably all agree that it is morally wrong to drive drunk. So, even if it is obvious that there is some sincere moral disagreement, it may not be so obvious that there is **more** disagreement than there is agreement. Indeed, it might even be that while there is a lot of disagreement about just what it is that morality requires, there is at the same time just as much or even more agreement about what morality requires. This suggests that it is not so clear that the premise (i) in the Argument from Disagreement really is true.

What about the premise (ii) in the Argument from Disagreement? It says that if there is considerable sincere disagreement over the facts in some area, then Relativism is true of that area. Is this true? We can begin by noting that the mere existence of **some** disagreement would not all by itself show that Relativism is true of an area. There is, after all, disagreement about whether Barack Obama was born in the United States, but surely Realism is the right attitude to take to that question. Either he was born in the United States or he was not, and whether he was has nothing to do to anyone's beliefs about it. So mere disagreement cannot, all by itself, show that Relativism is the right attitude to take to a subject matter.

But what if there is **considerable** disagreement? Here too, it is hard to see why that should be a reason to think that Relativism is the right attitude to take to a subject matter. There is, after all, lots of disagreement among physicists over the fundamental features of our Universe. There are still deep disagreements about quantum mechanics, and about the natures of space and time. It seems unlikely that this disagreement will go away anytime soon. But none of this inclines us to be relativists about physics. Indeed, this amount of disagreement is exactly what we expect from a subject as complex and difficult to understand as physics. One reason we continue to be realists about physics is that there is also considerable agreement (at least among experts) about the physical facts, in fact there is far more agreement than there is disagreement. Moreover, as hard and complex as physics is, it still seems that we are making progress. So the mere existence of considerable disagreement does not obviously show that Relativism is the right attitude to take. So we have some reason anyway to doubt whether premise (ii) in the Argument from Disagreement is true.

But what if after a long and exhaustive attempt to reach agreement in some field, we found only widespread and sincere disagreement with little or no agreement at all and no sense that progress was being made? (Just to be clear: this is not, as we have seen, the situation with respect to morality, since there is considerable agreement about moral facts, even though there is also considerable disagreement. Question: Is there also reason to think we are making progress in morality?) Would this justify being a relativist about that subject matter? Or would it instead justify being a nihilist about that subject matter? If we could never reach any substantial level of agreement, should we say that the facts depend on us, or should we say that there are no facts? Under what conditions would it be right to conclude, with the nihilist, that there are no facts at all, that we have been misled somehow into thinking there are facts when there really are not? I am not sure how to decide this question. I find it hard to know when to be a relativist instead of a nihilist. In any event, it seems clear that the existence of considerable sincere disagreement in some subject matter would not necessarily show that Relativism is true of that area. So it is not obvious that premise (ii) in the Argument from Disagreement is true.

We have seen that there is good reason to doubt the truth of both premises in the Argument from Disagreement. It is not obviously true that there is more disagreement about moral facts than there is agreement. And even if there were, it is not clear that this would show that Relativism is true of morality. So the Argument from Disagreement does not show that Moral Relativism is true; the argument is not successful. But the fact that the argument is not successful does not show that Moral Relativism is false. The conclusion of a bad argument might still be true. All we have shown is that one set of reasons for believing in Moral Relativism are not good ones. It might be that there are other, much better reasons for thinking that Moral Relativism is true. And of course it might be true even if we cannot find any reasons to believe that it is true. Still, as a good critical thinker we ought not to believe that Moral Relativism is true unless we have good reasons to believe that it is true. The same is true, of course, for the realist or the nihilist; we all need to have good reasons for our beliefs.

EVALUATING AN ARGUMENT

When evaluating an argument there are only two sorts of questions to ask:

1. Is the argument valid?
2. Are its premises true?

The Argument of Disagreement is valid, but its premises are not true. So it is not a good argument.

Critical thinking assumes that truth is independent of our beliefs.

Nonetheless, the realist might have a slight **methodological** advantage over both Relativism and Nihilism. It is sometimes suggested that Relativism and Nihilism are obstacles or impediments to critical thinking. I do not think this is true. What is true is that **unjustified** Relativism and **unjustified** Nihilism are impediments to critical thinking. One should not be a relativist or a nihilist without good reasons. But perhaps in the absence of convincing reasons to be a relativist or a nihilist, we ought to work under the assumption that Realism is the proper attitude to take. Maybe Realism is the proper **default** view to take, so long as we take it with an open mind, until we are shown that it is wrong. Perhaps it is better to err on the side of Realism than to err on the side of Nihilism or Relativism. In any event, the critical-thinking strategies and standards we will be discussing in the following chapters will assume that Realism is the appropriate attitude to take. We will assume that truth is independent of our beliefs.

1.4   KNOWLEDGE AND BELIEF

The traditional philosophical analysis of knowledge says that knowledge is justified true belief. This means that to know something you also have to believe it. But what do we mean by belief?

Sometimes we contrast what we know with what we merely believe, and sometimes when we talk about our beliefs we have in mind our opinions on moral or religious topics, where it is hard to find general agreement. If you were asked to list your beliefs, you might describe your views on God, happiness, and justice, but not include your views on the day's weather, on your favorite sporting team's recent performance, or on arithmetic. It even sounds a bit odd to say that I believe that $2 + 2 = 4$. It is tempting to say, "I don't believe it; I know it." But one reason that we find this odd to say is that it leaves the mistaken impression that we do not also feel quite confident that we know it. To say that I *believe* that $2 + 2 = 4$ would be to say something weaker than what I could say, and that is what makes it a misleading way to put it. But it might be true that I believe it, even if it would be misleading to say it. In any event, in this book we will follow the philosophical tradition and assume that to know something you must also believe it. Our real concern is with justification anyway and not with belief. Critical thinking is concerned with the **kind of reasons** that a true belief must be based on in order to count as knowledge.

> Freedom of belief does not mean that it is reasonable to believe without good reasons.

Believing something to be true is taking a certain attitude toward it. It is an attitude of acceptance: when we believe that there is milk in the refrigerator, then we accept that there is. But belief is not the only form of acceptance. Instead of believing that there is milk in the refrigerator, we can suppose that there is, or assume that there is, or presuppose that there is. These too are ways to accept that there is milk in the refrigerator, but they do not require the same sort of evidence as belief does. Belief is special in that it requires reasons of a special kind. I do not need any evidence or reasons to suppose that there is milk in the fridge. I can simply suppose it for the sake of an argument, or for fun! But to be rational, belief requires good reasons.

FREEDOM AND RESPONSIBILITY

We have and value freedom of action, as well as freedom of belief. It is important that it be, in some sense, up to us what we do and where we go. But this freedom is **limited**: no matter how much I might want to or how hard I try, I am not free to jump to the moon or grow 10 inches in a day. And freedom of action brings great **responsibility** too: I am not free to torture or hurt people for the fun of it.

Are there also limits to what you can believe? Could you now, at this very instant, voluntarily **make** yourself believe that $2 + 2 = 27$, or that the Earth really is at the center of the Solar system? Or are your beliefs not under your immediate voluntary control? Would you like them to be?

Are there also **responsibilities** that come along with having beliefs? Would it be irresponsible for you to believe that the Earth is at the center of the solar system? Why or why not? What would make it irresponsible?

We often speak of **freedom of belief**. Being able to form our beliefs free from outside interference and coercion is often held to be fundamental to human fulfillment. The idea is that we should be permitted to make up our own minds on religious and moral topics. This means that there are limits to the kinds of criticism that can be directed at our beliefs on such topics. But, and this is the crucial point, it does not necessarily mean that there are no epistemic standards against which our beliefs on these topics can be assessed. After all, freedom of belief is not restricted to moral and religious topics. We should also be free to make up our own minds about the weather, arithmetic, human evolution, and the best use of scarce public resources. Our beliefs about the weather and about human evolution still need to be based on good reasons, even if we ought to be allowed to make up our own mind on those topics. So freedom of belief does not mean that we do not need to have good reasons for our beliefs. In fact, as we will see in the next section, having good reasons for our beliefs is essential to genuinely making up our own minds. Critical thinking is appropriate not just when we think about the weather or about public policy. The standards and methods that are central to critical thinking are also appropriate when we decide what to believe about God, justice, or morality.

A good critical thinker withholds belief until enough evidence has been collected.

When we do not have enough evidence, the reasonable thing to do is to withhold belief, to be agnostic. We do not always have to have an opinion on every matter, and often it is better for us to keep an open mind. Keeping an open mind will make it easier for us to look for and appreciate new evidence. And it will make it easier for us to take seriously the opinions of other people. Of course, it is not always easy to stay open-minded, and we do not ordinarily have voluntary control over what we believe or do not believe. But a good critical thinker tries hard to remain agnostic until enough evidence has been collected to justify a belief.

1.5   KNOWLEDGE AND JUSTIFICATION

We have seen that knowledge is justified, true belief. To say that a belief is justified is to say that it is based or grounded on good reasons, that the believer has adequate or satisfactory reason to have that belief. But there are lots of different kinds of reasons to believe something, and it is worth distinguishing some of them so that we can focus on the kinds of reasons that critical thinking is concerned with.

It will help to have an example, so let us suppose that Jones believes that humans evolved from other living species, in something like the way current theories of evolution describe. We can ask three questions. (i) What kinds of reasons does Jones have for believing this? (ii) What kind of reasons is critical thinking concerned with? (iii) What is it for reasons of that kind to count as **good** reasons?

We should start by noticing a distinction between **producing** reasons and **sustaining** reasons. The producing reasons are the ones that made Jones believe it in the first place, whereas the sustaining reasons are the ones that his belief is now based on. The producing reasons need not be the same as the sustaining reasons. Perhaps Jones first came to believe that humans evolved from other species because he heard it on a TV show that he has now long forgotten about, but continues to believe it because of the evidence he has since acquired in various science classes. In that case, the producing reasons are not at all the sustaining reasons. It is of course possible for the producing reasons to also be the sustaining reasons. No doubt, for the first few days after watching that show, the reasons that produced his belief also sustained it. But this does not have to be the case. I suspect that for many of our beliefs, the reasons that we had for forming them are not those that now sustain them. There is nothing wrong with this. Indeed, it is to be expected, I think, that as our evidence changes and grows this will affect the reasons we have for what we believe. But it is still important to keep the difference in mind when we are asking why someone believes something, since criticizing the reasons he originally had might be beside the point if those are no longer his reasons.

1.5.1 Emotional and Pragmatic Reasons

As I said at the outset, there are many different kinds of reasons to believe something. One can have **emotional** reasons to believe something. Maybe Jones believes that humans evolved from other species in part because believing it helps him feel at one with his natural environment, and this feeling brings him a deep sense of connectedness and meaning. Giving up that belief might cause a sharp emotional pain or rupture. Or maybe he believes it because he knows that believing it upsets his religious father, and he derives satisfaction in being rebellious. Or maybe that belief fits into a larger web of beliefs he has about his place in the Universe, and giving it up would damage the integrity or coherence of that web of belief in a way that would be hard for him to accept. Some of our beliefs are simply so fundamental that giving them up would cause a huge and unpleasant upheaval in our personal worldview, and the desire to avoid this can itself be a reason to keep the belief.

Some people have suggested that emotional reasons play a fundamental role in producing or even sustaining our moral or religious beliefs. Perhaps Jones' belief that lying to others is wrong stems from feelings of guilt he has when he lies, or from feelings of shame he has when he has to admit to others that he has lied. Perhaps he believes that God exists partly because it brings him deep comfort. Moral and religious beliefs do not have to be produced or sustained by emotional reasons. And I suspect that emotional reasons play a role in many of our ordinary "factual" beliefs. It is important to us to feel balanced, and sometimes the need to continue to feel balanced plays a role in explaining why we continue to believe what we do.

We have been considering emotional reasons to believe something that involves only the believer himself. But one can also believe something because of the way that belief relates one emotionally to one's **community, culture, or heritage**. Having a strong sense of community and tradition is extremely important to us, and we should not underestimate the way it can influence and shape our view of the world. Perhaps Jones identifies with the scientific community and tradition and thinks that not believing in human evolution would force him to break with that community and that this break would be bad or painful. It is certainly true that many of the practices we currently have are sustained, at least in part, in order to strengthen and nourish strong community bonds. Sometimes, our practices and beliefs are so fundamental not only to our own personal worldview but to our cultural and ethnic heritage that it is hard to see them as anything but natural and inevitable. It may seem to us that not maintaining them would be a kind of lunacy. (Sometimes, it is only by studying foreign practices and traditions that one can really appreciate and even identify one's own heritage and practices for what they are.) In this kind of case, it might be impossible to even question the beliefs or practices without causing substantial emotional pain.

> Unlike epistemic reasons, emotional and pragmatic reasons for believing something are not reasons to think that the belief is true.

We can also have more purely **pragmatic** reasons to believe something. We might believe something because believing it makes it easier for us to achieve our goals or objectives. It might be that abandoning the belief would not cause us serious emotional pain of any kind, but that we find that maintaining the belief simplifies some part of our practical life. It is easier to get along if we believe it than if we question it, and so we continue to believe it.

1.5.2   Epistemic Reasons

We have been discussing reasons to believe something. But so far we have not discussed reasons to believe that something is true. Let us call reasons of that kind, ones that indicate that what we believe is true, **epistemic** reasons. Emotional reasons and pragmatic reasons are not epistemic ones. Even if it is true that abandoning some belief would cause substantial pain or practical difficulty, it does not follow that these reasons for sustaining the belief are also reasons to think that the belief is true.

This is clear, I think, in the case of Jones' belief that humans evolved from other species. The emotional or pragmatic reasons he has to believe that have nothing at all to do with whether the belief is true. Indeed, the truth of his belief has nothing at all to do with his emotions, or his community, or even with him. If it is true that humans evolved from other species, then this is true regardless of whether Jones even exists. Whether it is true depends on events that occurred long before he was born. Epistemic reasons are reasons to think that a belief is true or accurate, that it captures the facts properly, and they need to have no special bearing on our emotions or practical challenges. Indeed, as we all know, sometimes the truth is painful or uncomfortable.

CRITICAL THINKING AND THE PRACTICE OF MEDICINE

In an article in *The New Yorker*, Dr. Jerome Groopman wrote about how doctors sometimes let emotions get in the way of their examinations. He described a case in which he missed a patient's serious infection because he did not want to embarrass his patient by doing a thorough physical examination. Had he looked carefully, he would have found a serious infection. Luckily, another doctor discovered the infection and it was treated. Groopman's mistake, in this case, was not that he based his beliefs on his emotions, but that he allowed his emotions to get in the way of performing the kinds of tests and examinations he knew were needed before he deciding whether the patient was healthy. He allowed himself to form a belief that he knew was based on incomplete evidence. The consequences of this mistake might be just as bad as the consequences of forming beliefs on the basis of emotions. He wrote that this case illustrates an important lesson, neatly summarized by his friend Pat Croskerry: "Currently, in medical training, we fail to recognize the importance of critical thinking and critical reasoning. The implicit assumption is that we know how to think. But we don't."

Epistemic reasons are at the heart of critical thinking. Think back to the traditional philosophical definition of knowledge as justified true belief. Since knowledge requires *true* belief, the kinds of reasons involved in justification are epistemic ones, not emotional or pragmatic ones. The requirement that to know something one's belief must be justified means that one must have good epistemic reasons for the belief. That means that one must have **sufficient** and **acceptable** evidence—we will look much more closely at what each of those things mean in later chapters. Basing or sustaining a belief on emotions or on practical considerations cannot lead to knowledge, since these kinds of reasons to believe something are the wrong kind. To know whether humans evolved from other species, it is not enough to have strong emotional or pragmatic reasons; one must have strong reasons for thinking *that it is true* that humans evolved from other species. This does not mean that one cannot also have emotional or pragmatic reasons. Jones' belief that humans evolved from other species might be justified enough for knowledge even if it is sustained in part by emotional or pragmatic reasons, so long as he also has sufficient epistemic reasons to believe it. But if one is striving for knowledge, then one cannot rest content merely with emotional or pragmatic reasons, since they have nothing essentially to do with whether the belief is true, and truth is essential to knowledge. A belief that is based solely on emotional or pragmatic reasons cannot possibly count as knowledge, even if the belief is true. Knowledge requires strong epistemic reasons.

A belief that is based solely on emotional or pragmatic reasons cannot be knowledge, even if the belief is true. Knowledge requires epistemic reasons.

Deciding what to do: deciding on means and deciding on ends

Deciding what to do involves two separate decisions. The action's intended goal—its **end**—is one thing and the steps to achieve that goal—the **means**—are quite another. Here are some examples.

I will enroll in University in order to get an education.

I will dedicate all of June and July to writing my book in order to get it done.

I will put a pot of boiling water on in order to make dinner.

Thinking critically about what to do requires having reasons to pursue those ends and reasons to choose those means.

Reasons for pursuing some end are reasons for thinking that the end is good, or valuable, or worthwhile. I decided to write this text book because I believed that writing it would be a good thing to do, and I had reasons for this. You decided to go to college or university because you thought it would be a good thing to do, and you surely had some reasons to think that. Reasons to think that something is good are a special kind of reason, and we will look at them in more detail in a later chapter.

Once you decide on your goal or your end, you need to decide how to make it happen. This is deciding on the means to achieve that end or goal. Reasons to adopt some means are reasons for thinking that those means will succeed. I decided to dedicate one summer to working on the book because I thought this would be a good way to get the writing done. I decided on that means because I thought it would succeed. You decided to enroll in university because you believed it was an effective means to your goal of getting a university education.

1.5.3 Emotions and Evidence

Being a critical thinker means that our beliefs should be based on epistemic reasons, and not on emotional or pragmatic ones. Basing one's beliefs on emotions rather than on epistemic reasons is a mistake. Emotions can also make it difficult to collect the evidence we need for our belief to be justified, or even from investigating further. Emotions can also get in the way when we identify too much with our own opinions and beliefs or with our own methods for collecting or evaluating evidence. If I become too emotionally attached to my beliefs and opinions, then I may react negatively when someone asks me for my reasons, or when they raise objections to my belief or when they state their own alternative beliefs. I might feel that they are criticizing me and not just my beliefs. The same is true if I am asked to defend my assessment of the evidence or my use of different methods for collecting evidence. If I come to identify too closely with these particular methods for assessing and collecting evidence, if I come to think of my value as a researcher as tied into their value, then I will react to criticisms of them as if they were criticisms of me and my judgment. This feeling of being under attack might make me feel defensive, and this can prevent me from thinking critically about the issue at hand. The same is true when I ask someone for his or her reasons. This sort of question is easily taken as aggressive or combative, even when the intention is simply to consider the issue from all sides as thoroughly as possible.

PRACTICAL STRATEGY: DO NOT PERSONALIZE REASONS

Reasons and evidence do not belong to anyone; they are **universal**. And whether they are good has nothing to do with who accepts them; they are **objective**. To avoid personalizing reasons, replace the following:

   a. What evidence do you have?

   b. What are your reasons?

   c. Why do you believe that?

with the following impersonal ones:

   a'. What evidence is there?

   b'. What reasons are there to believe that?

   c'. Why should we believe that?

Knowing how to **distance** oneself from one's beliefs and opinions in order to think critically about them is not easy. It is one of the hardest things to achieve. But the best way to avoid this feeling is making sure that one's beliefs and opinions are based on sufficient evidence. Again: **think twice; decide once**. Another strategy is to avoid talking about "my reasons" or "your reasons" and to talk instead of "the reasons" or "some reasons." This makes sense anyway, since reasons and evidence are not owned or possessed by anyone: they are universal and objective. Instead of asking "What are your reasons for believing that?" which can come across as confrontational, ask, "What reasons are there to believe that?" which makes the question sound less confrontational. Instead of asking, "What is your evidence?" you can ask, "What evidence is there for that?"

Critical thinking requires that we have good epistemic reasons for our beliefs and decisions. Sometimes, in order to decide what to believe or do, we need to **acquire new evidence**. We have several sources of evidence at our disposal, several ways of gaining new information on which to base our decisions about what to believe or what to do. We can gain new evidence through direct observation, testimony, measurement, testing, and experiment. In Chapter 4, we will compare these different sources of evidence and consider when they provide evidence or information that is acceptable. Sometimes, we can decide what to believe or what to do by **drawing conclusions from the evidence we already have**. We can rely on what we already know to compare things or groups of things to see how they are analogous. We can reason about what else has to be true given what we already know or believe that we know, and we can reason about what alternatives the evidence that we have rules out. In Chapters 5 and 6, we will compare these different ways of drawing conclusions from the evidence we already have, and study some methods for telling when our reasoning is good.

1.6 GOOD REASONS ARE SUFFICIENT AND ACCEPTABLE

A belief is justified enough for knowledge only if it is based on good reasons. Two features are essential to good reasons. First, the reasons have to be **sufficient** to support the belief. Second, the reasons have to be **acceptable**. In later chapters, we will have a lot to say about both these features of good reasons. But let us now take a quick look at each element.

Imagine that you were on a jury for a murder trial. Suppose that Jones has been charged with the murder of Smith. During the trial, the prosecution brings forward several witnesses who give testimony about what happened the night of the murder. As a member of the jury, you have to decide whether the testimony really proves, beyond a shadow of a doubt, that Jones murdered Smith. There are two very different questions you need to ask about the evidence the prosecution has presented. First, you need to ask whether the evidence, if true, would prove that Jones murdered Smith. That is the question of whether the evidence is sufficient. Second, you need to ask whether the evidence is accurate, whether it comes from trustworthy sources. That is the acceptability question.

Suppose, in particular, that Hamish testifies that he saw Jones holding the murder weapon and standing over Smith's body. You need to ask yourself two questions about Hamish's testimony: first, would it (together with the rest of the evidence the prosecution put forward) show that Jones really did murder Smith; second, is Hamish a reliable witness? These two questions are independent of one another, in the sense that you can answer Yes to either one while answering No to the other. Let us look at these in more detail.

First, a belief is justified enough for knowledge only if it is based on **sufficient** evidence; this just means that it has to be based on **enough** evidence. In deciding what to believe or do we need to make sure that we have collected enough evidence. This is the idea behind the legal requirement that a jury can find the defendant guilty only if they have proof beyond a reasonable doubt. In deciding whether a defendant is guilty, it is not enough that the prosecution present *some* evidence of guilt. It needs to present enough evidence. Ideally, it should provide enough evidence to guarantee that the verdict the jury reaches is the right one. The evidence, in that case, would make it impossible for the verdict to be mistaken. The jury could not go wrong if it made its decision on the basis of that evidence. What is true of juries is just as true of us as we try to decide what to believe and what to do. We can sometimes collect this ideal amount of evidence, but we often have to make do with less than this. In chapter 3, we will study the ideal amount of evidence and consider some strategies for telling how close we are.

A belief is justified enough for knowledge only if it is based on evidence that is both sufficient and acceptable.

Second, a belief is justified enough for knowledge only if it is based on **acceptable** evidence. In a perfect world, we would only rely on evidence that we knew for a fact was true or accurate. But we are rarely in that kind of situation. Usually, we have to make our decisions on the basis of information that we are pretty sure about, but not one hundred percent convinced of. Usually, the acceptability of some piece of evidence depends on where it came from, on its source. Some sources of evidence are better than others for certain kinds of beliefs, and it is always an important question whether a given source of evidence is trustworthy in a particular case. Direct visual observation is a good source of evidence for beliefs about the colors of objects but it is not a good source of evidence for beliefs about other physical properties of objects. You can often tell just by looking whether something is brown or red, but it is pretty much impossible to tell just by looking whether something will dissolve when placed in water. You can tell by looking whether someone is tall or male, but not whether they are a lawyer or a doctor. You can sometimes tell by looking whether a bridge needs to be repainted but not whether the bridge is at risk of collapse. A lot of care is needed when we are deciding what to believe or what to do to ensure that our decisions are based on acceptable evidence.

1.7   WHEN EVIDENCE CONFLICTS

Sometimes, one piece of evidence we have conflicts with another piece of evidence we have. There are two ways that evidence can conflict and a good critical thinker keeps an eye out for both sorts of conflict.

> Two pieces of evidence **directly** conflict when one indicates that something is true and the other indicates that it is false.

Sometimes, two pieces of evidence point in opposite directions. Let us call that a **direct** conflict. Here is an example. Suppose Susan sees what look to her like bear tracks on the riverbank. This is evidence that a bear is nearby. But suppose that her very experienced guide says that no bears have been in the area for 20 years. The guide's testimony is evidence that no bear is nearby. In this case, there are two pieces of evidence that conflict: one indicates that a bear is nearby and the other indicates the opposite. Or imagine that during a trial one witness says that Jones was at the hotel, where the murder occurred and another witness claims that Jones was at home that night. Again, these two pieces of evidence conflict, since they point in opposite directions. These are examples of direct conflict between pieces of evidence.

In this sort of case, one of the pieces of evidence will have to be misleading. Either the tracks are not bear tracks, or else the guide is mistaken. But since Susan does not know, the wise thing is to withhold judgment about whether a bear definitely is present. Likewise, at least one of the two witnesses is mistaken—they cannot both be right. But if the members of the jury cannot figure out which one is mistaken, the wise thing to do is to withhold judgment.

Here is another case where two pieces of evidence are in direct conflict. Consider a case of a persistent visual illusion, like the Müller-Lyer Illusion, presented below.

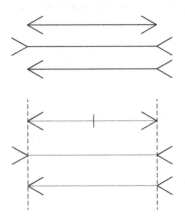

When we look at the drawing, it looks like the middle line is quite a bit longer than either the top or the bottom lines. But if we measure them with a ruler, we will find that they are in fact of the very same length. We are now in a situation where our evidence conflicts. Our eyes tell us one thing; our measurement tells us another. The observational evidence directly conflicts with the measurement evidence. Something has to give. In this case, we have figured out that the evidence we get from observation is misleading, and that the evidence we get from measurement is accurate. (Part of what is fun about this illusion is that it is *persistent*: the middle line still looks longer even when we know that it is not!)

Sometimes when a piece of evidence we have is in direct conflict with another piece of evidence we have, one of the pieces of evidence will be stronger than the other. In that case, let us say that first piece of evidence **overrides** the second. It is not easy to say what makes one piece of evidence stronger than another, but we will return to this question later on. But this is what happens in the illusion case. For the measurement evidence is stronger than the observational evidence. This means that it would be wrong to rely on the observational evidence in this case, since we know we have better evidence from measurement.

When two pieces of evidence directly conflict, if one is stronger than the other, then the stronger evidence **overrides** the weaker evidence. It is unreasonable to rely on overridden evidence.

When we decide what to believe or what to do, we have to make sure that we consider all of the evidence we have or can get and we have to make sure that the evidence we decide to go with is not overridden by other evidence.

> **CRITICAL THINKING MISTAKE: PRIVILEGING CONFIRMING EVIDENCE**
>
> It is a mistake to assume that evidence that confirms what we already believe is better than new evidence that conflicts with it. This is a mistake because what we already believe may be false, and if we were to consider the disconfirming evidence more carefully we would see this and change our minds. A critical thinker is always willing to reflect on whether her beliefs are based on sufficient and acceptable evidence.

One piece of evidence **indirectly** conflicts with another when the first indicates that the second is from an unreliable source.

Evidence can conflict in another way. To see it, let us consider a different story. Suppose that Mark takes his daughter's temperature using an electronic thermometer. The thermometer reads 98°F. This is some evidence that the daughter does not have a fever. But suppose that Mark them remembers that the batteries are dying in the thermometer. This is some evidence that the thermometer might be giving a misreading, that maybe the thermometer is not working properly. Here again, we have a case where the evidence conflicts. But the two pieces of evidence here are not in direct conflict. For the evidence that the thermometer is broken is not evidence that the daughter **does** have a fever. Rather, it is evidence that the reading is not acceptable evidence. When one piece of evidence indicates that another piece of evidence is not acceptable, let us call that an **indirect conflict**.

When one piece of evidence indirectly conflicts with another, if the first is stronger, then it **undermines** the second. It is unreasonable to rely on undermined evidence.

If one piece of evidence indirectly conflicts with another, and the first piece is stronger than the second, then the first piece of evidence **undermines** the second piece of evidence. For example, suppose that Wayne testifies that he saw Jones pull the trigger. That is some evidence that Jones is guilty. But suppose that Simon testifies that Wayne has a grudge against Jones and would lie on the witness stand. In this case, Simon's testimony indirectly conflicts with Wayne's. Suppose, further, that we have really good reason to trust Simon. In that case, his testimony is stronger than Wayne's testimony. So Simon's testimony undermines Wayne's testimony. This does not mean that we think that Wayne testified *falsely*. It just means that we should not trust what he says. We should remain agnostic, undecided. We should withhold judgment until more evidence is in.

CRITICAL THINKING MISTAKE: PRIVILEGING AVAILABLE EVIDENCE

It is a mistake to assume that evidence that we currently have is better than evidence that we might collect. This is a mistake because if we were to collect more evidence we might discover some that overrides or that undermines the evidence that we have. It might be that our current evidence is the best we can get, but we will not know this until we try to collect more. Crucially, even if we have excellent reason to rest content with the evidence we have, we should always keep an open mind that we might uncover new evidence that will override or undermine the evidence we now have.

A good critical thinker withholds belief until enough evidence is collected.

Sometimes we may have reason to question all of the evidence provided by some source. For example, the Müller–Lyer illusion shows that we have to be very careful when we rely on evidence provided by our vision, at least when we are trying to decide when two lines are of the same length. Vision, it seems, can be quite unreliable on this kind of topic. But it would be wrong to respond to the Müller–Lyer illusion by believing the opposite of what our eyes tell us. The proper response is to withhold judgment until more evidence is in. "It looks like the middle line is longer, but let's measure it just to make sure." When we decide what to believe or what to do we need to make sure that the other evidence that we have does not undermine the evidence we are relying on. Once again: think twice, decide once.

EXERCISE 3

A. Comprehension questions. (When you answer these questions, pretend that you are explaining or teaching the answer to a friend who is not in the class. Doing that will force you to put in LOTS more background information than you would if you were trying to answer them for your instructor.)
   1. What is the traditional definition of knowledge?
   2. What is the difference between Realism and Relativism?
   3. Could one be a realist and a relativist about biology? Why or why not?
   4. Why does the existence of disagreement in some subject area not show that Relativism is true of that area?
   5. Why is Realism the default attitude to take in a subject area?
   6. How are freedom of action and freedom of belief alike? How are they different?
   7. What is an example of an emotional reason to believe something?
   8. Why are emotional reasons not good enough for knowledge?
   9. List two ways in which emotions can be obstacles to critical thinking.

10. What is the difference between acceptable reasons and sufficient reasons? Give an example of reasons that are sufficient to believe something but not acceptable.

11. Could evidence be overridden without being undermined? Explain using an example.

12. The traditional philosophical definition of knowledge says that knowledge is justified true belief. When presented with a definition that analyzes some idea or concept into several parts or elements, it is a good idea to investigate how those elements are related to one another. To do this, one asks whether it would be possible to have two of the elements without the third. Is it possible for someone to have a belief that is justified (i.e., based on epistemic reasons) even though the belief is not true? Try to construct stories to test whether these elements are independent?

1.8   CRITICAL THINKING AND PERSONAL AUTONOMY

We have seen that critical thinking is aimed at knowledge. It pretty much goes without saying that knowledge is valuable. For one thing, since knowledge requires truth, if we know something then we have the truth on our side. So critical thinking, to the extent that it can help us gain knowledge, can also save us from making mistakes. And that is a good thing. But thinking critically as we decide what to believe or do is valuable for a different, and in some ways more important, reason. Thinking critically is essential to making up one's own mind, and this is fundamental to being an autonomous person. Let us explore this by looking first at the differences between a belief and a prejudice.

1.8.1   Belief and Prejudice

Knowledge is valuable because of its links to truth. But as we saw, knowledge also requires justification, and justification is valuable because it makes the difference between having a well-reasoned belief and having a **prejudice**. And no one wants to be prejudiced. But what exactly is it to be prejudiced, and why is it so bad?

Usually when we talk about prejudices we have in mind hurtful views about race, religion, or ethnicity. We say that people who treat Asians or Catholics less well than they treat Europeans or Episcopalians are prejudiced against them. Some people used to believe that Irish immigrants were lazy, could never keep a job and did not care about supporting their families. Irish immigrants were discriminated against as a result of these prejudicial views. Of course, those beliefs about Irish immigrants were totally false, and it is even hard for us now to imagine how anyone could have believed them in the first place. (Unfortunately, it is always easier to spot someone else's prejudices than it is to notice one's own, and there is little reason for optimism that we are any less prejudiced than are the rest of our fellow humans.)

But what made those beliefs prejudices was not that they were false. There has to be a difference between a belief that is false and belief that is a prejudice. Not every false belief is a prejudice. People used to believe that the Sun orbited the Earth, but we do not think that this false belief made them prejudiced. This was a mistake, not a prejudice. And isn't it possible that a prejudicial view could actually turn out to be true? Suppose I see in the newspaper a picture of someone who has been arrested for some crime and I immediately conclude that he is guilty just from the look on his face. I think we would say that my belief in his guilt was a prejudice. But what if it turned out that he was in fact guilty? Wouldn't we still say that my belief was prejudicial even though it was true? So it seems that whether a belief is a prejudice has nothing to do with whether it is true or false.

One clue to the nature of prejudice comes from the word itself: a prejudice is a **pre**judgment. To prejudge someone or something is to form a judgment or belief about them before enough of the facts are in, before one has enough evidence. Taken literally, a belief is a prejudice when it is not based on good epistemic reasons. My belief in the defendant's guilt was a prejudice because it was not based on good enough reason, and this is so even though the belief was in fact true. The members of a jury are asked not to prejudge the question—not to decide whether the defendant did it—before all of the evidence has been presented. Since critical thinking can help us to make sure that our beliefs are based on good epistemic reasons, critical thinking can also help us to avoid being prejudiced.

1.8.2   Making Up Your Own Mind

But why should we avoid prejudice, especially if prejudice is compatible with being right? This might sound like a silly question, but answering it can help us to see one of the deeper values to critical thinking. One reason to avoid prejudice is that we want to make up our own mind and being prejudiced is the very opposite of making up your own mind.

If we let our beliefs get formed before we have had a chance to examine all the evidence, then it is as if we have lost control of our beliefs and views. Forces and influences that are outside of us would in that case form our beliefs and opinions for us. My spontaneous belief that the arrested man was guilty was not the result of careful deliberation by me. The belief just came over me. I was not responsible for it. In a real sense, I did not **make** up my mind to believe that he was guilty; rather, my mind was made up for me. But that is not how I want my beliefs and opinions to get made. I want them to be *my* beliefs and opinions, ones that I choose and can take responsibility for having, not ones that were simply given to me or (even worse) forced on me. And this is so even if the prejudicial beliefs turn out to be true.

Making up one's own mind is part of what it is to be **autonomous**. Being autonomous means exercising the power to determine one's self, to decide on one's own what to do or what to believe, what kind of life to live. Because critical thinking demands reasons and requires us to be reflective as we decide what to believe and what to do, thinking critically is crucial to exercising our ability to determine our own minds, to decide for ourselves.

Sometimes, making up one's own mind can mean disagreeing with others or even abandoning beliefs and practices that one was born into. Making up one's own mind about religion or politics can sometimes cause pain and lead to separation from those we love. This may be unavoidable if one finds that those practices are not based on good enough reasons, and making the break can require a good deal of courage. But it is not inevitably like that. Examining one's beliefs and practices can also reveal deep and even new reasons for keeping them, and this process can strengthen one's allegiance to them and deepen one's bonds to others who share those beliefs and practices. The benefits of making up one's own mind far outweigh the risks.

We have been discussing the responsibility that we have to make sure that our beliefs and practices are grounded in good reasons. In a famous essay, William Clifford argued that we also have a responsibility to others to make sure that we have good reasons to believe what we do. His reason was that beliefs make a difference to action. We act on our beliefs, and if our beliefs are not based on good enough reasons, then we run the risk that our actions will cause unintended harm. Clifford illustrated this point with a story about a wealthy but penny-pinching shipowner, whose ship full of immigrants was ready to set sail. The shipowner had good epistemic reason to think that the ship was not sea-worthy but was reluctant to pay for the needed repairs and to put up with costly delays. Eventually, he convinced himself that the ship was safe. He let his pragmatic and emotional reasons overpower his epistemic ones. Tragically, he was mistaken and the ship sank, killing everyone on board. Clifford argued that not only was it wrong for the shipowner to let the ship sail, it was wrong for him to believe as he did that it was safe, since his belief was not based on adequate grounds. It is wrong, Clifford insisted, to believe something on the basis of wishful thinking, or for nothing but self-interested reasons.

But suppose that the ship had not sunk. Suppose that the crew and passengers had gotten lucky and the ship made it safely to America. Still, Clifford argued, it would have been just as wrong for the shipowner to allow the ship to sail and to have believed as he did that the ship was safe. Suppose finally that the ship was in fact quite safe, and that the shipowner's initial concerns about its safety were not well founded. Still, if the shipowner ignored those concerns and convinced himself that the ship was safe in hopes of saving a few dollars, Clifford argued, it would still have been just as wrong for him to have allowed the ship to sail and for him to have believed as he did that the ship was safe. It would have been wrong for him to have believed that even though his belief would have been true. It would have been wrong because his belief would have been based on inadequate evidence. It is, Clifford concluded, "Always and everywhere wrong to believe on inadequate evidence." To the extent that critical thinking can help us to ensure that our beliefs are based on strong epistemic reasons, it can help us to fulfill the obligations that derive from the ethics of belief.

CHAPTER SUMMARY

Critical thinking is reasonable and reflective thinking aimed at deciding what to believe or what to do. When we try to decide what to believe or what to do, we are trying to gain knowledge. We want to know the facts or the best way to achieve our goals. Knowledge is justified true belief. A belief is justified only when it is based on sufficient and acceptable evidence. Relying on such evidence not only reduces the risk of error; it also helps us to avoid prejudice. Avoiding prejudice is essential to making up one's own mind about what to believe and what to do. Critical thinking provides practical methods and standards for helping us to make sure that our beliefs are based on adequate epistemic reasons. In this way, critical thinking helps us to become autonomous.

CHAPTER EXERCISES

A. Comprehension Questions. (When you answer these questions, pretend that you are explaining or teaching the answer to a friend who is not in the class. Doing that will force you to put in LOTS more background information that you would if you were trying to explain the material to your teacher.)

   a. What is the difference between a prejudicial belief and a false belief? Use an example to illustrate your answer.

   b. Could a prejudicial belief be true? Explain, using an example.

   c. Could believing something on the basis of emotions alone make one autonomous? Why or why not? Use an example to illustrate your answer.

   d. List five character traits that you think are characteristic of an ideal critical thinker. Give an example of each one.

   e. Suppose that Jones is a universal relativist (i.e., a relativist about all subject matters) and that Smith is a universal realist (i.e., a realist about all subject matters). Could they nonetheless agree on all the facts? What exactly would they disagree about?

   f. Consider the following proposed definition: to lie is to deliberately say something that is false and that one believes to be false in order to mislead another person. What are the elements of this proposed definition? Are those elements independent of one another?

   g. Some philosophers claim that it is wrong to lie to someone because it prevents them from making up their own mind. Construct a story about Jones (or your favorite character) to illustrate this point. Do you agree that this is part of what makes lying wrong?

   h. Thomas Jefferson is supposed to have said that all knowledge begins with book knowledge; that is, with knowledge that we get from reading books or from trusting what other people say. Could this be right?

B. In the following texts, reasons are given for some belief or practice. Explain whether the reasons are epistemic ones.

   a. Sally believes that it is wrong to eat meat. She once watched a documentary on the methods used to kill cows, and it made her so sad that she immediately became opposed to eating meat.

   b. The glass of milk is empty. I can see it with my own eyes that it is.

   c. The glass of milk is empty. I cannot see it, but my mother just told me that it is.

   d. We have to hold the party on Christmas Eve, because we have always held it then.

e. John believes that the sofa will fit up the stairs. He first measured the sofa and then the stairs, and decided that it would go up easily if tilted on its side.

f. Ashanti believes that Senator Doolittle's proposal is not cost effective. She finds that politicians are such hypocrites that she disagrees with everything they propose.

g. Robert believes that his car will not last much longer. He knows several people who own the same make of car and none of them lasted as long as his has lasted. So he figures that his car will not last much longer.

h. Susan believes that birds are a kind of dinosaur. She does not remember how she first came to believe it, but has decided to believe it until she finds some contrary evidence.

i. John thinks that smoking causes cancer. He believes it because his mother and two aunts died of cancer after smoking all of their lives.

C. In each of the following, several epistemic reasons are given to believe something. Which is the strongest reason? What makes it stronger?

a. John, Susan, and Terry all believe that the bank robber was a male. John was there during the robbery and saw the robber. Susan read about the robbery in the newspaper. Susan told Terry about the robbery.

b. John and Susan both believe that the acid caused the chemical reaction. John read in a textbook about the likely causes of such a reaction. Susan performed several experiments to rule out other possible causes.

c. Susan and Terry both believe that their checking accounts are overdrawn. Terry got a phone call from his bank telling him about his balance. Susan noticed it when she was balancing her checkbook last night.

d. John and Susan believe that some early settlers in New England suffered real hardships. John read some original diaries written by early settlers. Susan saw a documentary on TV.

e. John and Susan both believe that building a new bridge will greatly reduce the current traffic problems. John based his belief on a comparison of the proposed bridge and the traffic problems to those in other cities. Susan believes it because she heard the city planners claim that the bridge would reduce traffic problems.

f. John and Susan both believe that raising the minimum wage would lead to higher unemployment among the very poor. John believes it because he thinks that it follows from what he learned in his economics class. Susan believes it because she works in an unemployment office and has seen the unemployment lines grow after the wage has been raised in the past.

D. In (a) in exercise (C), if the belief had been that the robber was a male with a long criminal record, then Susan's belief would have been better justified than John's, since it is hard to tell just by looking whether someone has a criminal record, but this is the kind of information a newspaper report would get right. For each of the other questions in (C), change the shared belief but not the kind of evidence each character relied on, so that the other person's reasons are stronger.

1.9 CRITICAL THINKING IN PRACTICE

1.9.1 Critical Thinking Mistakes

This book is intended as a practical guide to deciding what to believe. In later chapters we will discuss some strategies and standards that can help us to make sure that our decisions about what to believe or do are based on good epistemic reasons. As we go along, we will draw attention to some familiar mistakes, sometimes called "fallacies." Identifying them will help us to avoid them in our own thinking and to spot them in other people's thinking. Seeing why they are mistakes will help us know what to look for as we try to find good epistemic reasons for our decisions. All of the mistakes are collected together at the end of the book, for quick and easy reference.

Personalizing Reasons.   It is a mistake to personalize reasons by treating them as if they belonged to someone. That is a mistake for two reasons. First, epistemic reasons are universal: if they are reasons for me to believe something then they are equally reasons for anyone else to believe it too. Second, epistemic reasons are objective: whether a piece of evidence is sufficient or acceptable is an objective matter. It has nothing to do with me or with anyone else. Personalizing reasons can obscure the fact that they are universal and objective. It can also allow emotion to get in the way of thinking critically if one identifies too much with one's own reasons or if one rejects reasons just because someone else accepts them.

Appeal to Relativism.   It is a mistake to just assume that truth is relative. This is a mistake because we always need to have good reasons for our beliefs, including our belief that Relativism is the right attitude to take toward some subject matter. Relativism with respect to some subject matter is the view that the facts in that area are in some way dependent on our beliefs about them. Relativism might be the right attitude to take toward such topics as what is humorous or what is tasty. But for most topics, even religious and moral ones, it is best to assume that Realism is the appropriate attitude, unless one has powerful reasons not to. For most topics, in other words, it is wrong to assume that what is true for me might not be true for you, or that what is true for our community or culture might not be true for others. Truth is the same for everyone.

Sometimes, an appeal to Relativism will be used as attempt to bring a discussion to an end. One person, perhaps tired of the debate or feeling that they are on the losing side, will say to the others: "Well, I'm entitled to my view and you are entitled to yours." This kind of response is fine if what is intended is that everyone is allowed to make up their own minds about what to believe or do. But if the point is that we can both be right even when we disagree, then this is a mistake that we should avoid, unless there is excellent reason to think otherwise.

Appeal to Emotion.   It is a mistake to base our beliefs only on our emotions. This is a mistake because how a belief makes us feel is not evidence that the belief is true, and a belief should be based on evidence that it is true. For a belief to be justified enough for knowledge it must be based on good epistemic reasons. Epistemic reasons are reasons to think that the belief is true. Emotional reasons are not epistemic ones. How a belief makes us feel has nothing to do with whether the belief is true. As we have already noted, critical thinking does not aim to eliminate emotion from our decision-making. I doubt this would be worthwhile even if it were possible. Many of our beliefs are so fundamental to our deepest conceptions of ourselves, of our culture or our place in the Universe that the pain involved in abandoning them would be too great to bear. It is fine for our beliefs to have or even constitute these emotional supports, so long as they also have sufficient support from epistemic reasons. But it is a mistake to base our beliefs on nothing but emotional reasons. We also saw that it is a mistake to allow emotions to prevent us from collecting or assessing the evidence we need to make the decisions we must.

Privileging Confirming Evidence.   It is a mistake to assume that evidence that confirms what we already believe is better than evidence that conflicts with it. This is a mistake because what we already believe may be false, and if were to consider the disconfirming evidence more carefully, we would see this and change our minds. A critical thinker is always willing to reflect on whether her beliefs are based on sufficient and acceptable evidence.

Privileging Available Evidence.   It is a mistake to assume that evidence that we currently have is better than evidence that we might collect. This is a mistake because if we were to collect more evidence we might discover some that undermines or overrides the evidence that we have. It might be that our current evidence is the best we can get, but we will not know this until we try to collect more. Crucially, even if we have excellent reason to rest content with the evidence we have, we should always keep an open mind that we might uncover new evidence that will override or undermine the evidence we now have.

AN EXAMPLE OF APPEALING TO TRADITION

When I was a child, my family lived in England. The houses in our neighborhood all had their water pipes running up the outside of the house, instead of inside the exterior walls. Predictably, the pipes froze and burst every winter and workmen had to be called to repair them. My father asked the landlord why the pipes were on the outside instead of inside the walls. The landlord explained: Well, if they were on the inside, then we could not get to them when they froze. The landlord had accepted the traditional way of thinking of the problem: he saw it as an access problem, best solved by putting the pipes on the outside walls. Having been raised in Canada, my father saw it as a freezing problem, best solved by putting the pipes inside the heated space of the house. The landlord's mistake was in not asking whether the traditional way of thinking was the right way.

Appeal to Tradition.   It is a mistake to believe something just because that belief is traditional. This is a mistake because the fact that a belief has a long history is not evidence that it is true, and it is a mistake to believe something without evidence that it is true. Being a critical thinker does not mean abandoning all of our traditional beliefs. It just means that we need to have good reasons to continue holding them.

1.9.2 Critical Thinking Strategies

This book is intended as a *practical* guide to deciding what to believe. As we go along, we will draw attention to some useful practical strategies or methods. These will all be collected into an appendix at the end, for quick and easy reference.

Look for Conceptual Relations. It is good to know how to look for relations among our concepts and ideas. We did this with Robert Ennis' definition of critical thinking as reasonable, reflective thinking aimed at deciding what to believe or what to do. The other was the standard philosophical definition of knowledge as justified, true belief. When an idea or concept is analyzed into several parts or elements, it is always a good idea to ask how those parts or elements are related to each another. To do this, simply ask yourself whether you can think of an example of something that has some of the elements but not others. For instance, we noticed that simple arithmetical calculations are a kind of thinking aimed at deciding what to believe but are not reflective because they do not require thinking about the method one uses. Whenever a concept or problem has elements or parts, ask: how are those parts related to one another?

Think Twice; Decide Once. To paraphrase the old carpenter's motto (measure twice and cut once): it is best to think twice and decide once. We know from psychological experiments that people are reluctant to change their minds. Once our opinions are set, it seems to take a lot to revise them. For one thing, people tend to privilege evidence that confirms their already existing beliefs over evidence that conflicts with it. They assume that evidence that conflicts with what they already believe is probably not reliable. For another thing, people tend to prefer the evidence they have to the evidence they would have to do something to get. To protect against these built-in obstacles to critical thinking, it is better to make sure that one has enough of the right kind of evidence before one makes a decision. It is better to think twice and decide once, than to have to go back and revise one's decisions.

1.9.3 From Theory to Practice: Applying What We Have Learned

One goal of this book is to provide you with the conceptual tools and the practical strategies you need to become a strong critical thinker. Thinking critically requires having an appropriate vocabulary for describing and evaluating the decisions we need to make, as well as having the strategies and methods needed to make sure that our decisions are based on the right kind of evidence. But book learning only goes so far. Becoming a critical thinker requires using these concepts and skills in our own life. We can and should think critically about our own decisions and values, about our classes and studies and about our workplace experiences. The following set of exercises will continue throughout the book, as we acquire new concepts and learn new strategies. They are designed to help you "transfer" what you learn in this class to the rest of your life. And as with everything, the more you put into them, the more you will get out.

1.9.3.1 Thinking Critically about Ourselves Good critical thinking begins at home. This means that we can practice the skills and strategies involved in thinking

critically by reflecting on ourselves and our own decisions and values. The self-examination exercise—which continues throughout the book—asks you to examine your conception of a good person. In this chapter, we will begin by outlining the exercise.

a. List five or six traits that you think are essential to being a morally good person. You can be as specific or as general as you like. But it is good to pick traits that are varied as you can. Some examples: honesty, loyalty, generosity, and faithfulness.

b. Pick one of them to work on for the remainder of the text. Try to define it in other terms, as if you were explaining it to someone who was unfamiliar with it. Think up a story in which it is illustrated.

c. Explain why you think that trait is essential to being a morally good person. Try to make sure that your reasons are epistemic ones, as opposed to emotional or pragmatic ones.

1.9.3.2   Thinking Critically in the Classroom   Every university and college is in the business of producing critical thinkers, and each of their departments and programs are charged with trying to improve the critical-thinking skills of its students. Geology departments want to do more than just teach their students geological facts; they want to teach them how to think critically about geology. Business programs want to help their students become adept at thinking critically about business problems and solutions, and not just to teach them business concepts and practices. This exercise, which will continue throughout the text, is designed to help you see where critical thinking can fit in with your studies.

a. In your own words, and with as much detail as you can, list five or six things in your program where critical thinking is required in learning. Some examples: memorizing definitions and concepts; learning historical events and explanations; performing measurements; collecting evidence; doing factual research; writing essays; performing experiments; evaluating performances and works of art; analyzing texts and arguments. As clearly as you can, and using the concepts we have studied in this chapter, explain in what way critical thinking is required in each of them.

b. Using the textbooks for your courses as a guide, compile a list of the five or six most important concepts for your field of study. These will be the concepts that are used most broadly to formulate the claims and to frame the subject matter. They should not be the same as the concepts in another field. For example, the concept of a cell is essential to biology, but not to economics; the concept of demand is crucial for economics, but not to history.

c. The only way to succeed in your studies is to study hard. Critical thinking can help with this. List five or six things that you do as part of your studying and describe how they involve critical thinking, in the sense that we have been discussing in this chapter. Some might involve decision making while others involve reflection.

1.9.3.3 Thinking Critically at Work   Studies show that employers value an ability to think critically more than just about any other trait in an employee. They want their workers to be able to think critically about both day-to-day problems as well as about broader organizational performance and plans. Many employers even provide critical-thinking training as an element in management development. This exercise, which will continue throughout the text, is designed to help you see where critical thinking can be applied at work.

a. Thinking about your workplace, list five or six tasks that you or your co-co-workers are regularly asked to perform that require thinking critically in the sense that we have been discussing. They can be as simple or complex as you like, but again it is best to make the list as varied and specific as possible. (A hint: start with very general tasks, and then analyze them down into smaller more discrete tasks.) Some examples: dealing with customer complaints; regular communicating with co-workers and supervisors; ordering and stocking inventory; dealing with late or delinquent bills; implementing or evaluating systems and procedures.

b. Pick one of those tasks, and answer the following.

   (i) What is the task? Be as detailed and specific as you can.

   (ii) In what ways does it require critical thinking? Which of the elements of critical thinking does it require?

   (iii) What information do you usually need to perform the task and how do you usually collect and assess that information?

   (iv) If you could implement a change that would improve or enhance your performance of that task, what would it be?

   (v) What obstacles are there to thinking critically in the performance of that task? Be as specific and detailed as you can.

2

CLARIFYING MEANING

Critical thinking is reasonable, reflective thinking aimed at deciding what to believe and what to do. Knowing how to reflect critically on meaning is fundamental to critical thinking. Before we decide what to believe or what to do, we need to make sure that we have clearly defined the words and concepts that we use to formulate the beliefs that we are assessing, to describe the proposals we are considering, and to frame the problems we are facing and the solutions we are contemplating. Otherwise, we run the real risk that we will end up believing something we should not, doing something that will not succeed, or failing to solve the problems we tackle. In this chapter, we will study some practical strategies for constructing and evaluating definitions. But let us start by discussing in a bit more detail where definitions fit into critical thinking.

2.1 THE PLACE OF DEFINITIONS IN CRITICAL THINKING

Knowing how to construct and evaluate definitions is fundamental to critical thinking itself. If we are trying to decide whether to accept or believe some claim or statement, then we need to make sure that we fully understand what the claim or statement means. We may need to analyze it into elements, contrast and compare it with similar claims, and determine what else accepting or believing it would commit us to. If we are presented with several proposals or plans of action, several options for reaching some end, then before we decide on one of them we need to make sure that we understand how the plans differ and how they are similar. What would be

A Practical Guide to Critical Thinking: Deciding What to Do and Believe, Second Edition. David A. Hunter.
© 2014 John Wiley & Sons, Inc. Published 2014 by John Wiley & Sons, Inc.

involved in adopting one of them over the others? What other possible courses of action are there and what would be involved in adopting them instead? Knowing how to clarify meaning by reflecting critically on it is thus fundamental to being a critical thinker.

Second, knowing how to construct and evaluate definitions is fundamental to understanding and fully engaging in an academic discipline. Every discipline or field of study has its own **fundamental concepts**, ideas, and technical terms. The concepts that are basic to biology, for instance, are very different from those that are basic to chemistry or physics. The concepts and ideas that are characteristic of archaeology are very different from those that are fundamental to anthropology or to the literary analysis of drama. These fields of study all have different fundamental concepts even though they may study the very same phenomena. Biology, chemistry, and physics all study living systems (among other things), just as archeologists, anthropologists, and literary theorists might all study ancient Greek tragedy. Different disciplines approach the same phenomena from different perspectives, and these perspectives are defined—or **framed**—by the concepts that are fundamental to each discipline. This difference is part of what makes thinking about living things from a "biological" perspective so different from thinking about them from a physical or sociological one. The same is true of business organizations. Each organization has its own ways of describing its structure and its operations and goals. Participating successfully in an organization requires understanding these concepts, and this requires knowing how to think critically about meaning. Knowing how to critically reflect on the meaning of a discipline or an organization's fundamental concepts is thus fundamental to being able to participate in that discipline or organization.

Finally, knowing how to construct and evaluate a definition is often a fundamental step in solving problems and evaluating reasons for believing something. Sometimes, knowing how to frame or define a problem is half the work needed to solve it. Some problems are so clearly defined from the start that little or no critical refection is required to solve them. Simple arithmetical calculations are like this. We know up front what the problem is (e.g., find the square root of some number), we know what methods are to be used, and we know what kind of answers we are looking for. But for other kinds of problems, it is not clear at the start just what the problem is, or what the best method is for approaching or solving it. With such **open-ended** problems, it might not even be clear what will count as an acceptable solution, and to solve them we may need to think hard about how to formulate the problem. The problems of ending poverty, of rejuvenating American cities, or of designing a university's curriculum to improve student performance are open-ended problems, not because they cannot be solved, but because part of the problem is getting clear on what the problem is. Knowing how to reflect critically on problems with the goal of defining them clearly is thus central to problem solving.

In this chapter, we will study what is involved in reflecting critically on meaning. We will study a practical strategy for constructing and evaluating definitions, whether of concepts, plans, or problems. We will see how this method can be used to understand the fundamental concepts that disciplines use to frame the phenomena they study.

2.2   ASSERTION

It will be helpful to start by drawing attention to some basic facts about language, since we use language to formulate our claims and proposals. Some of the facts we will discuss may seem quite straightforward, but that is OK, since others of them are among the more difficult concepts in this whole book. Discussing them will provide a secure foundation for our later discussions about definitions and fundamental concepts.

Ordinarily, we use complete declarative sentences to say what we believe, to list and present our evidence, and to give our reasons. Here are some examples of complete declarative sentences.

Jones was at the scene of the crime.

Building a bridge across the river will be too costly.

Samantha ought to eat more vegetables.

Rising inflation causes unemployment.

What makes them **declarative** sentences is that they can be used to say something true or false. But not all complete sentences can be used to say something true or false. Here are some complete sentences that cannot be used to say something true or false.

Are oysters delicious?

I baptize you, "David."

I promise to pay you back next week.

Stop!

These are perfectly fine sentences and have their uses, but they cannot be used to claim that something is or is not true. They are used to ask something, to perform a baptism, to make a promise or to issue a command. They cannot be used to state truths. Since our interest in this book is with reasoning that is aimed at truth, we will focus on sentences that can be used to say something that is true.

> To assert something is to claim that it is true. We use a complete declarative sentence to make an assertion.

When we use a complete declarative sentence to say something, we are making an **assertion**. To **assert** something is simply to claim that it is true. If I assert that Toronto is a city in Canada, then I am claiming that it is true that it is a city in Canada. I am, as it were, going out on a limb and making a claim about how things are. But it is important to keep in mind that just as a complete declarative sentence can be false, an assertion can also be false. If someone were to assert that Toronto is a city in the United States, then her assertion would be false. So, an assertion can be true or false.

We make an assertion when we tell someone what we believe. If the witness testifies that Jones was at the scene of the crime, then the witness is expressing his belief by asserting that Jones was there. Of course, one can also assert something without believing it; this is what makes lying possible. When a person knowingly lies, she asserts something that she knows is false: she knowingly making a false assertion. And we assert things when we provide our reasons for our beliefs too. When we state our reasons for believing something, when we collect together our evidence in support of a point of view or proposal, we are making assertions.

Different declarative sentences can be used to assert the very same thing. If I want to assert that John is a liar, I could do it using either of the following sentences.

John is a liar.

John is mendacious.

These sentences are simply different ways of asserting the same thing. They are synonymous. It is a good thing that different sentences can be used to assert the very same thing, since otherwise people who spoke different languages could never say the same things! But it does make our work as critical thinkers a little bit more difficult. For it means that we cannot keep track of what someone is asserting just by keeping track of what sentences they are using. We need to keep an eye on the possibility that they are simply repeating themselves in other words.

A complete declarative sentence can also be used to assert more than one thing. Suppose Jones used the following sentence to make an assertion.

Bill's wife is mad at him.

If we wanted to analyze what Jones asserted, we might come up with the following list.

Bill has a wife.

Bill's wife is mad.

Bill's wife is mad at him.

Each of these things is on our list because each of them is something that Jones was claiming to be true. In saying what he did, Jones asserted several things. Of course, rather than use three sentences, Jones did what we would all do and used a single sentence to assert all of them at once. This is another handy trick made possible by language. But it too makes our work as critical thinkers a bit more difficult, since (as before) it means that keeping track of what someone is asserting is not the same as keeping track of what sentences he is using. If we want to make sure that we know what someone is asserting and—what is just as important—what they are not asserting, we need to know how to analyze their assertions into their parts. After all, if they are giving us reasons to believe something, then each part might be a separate reason, even if they are all packed neatly into one long sentence.

If we do not distinguish one from the other, then we will not really appreciate their reasons. We will return to this important point in a later chapter.

EXERCISE 1

Comprehension Questions (When you answer these questions, pretend that you are explaining or teaching the answer to a friend who is not in the class. Doing that will force you to put in LOTS more background information than you would if you were trying to answer them for your instructor.).

 A. What is it to assert something?
 B. Is a prediction of some future event an assertion? Explain using an example.
 C. Could the word, "Yes," be used all on its own to make an assertion? If so, use an example to illustrate.
 D. Could a false sentence be used to make an assertion? Use an example to illustrate.
 E. Do you have to believe what you assert? Explain using an example.
 F. Compose a sentence that asserts more than three things.
 G. Compose a sentence that asserts only one thing.
 H. How many things are asserted in the following sentences:
    a. The Earth orbits the Sun quickly.
    b. Can I have another cookie?
    c. I think that cookies are delicious.
    d. I love you!

2.3   THE ASSERTION TEST

We saw that a person can assert more than one thing when they use a declarative sentence. If the sentence is complicated enough, they can be asserting lots and lots of things. It will be helpful to have a way to figure out exactly which things a person is asserting when they say something. In this section we will study a simple strategy for figuring this out. We will call it the **assertion test**.

We know that to assert something is to claim that it is true. So if we want to figure out how many things a person is asserting we need to ask how many things she is claiming to be true. It will be useful to have a bit of terminology. Instead of saying that the person would be asserting some "thing," let us say that she would be asserting a **proposition**. A proposition is something that is true or false, that can be believed or denied, that one can know to be true, or that one can imagine, suppose, wonder or consider to be true. We can use complete declarative sentences to formulate propositions—that means, we put propositions into linguistic form using complete declarative sentences. Using this terminology, we can now put our question this way: how can we figure out which propositions a person is asserting when she says something (or: how many propositions does a certain sentence formulate?).

Let us start with a relatively easy case. Consider the following sentence.

Toronto is in Canada and Buffalo is in the United States.

This sentence is a **conjunction**. That means that it is a sentence containing the word "and." In this conjunction we can identify two complete declarative sentences joined by that "and."

(i) Toronto is in Canada
(ii) Buffalo is in the United States.

We can call the sentences connected by the "and" the "conjuncts" of that conjunction and each conjunct formulates a proposition. Someone saying this complex sentence would be asserting two propositions, one for each conjunct. She would be asserting both the propositions that Toronto is in Canada and that Buffalo is in the United States. She would be claiming that both those propositions are true. This means that the conjunction she is asserting would be false if either of those propositions were false. Since she is asserting both, both have to be true for her overall assertion to be true.

We can use this example to introduce the assertion test. Suppose that someone is saying something and we want to figure out whether she is asserting a certain proposition. Let us call that proposition "P." To decide whether she is asserting P, we start by supposing that the proposition that P is false. This can be tricky, because sometimes when we use this test, we may already believe or even know that P is in fact true. Still, we want to suppose *for the sake of figuring out what the person asserted*, that the proposition is false. Next, we ask the following question: *could her assertion be true if P were false.* If the answer is Yes, then she did not assert P. If the answer is No, then she did assert P.

The idea behind the test is this. To assert a proposition is to claim that it is true. So if a person's assertion could be true even if a certain proposition were false, then she did not assert that proposition. That proposition could not be part of what she asserted if her assertion could be true even if that proposition were true. On the other hand, if the answer is no—that is, if her assertion would be false if that proposition were false—then that proposition was one of the things that she asserted.

To tell whether a person asserted a proposition, ask whether what she said could be true even if that proposition were false.

If Yes, then she did not assert it.
If No, then she did assert it.

The assertion test will prove enormously useful not only with definitions but in later chapters too. But it is a bit tricky to use. For it requires us to first suppose that one proposition is false and then consider whether another proposition could be true.

This little bit of mental gymnastics is tricky. But it is enormously valuable, and will come in handy in several different sections of this book. In fact, after teaching critical thinker for over a decade, I am inclined to think that being able to do this bit of mental gymnastics is the single most important critical thinking skill there is.

Let us see how the assertion test works in the conjunction case. Recall that we had the following conjunction.

Toronto is in Canada and Buffalo is in the United States.

> When we use a conjunction to make an assertion, we assert all the conjuncts.

Suppose that Jane said this, and suppose that we wanted to know whether in saying this she was asserting the proposition that Toronto really is in Canada. To use the assertion test, we first suppose, *just for the sake of the test*, that the proposition that Toronto is in Canada is false (To help with this, let us suppose that Toronto is a city is Mexico.). Now we ask the following: could what Jane said be true even if the proposition that Toronto is in Canada were false. (That is, could what Jane said be true even if Toronto were a city in Mexico?) The answer is No. If that proposition were false, then what she said would be false too. For she is claiming that Toronto is in Canada. In other words, the assertion test confirms what we already knew about this case: Jane asserted the proposition that Toronto is in Canada.

That case was relatively straightforward. Here is a slightly more difficult one. Suppose that Emily said the following.

Either Calgary is in Alberta or Calgary is in Saskatchewan.

This sentence is a **disjunction**, which just means that it is a sentence containing the word "or." We can again identify two complete declarative sentences, though in this case they are joined by an "or." We call them *disjuncts*. For each declarative sentence we can identify a proposition: the **proposition that Calgary is in Alberta** and the **proposition that Calgary is in Saskatchewan**. Let us use the assertion test to see whether Emily asserted those propositions.

> When we use a disjunction to make an assertion, we do not assert either disjunct. Rather, we assert that at least one of the disjuncts is true.

Start with the proposition that Calgary is in Alberta. To use the assertion test, we first suppose that it is false. Now we ask: could what Emily said be true even if that proposition were false? The answer is Yes. All it takes for what she said to be true is for *one or the other* of its disjuncts to be true. **They do not both need to be true**. The same goes, of course, for the other disjunct. So in saying what she did, Emily did not assert either of those two propositions. She did not claim that Calgary is in Alberta and she did not claim that Calgary is in Saskatchewan. Instead, she asserted something much more complicated: she asserted that one or the other (or perhaps both) of the disjuncts is true, but that is not the same as asserting either disjunct.

Now consider the following **conditional**.

If Stephen Harper is the Prime Minister of Canada, then the Prime Minister of Canada is male.

A conditional is a sentence containing an "if." As with "and" and "or," we use "if" to connect together two declarative sentences, each of which formulates a proposition. The sentence following the "if" formulates the *antecedent* (in this case, the antecedent is the proposition that Stephen Harper is Prime Minister (PM) of Canada.). The proposition following the "then" formulates the *consequent* (in this case, the consequent is the proposition that the PM of Canada is male.).

Suppose that Miranda says that sentence. Let us use the assertion test to see whether she asserted the antecedent. To use the test, we first suppose that Stephen Harper is not the PM of Canada. Next, we ask the following: could what Miranda said still be true, even if that antecedent is false? In other words, could it still be true that if Stephen Harper is the PM of Canada, then the PM of Canada is male? The answer is Yes, and that could still be true. Even if he were not in fact the PM, it would still be true that *if he were, then the PM of Canada would be male.* So this shows that in saying what she did, Miranda did not assert that Stephen Harper is the PM of Canada.

Now let us consider the consequent. Suppose that the PM of Canada is not male. Would it still be true that if Harper had been the PM, then the PM of Canada would in that case have been male? Again, the answer is Yes.

> When we use a conditional to make an assertion, we do not assert the antecedent or the consequent. Rather, we assert that the truth of the antecedent is sufficient for the truth of the consequent.

This shows that when we say something with a conditional we do not assert either the antecedent or the consequent. Rather, we are asserting that a complex logical relation holds between the antecedent and the consequent; roughly, that if the antecedent were true, the consequent would be true too. In Chapter 5 we will look in a lot more detail at this logical relation. Conditionals play an essential role in our reasoning using definitions and in our reasoning about causal relations among events (which we will study in Chapter 5). But for now, keep in mind that when we say something with a conditional we are not claiming that the antecedent is true and we are not claiming that the consequent is true.

So far, we have seen that disjunctions and conditionals do not assert all of the propositions we are formulated in them. There is a final case that is worth noting. Consider the following two sentences.

Joan believes (said) that Stephen Harper is the PM of Canada.

Joan knows that Stephen Harper is the PM of Canada.

Both sentences contain **propositional noun clause**. A propositional noun clause is just a complete declarative sentence prefixed with the word "that." We use noun clauses like that to talk about propositions. We do this when we want to say, for instance, what a person said, or believes, or knows, or remembers.

Our two examples involve the same propositional noun clause. The proposition is that Stephen Harper is the PM of Canada. Now we can ask our question: Is that proposition asserted in either sentence? Again, we can use our assertion test to answer the question.

Let us start with the first sentence. Suppose that Ethan says it. Did he assert that Stephen Harper is the PM of Canada? That is, in saying that, did he claim that it is true that Stephen Harper is PM of Canada? Using the assertion test, let us first suppose that the proposition that Stephen Harper is PM of Canada is false. Next, we ask the following: could what Ethan said be true even if that proposition is false? That is, could it still be true that Joan believes (or said) that he is? The answer is Yes. She might believe it or say it even if it was not true. We all know from personal experience that it is possible to speak or believe false things, though we all try to avoid this. So in using this sentence, Ethan was asserting that Stephen Harper is the PM of Canada.

An assertion made with a sentence containing a propositional noun clause does not always assert that proposition.

With the following verbs, the proposition is **not** asserted:

"believes that," "hopes that," "thinks that," "says that," "asserts that."

With these verbs, the proposition **is** asserted:

"knows that," "remembers that," "proves that," "sees that."

What about the second sentence? Suppose that Artemis says it. Did Artemis assert that Stephen Harper is the PM of Canada? Artemis said that Joan knows that Stephen Harper is the PM of Canada. Could it be true that Jane *knows* that Harper is the PM of Canada even if, as we are supposing, he was not the PM of Canada? Here the answer has got to be No. If a person knows something, then she is right. So in using that second sentence, Artemis did assert that Stephen Harper is the PM of Canada.

The assertion test is a bit tricky to use. It requires supposing something to be false, and then asking whether something else could still be true. This requires imagination and flexibility. But knowing how to tell what is being asserted and what is not is fundamental to critical thinking.

EXERCISE 2

A. Comprehension Questions. (When you answer these questions, pretend that you are explaining or teaching the answer to a friend who is not in the class. Doing that will force you to put in LOTS more background information than you would if you were trying to answer them for your instructor.).

  a. What is an assertion?

  b. What is a conditional?

    c. What is the difference between a disjunction and a conjunction?

    d. What is a non-asserted noun-clause?

    e. Can you use a disjunction to make an assertion? Give an example?

    f. Could a disjunction be true if both of its disjuncts were false?

    g. Could a conjunction be true if one of its disjuncts was false?

    h. Using the concepts we have been discussing, explain why there is something wrong with using the following sentence to make an assertion: "It is now raining, but I do not believe that it is now raining."

B. What is asserted in the following?

    a. Susan sold Peter the chips and he ate them all.

    b. Either the cook is angry or her spices are hooter than usual.

    c. The restaurant was pretty disappointing: the fish was overcooked, the sauces were boring and the service was terrible.

    d. Padma told me that her mother is coming to town.

    e. Harry knows that Voldemort is back.

    f. The First City Bank has gone bankrupt and will be closing its doors next Monday, according to bank officials.

    g. The United Nations military intervention in Africa has produced more harm than good and has not achieved any of its main objectives, reports a local think tank.

C. For each of the following propositions, construct three complex sentences that formulate it but do not assert it.

    a. Oysters are delicious.

    b. Sam believes that oysters are delicious.

    c. Johannes knows that oysters are delicious.

D. Look at today's newspaper and find three letters to the editor. List all of the assertions made in each one.

2.4 CONSTRUCTING AND EVALUATING DEFINITIONS

Knowing how to construct and evaluate definitions is crucial to critical thinking. We are all familiar with what happens when people mean different things by their words. If two friends are having a discussion about whether it is bad to be jealous, but they mean different things by "jealousy," then their discussion is not going to be very productive, especially if they do not even realize they mean different things. For maybe if each realized that the other means something different by it, then they might discover that they in fact agree on more than they thought. Thinking critically about political speeches and about advertisements regularly requires thinking about the meanings of the being words. Words like "unemployment" and "productivity" are technical words with very special definitions. In this section we will study a method for constructing and evaluating definitions. We will call it the SEEC method.

When we think of definitions we probably think first of the definitions of words and ideas. But we can also define plans and problems. To define something is just to make it clear, to distinguish it from other things with which it might be easily confused, and we can make just about anything clear. As we noted at the outset of this chapter, knowing how to construct and evaluate a definition is fundamental to critical thinking. Whether we are trying to decide whether to believe some assertion, whether to adopt some course of action, or how best to solve some problem, we have to make sure that we have a clear understanding of what the claim, course of action or problem is. And this means that we have to know how to define it. In this section we will study a practical, SEEC method for constructing a definition and we will apply it in several cases.

CRITICAL THINKING IN CRIMINAL JUSTICE

How many child kidnappings would you say there are every year in all of the United States? According to the National Criminal Information Center (NCIC) database, over 800,000![1] That is 2,000 kidnappings every week. That is more than the population of many American towns. Indeed, it is more than the entire population of Vermont, Wyoming, South Dakota, North Dakota, and Alaska. But what do they mean by "child kidnapping." It turns out that according to the NCIC definition, child kidnapping includes: abductions by a family member, abductions by someone other than a family member, runaways, abandoned children, and lost or otherwise missing children. Most of these would not ordinarily be counted as kidnappings. In fact, of the cases that NCIC included as child kidnappings, only 115 were stereotypical kidnappings: a non-family abduction perpetrated by a slight acquaintance or stranger in which a child is detained overnight, transported at least 50 miles, held for ransom or abducted with the intent to keep the child permanently or killed. This puts a very different face on the facts. The point here is not that the 800,000 cases are not serious or troubling or even tragic, but only that if we do not know what is meant by "child kidnapping" we will not know what to make of that number.

Here is a four-step method for constructing and evaluating definitions. First, a good definition will formulate the meaning as clearly and simply as possible. This can usually take the form of a short **slogan** composed of key words. Second, a good definition will **elaborate** on that slogan by filling in some of the detail that it will inevitably leave out. The elaboration might say something about how the different key words in the slogan are related one to another. This should take no more than a few sentences. Third, a good definition will provide an **example** or two, depending on the complexity of what is being defined. The example could be from real life or it could be fictional, so long as it is clear and uncontroversial. Fourth, a good definition will mention some **contrasting** ideas or concepts, one that might easily be confused for what is being defined. Put together, these four steps make up the SEEC method for defining something (We use it to SEEC clarity!). Let us look at each part in more detail.

2.5   GIVE A SLOGAN

Suppose that Matthias is trying to give a definition of an apple pie. (Maybe he had agreed to buy us one at the store, and he wanted to make sure he did not come home with the wrong thing.) So he wants to make sure that we mean by "apple pie" the same thing that he means by it. Using our SEEC method, he starts by giving us a slogan.

Ideally, the slogan should say, as clearly and briefly as possible, what it is for something to be an apple pie. We can think of the slogan as like a rule or a recipe that we can use to decide whether something is or is not an apple pie. In principle, we should be able to use the slogan as we walk through the grocery store to figure out, for each and every thing in the store, whether or not it is an apple pie. So it should be true of each and every apple pie, and it should not be true of anything that is not an apple pie. We can be a bit more precise about what this demand comes to.

Matthias' slogan should state what is **necessary** for being an apple pie. Something is necessary for being an apple pie when a thing has to have it to be an apple pie. Without it, the thing could not be an apple pie. For instance, containing apple is necessary for being an apple pie. Nothing has been, will be, or ever could be an apple pie unless it has some apple in it. The apple can be sliced, diced, or pureed. It probably does not matter what form the apple takes. But to be an apple pie, a thing has to contain apple. This just is part of what it is for something to be an apple pie. Maybe having a bottom crust is also necessary. Perhaps having a top crust is also necessary (My father used to claim that containing extra-sharp cheddar cheese was also needed—but I am not so sure he was right about that!).

Suppose that Matthias has listed several things that are needed for something to be an apple pie. Suppose he offers the following proposed slogan:

> An apple pie contains apple.

A definition's slogan is too broad when it leaves out a necessary condition.

Is his slogan correct? Has he given us enough information? Can we use that as a rule or a recipe to figure out which things in the store are apple pies and which things are not? Well, we can use it to figure out that a porterhouse steak is not an apple pie. But if that was all we had to go on, then we might come home with an apple donut, or a jar of apple sauce. So Matthias' slogan does give us enough information. Though it does state one necessary condition, it does not state enough of them. It leaves off some of the things that are needed for being an apple pie. In other words, his proposed slogan is **too broad**.

Suppose that Matthias revises his slogan to the following:

> An apple pie contains apples, a crust, and cinnamon

A definition's slogan is too narrow when it includes a condition that is not necessary.

He has added some more conditions to his slogan. But now we can ask the following: is containing cinnamon really necessary for being an apple pie? I do not think so. It seems to me that something could be an apple pie even if it did not contain any cinnamon at al. (It might not be a *delicious* apple pie, but that is a different matter.) So, Matthias' revised slogan includes something that is not necessary for being an apple pie. In other words, his slogan is **too narrow**.

Suppose, at last, that Matthias offers us the following slogan:

An apple pie is a baked pastry with a top and a bottom crust that contains apple.

And let us suppose that he is right, and that this is a correct definition of an apple pie. He has identified several things that are needed for something to be an apple pie: being baked; having a top crust; having a bottom crust; containing apple. Though each of these things is necessary for being an apple pie, none of them is enough all by itself. All four are needed for something to be an apple pie. And together, they are all that is needed. In other words, together, those four conditions are **sufficient** for being an apple pie. Anything that meets those four conditions is guaranteed to be an apple pie.

A definition's slogan should state conditions that are individually necessary and jointly sufficient.

We have seen that something can be necessary *without being sufficient*. Containing apple is necessary for being an apple pie, but it is not sufficient. It is not enough. Something can be both necessary and sufficient at once. To see this, let us change examples. Consider the concept of being a millionaire. Owning at least one million dollars is sufficient for being a millionaire. That would be enough money to make a person a millionaire. It is also necessary; to be a millionaire you need to own at least one million dollars. So owning at least a million dollars is necessary and sufficient for being a millionaire. Now, suppose that Sergio owns 100 million dollars. That would make him a millionaire. So owning 100 million dollars is sufficient for being a millionaire. But it is not necessary. Owning that much money is more than enough. So something can be sufficient and yet not necessary. (Here is another example: getting an A is sufficient to pass this course, but it is not necessary, since a student who gets a C will also pass.)

A slogan can be **both too broad and too narrow**. Consider again the definition the NCIC used when they reported that there were 800,000 child kidnappings in the United States during 2005. Many of us would say that their definition is too broad. We would not include running away from home as a kind of kidnapping. This means that the NCIC's definition left off something that we consider necessary for being a child kidnapping. But notice that their definition of a "stereotypical kidnapping" might be too narrow as well, for it requires that the child be transported at least 50 miles from home. I doubt that most of us would consider that really necessary for a kidnapping. The NCIC's definition of "child kidnapping" was, by ordinary standards anyway, both too narrow and too broad.

PRACTICAL STRATEGY: LOOK FOR COUNTEREXAMPLES

An important step in constructing or evaluating a proposed definition is looking for **counterexamples**. A counterexample is a case, either a real one or a fictional one, that shows that the slogan is either too broad or too narrow. If you think that someone's proposed slogan is too broad or too narrow, then you need to present a counterexample. If, someone presents a counterexample to a slogan you proposed, then you must either (i) show that it is not a genuine counterexample or (ii) revise the slogan.

How bad is it for a proposed definition to be too broad or too narrow compared with our ordinary standards? While it would be good if we all had exactly the same necessary and sufficient conditions in mind when we use our words, this is not very likely. Most of us use our words in **idiosyncratic** ways, ways that are just a little bit different from the way others use them. But for practical purposes, the existence of these differences is not important, so long as we are all aware of them. It is less important that we all agree that a definition captures our own idiosyncratic usage than that we all agree on what we will mean by it for **the purposes at hand**. If we can agree, either just for the sake of the discussion or for good, on what we mean by "child kidnapping," then this will make it easier to avoid misunderstandings when we start to say what the facts are. Definitions can report actual usage, but they can also help to standardize it. Both are worthwhile goals.

It is also good for our words to remain **flexible** to deal with new or unanticipated uses. Sometimes it is better to hold off on being too precise in specifying necessary and sufficient conditions because more research and investigation may be needed before we can decide whether something really is a referent of some word. It took biologists a long time to figure out whether whales fit the definition of a *fish*, and only recently did astronomers decide that Pluto does not fit the definition of *planet*. Making these decisions required finding out more about whales and planets, and thinking hard about what we *want* our words to mean. We usually want our words to leave room to deal with unanticipated uses. Laws, for instance, are usually written so as to leave room for unexpected cases. We rely on judges and lawyers to help us decide how best to apply our words and concepts in cases that the legislators who wrote the laws could not have anticipated. If the words had no flexibility at all, if we insisted on necessary and sufficient conditions from the very start, then we would not know how to describe these new cases. Biologists want their concept of a *species* to be flexible enough to let them describe new phenomena in terms of species. Astronomers decided to adjust the definition of "planet" even though it meant deciding that Pluto was not a planet after all, because they believe that the new definition allowed them to better say the things they wanted to say all along.

EXERCISE 3

Comprehension Questions. (When you answer these questions, pretend that you are explaining or teaching the answer to a friend who is not in the class. Doing that will force you to put in LOTS more background information than you would if you were trying to answer it for your instructor.)

a. What is the difference between a necessary and a sufficient condition?

b. Could a necessary condition also be a sufficient one? If so, give an example.

c. Could a sufficient condition also be necessary? If so, explain using the concepts we have discussed in this chapter, and give an example.

d. Explain how a condition that is sufficient might not also be necessary. Give an example to illustrate your answer.

e. If you assert that Jones is a millionaire, are you also asserting that Jones meets all of the conditions that are necessary for being a millionaire? Are you asserting that Jones meets all of the conditions that are sufficient? Explain.

f. What conditions are necessary and sufficient for a conjunction to be true? What about for a disjunction to be true?

2.6   EXPAND ON THE SLOGAN

The initial statement of the meaning should be as succinct as possible. Look back at the definition we discussed in Chapter 1 of "knowledge." We said that according to the traditional philosophical definition, knowledge is justified, true belief. This is about as succinct and slogan-like as possible. We could even make it into a bumper sticker! But it would be wrong to leave it at that, since there is still plenty of room for misunderstanding. It would be good to expand on the slogan by filling in details and by saying how the concepts used in the slogan are related to one another.

In the case of the definition of *knowledge*, it would be especially helpful to say more about what belief, justification, and truth are, and how they are related to the other two. We discussed these issues at great length in Chapter 1. But in a brief definition, it might be enough simply to say something like this:

> Knowledge is justified, true belief. To know something, you have to believe that it is the case; if you do not believe it, then you do not know it. But to count as knowledge, your belief also has to be based on enough evidence. That is, it has to be justified. Finally, your belief has to be true. These three necessary conditions are independent of one another. A true belief might be unjustified; a justified belief might be false; and a person might fail to believe something true even though they have excellent reason to believe it. All three are needed, and together they are sufficient, for knowledge.

This elaboration of the brief statement of the meaning of *knowledge* fills in the missing details, by making it clearer what is meant by "justification," and by saying something about how those three key terms are related one to the other.

2.7   GIVE EXAMPLES

It is almost always helpful to provide some examples. But it is not always easy to know which examples to select. Since the goal of providing a definition is to secure common understanding, the example has to be as non-controversial as possible. This means that it has to be one that everyone involved in the discussion will agree fits the slogan provided. If in constructing a definition you use an example that some people think does not fit, this will only make it harder to secure shared understanding. Remember that the goal is to reach agreement on how to talk about the facts in order to focus on disagreements about the facts themselves.

If the elaboration involves identifying and relating several concepts, as our example above does, then it would be useful to provide examples showing how the concepts are related. For instance, it would be good to supplement the elaboration of our definition of knowledge with an example of someone who has a true belief that is not justified enough for knowledge, or someone who has a false belief that is nonetheless based on pretty good evidence. The examples could be from real life, so long as everyone involves knows the story. But the example could also be fictional. The goal is always to secure mutual agreement on how the language is to be used.

With examples, more detail is almost always better. Suppose one wanted to give an example of a false but justified belief. Here is one.

A child's belief that Santa Claus exists.

We all recognize the idea. But there is not enough in it to make it clear that it really is a case of a justified false belief. It would therefore be better to say the following.

> Suppose that little Joan believes that Santa Claus exists, and believes it because her Mom and Dad have told her that he does, and that he brings presents every year. Joan's belief is justified, since it is based on her parent's testimony and, in general, it is reasonable to believe what your parents say unless you have good reason to doubt them. But her belief is false, since Santa does not exist. So, this is a case of a false but justified belief.

This example is laid out in much more detail, and the detail also makes it really clear how it is an example of what it is supposed to be an example of.

2.8   IDENTIFY CONTRASTING IDEAS

Finally, in giving a definition it is usually helpful to contrast the concept being defined with other related ones. It is best to focus on concepts that others are likely to confuse for the one you are defining. Since nobody confuses a concept for its opposite, it is usually not very useful to identify the contradictory concept. Indeed, it is not always very clear what the opposite is. What is the opposite of knowledge? Is it false belief, or is unjustified belief the opposite of belief? What is the opposite of murder? It is much likely that someone will confuse murder with killing in self-defense or with killing by mistake than with the opposite of murder. It is more likely that someone will confuse child kidnapping with a child's agreeing to run away with a non-custodial parent. Those are the misunderstandings and confusions that definitions are intended to prevent or remedy. In the case of our definition of knowledge, it is better to contrast knowledge with certainty or with consensus opinion, or with mutual agreement. Once again, though, if one chooses as contrasting concepts ones whose meaning is controversial, then the definition will fail to prevent or remedy misunderstanding. The point of working hard to develop a definition is to resolve and avoid misunderstanding, not to generate it.

EXERCISE 4

A. Comprehension Questions. (When you answer these questions, pretend that you are explaining or teaching the answer to a friend who is not in the class. Doing that will force you to put in LOTS more background information than you would if you were trying to explain it to your instructor.)

   a. What is the purpose of providing a definition?

   b. What is a counterexample? What are counterexamples used for?

   c. When is it acceptable for a definition not to identify necessary and sufficient conditions? Explain why.

   d. What is it for a slogan to be too broad? Give an example.

   e. What is it for a slogan to be too narrow? Give an example.

B. For the following proposed definitions, find a counterexample. Identify whether it shows that the definition is too broad or too narrow.

   a. Oxygen: a colorless and odorless gas.

   b. Apple pie: a dessert made with apples

   c. Triangle: a three-sided two-dimensional figure with a 90-degree angle.

   d. Violin: a stringed instrument

   e. Parent: the father or mother of a human.

   f. Stove: a kitchen appliance used for cooking.

C. Here is a definition of "murder" from the online dictionary **The Free Dictionary** by Farlex. (http://legal-dictionary.thefreedictionary.com/murder). (i) What does it claim is necessary and sufficient for first-degree murder? (ii) Identify the examples it provides. (iii) Identify the contrasting concepts it provides.

> **murder** n. the killing of a human being by a sane person, with intent, malice aforethought (prior intention to kill the particular victim or anyone who gets in the

way), and with no legal excuse or authority. In those clear circumstances, this is first-degree murder. By statute many states make killings in which there is torture, movement of the person (kidnapping) before the killing, as an incident to another crime (as during a hold-up or rape), and the death of a police officer or prison guard all first-degree murders with or without premeditation, and with malice presumed. Second-degree murder is such a killing without premeditation, as in the heat of passion or in a sudden quarrel or fight. Malice in second-degree murder may be implied from a death due to the reckless lack of concern for the life of others (such as firing a gun into a crowd, or bashing someone with any deadly weapon). Depending on the circumstances and state laws, murder in the first or second degree may be chargeable to a person who did not actually kill, but was involved in a crime with a partner who actually did the killing or someone died as the result of the crime. (Example: In a liquor store stick-up in which the clerk shoots back at the hold-up man and kills a bystander, the armed robber can be convicted of at least second-degree murder. To be murder the victim must die within a year of the attack. Death of an unborn child who is "quick" (fetus is moving) can be murder, provided there was premeditation, malice, and no legal authority. Thus, abortion is not murder under the law. (Example: Jack Violent shoots his pregnant girlfriend, killing the fetus). Manslaughter, both voluntary and involuntary, lacks the element of malice aforethought.

D. For the following concepts, compare and contrast the definitions provided in three dictionaries.

   a. Automobile

   b. Water

   c. Tiger

   d. Honesty

   e. Knowledge

   f. To eat

   g. The tango

E. Using the SEEC method, formulate definitions for the following.

   a. Donut

   b. Apple

   c. Honesty

   d. Regret

   e. Chair

   f. Planet

2.9 THINKING CRITICALLY ABOUT FRAMEWORKS

Different disciplines are in part defined by the concepts they use to describe, explain, and raise questions about the phenomena they study. Even though geologists and physicists are both interested in earthquakes, they think about earthquakes in different ways. Likewise, even though sociologists and psychologists are interested in family dynamics, they typically employ different concepts for describing, explaining, and raising questions about family life. They employ different **frameworks**, even though they are thinking about the very same phenomena. A framework is simply a set of concepts and methods that define a specific perspective or point of view. Different frameworks allow for different ways of describing, explaining, and raising questions about a phenomenon. Engaging in a discipline requires understanding and being able to think with its framework. Thinking critically while engaging in a discipline requires reflecting on that discipline's framework, on the way its set of concepts is used to describe, organize, and think about the phenomena it studies.

As we saw above in our discussion of necessary and sufficient conditions, it is not always possible to provide a neat definition of a technical term. Often, this is not even desirable. We often want some flexibility in our concepts, to allow us to respond to new evidence and new discoveries in new ways. This is one reason that it is helpful when providing a definition of a discipline's key concepts to provide examples and contrasts, since providing those can do as much as necessary and sufficient conditions to prevent or remedy misunderstanding.

Let us consider an example: the case of cancer. We can theorize about cancer from many different perspectives. If we think of it from a molecular perspective, then we need to use the concepts of molecular biology to describe cancer. This will include thinking in terms of genes and proteins, and the kinds of processes, structures, and chemical interactions that occur at that level. We can also think of cancer at the cellular level, in terms of the actions and processes that cancerous cells undergo, and how cancerous cells differ from other kinds of cells; or we can think of cancer at the level of the entire organism, in terms of the animal's internal, systemic responses to cancer and to the operation of the nervous, immune, and reproductive systems. We can also think of it from a sociological level, in terms of how cancer affects family, work, and community relations. In moving from one perspective to another, we are able to describe, explain, and understand aspects of the phenomena that we cannot "see" from the other levels. The other levels lack the vocabulary for describing those aspects.

The feature of frameworks that make them valuable—that they allow us to think about a phenomenon in one clearly defined set of concepts—is also the feature that makes them limiting. There is nothing inherently wrong with this. But it is a mistake to get **stuck in a framework.** This is the mistake of not realizing that there are other perspectives on a given phenomenon, problem, or issue. We need to keep in mind that there are always different perspectives on any phenomena, issue, or problem. Indeed, changing perspectives can sometimes lead to solutions to problems that were first identified but could not be solved at a different perspective. If we were not able to think about cancer at the genetic level, our understanding of the causes of cancer would be very much poorer than it is. This is so, even though not everything about its causes can be learned at that level. Sometimes, we need to think about a phenomenon from several different perspectives at once. A doctor who discusses a patient's cancer only at the cellular level and not also at the sociological or psychological perspectives will not provide a complete treatment. If we think of the problem of urban poverty only from a sociological perspective and not also from the perspective of criminal justice or micro-economics, we are likely to miss or overlook features of the problem that are hard to see from the sociological perspective alone.

PRACTICAL STRATEGY: RULE OF THREES

When trying to define a problem, it is helpful to think about it from at least three different perspectives. This is especially important when assessing the costs and benefits of a proposed course of action. Deciding how to respond to global warming requires thinking about the problem from economic, fiscal, environmental, employment, and political perspectives, just to name a few.

Sometimes, politicians and interest groups use one framework rather than another when describing a proposed or existing policy in order to influence the public's attitudes toward that policy. The very same policy is called by one side "drilling for oil" but the other calls it "energy exploration." In principle, there is nothing wrong with a policy's being described in different frameworks, since, as we have seen, most policies and problems are multi-dimensional. The search for oil reserves has environmental and economic aspects as well as impacts on employment, on pollution, on the broader economy, on energy conservation, and on national security, just to name a few. It would be wrong to decide on a policy without having examined it (and its alternatives) from all these sides. There is no privileged perspective. So there is nothing in principle wrong with a policy's being framed in different ways by different politicians or interest groups. But it is a mistake on our part if we fail to realize which framework the policy is being presented to us from within. It is always a mistake to get **stuck in a framework**.

EXERCISE 5

A. For each of the following familiar problems, frame them in the specified way. Your goal is simply to describe the problem using the concepts that are central to the relevant field, not to offer solutions to it.

a. The high rates of teenage pregnancy (economic and emotional).

b. Religious intolerance (economic and cultural).

c. Adolescent drug use (physiological and psychological).

d. Online file sharing of music and movies (economic and cultural).

2.10 CLARIFYING BELIEFS AND PROBLEMS

We sometimes have to clarify beliefs and opinions or get clearer about problems that we face. The need to define our beliefs and opinions and our problems is sometimes hidden by the fact that we so often use simple "Yes/No" questions to find out what other people think and we use simple sentences to tell them what we think, even on topics that we all know are very complicated and controversial. Public opinion surveys regularly ask people whether they support this or that government policy or proposal, and the pollsters are looking for a Yes/No answer. "Do you support the war in Iraq?" "Do you support a person's right to own guns?" But we know that our opinions on most topics are very complex. What is more, even when we agree, we might have different reasons for agreeing. On really complex topics—abortion, capital punishment, and teenage drug use—there is room for huge difference in what we believe. But there is just as much room for differences in our reasons even when we believe the same thing. One can support capital punishment for economic reasons, or for political reasons, or out of concern for deterrence or simply because one believes that it provides the most appropriate punishment. The same is true in the case of problems. People who agree that some phenomena is a problem might disagree about what makes it a problem, and in some ways this is even more important than their agreement on its being a problem. We hear people talk about "the problem of illegal immigration," or "the problem of underage drinking," as if everyone who agrees that those name a problem agree on just what the problem is. In this section, we will study ways to clarify our opinions and beliefs and our problems.

We can use the SEEC method to help us to clarify our opinions and the propositions we believe. The basic approach is the very same as with definitions of concepts. It is good to find a neat, brief way to formulate our opinion, and then provide an elaboration of it, focusing on some of the key words and concepts. In some cases, it will be helpful to provide some examples, though in others it will not. In all cases, or at least cases at all interesting, it will be good to mention a few contrasting propositions, ones that are likely someone might think is the one you have in mind even though it is not. Here is an example of the use of the SEEC method to define a proposition believed.

> I believe that lying to friends is always wrong. I think you have a moral duty to answer sincerely when your friends ask you questions. Telling them something that you do not really believe is just wrong. If a friend asks for my opinion on their career choice, I should take their request for my opinion and advice seriously, and tell them what I really think. If a friend asks me for my opinion on which flat screen TV to buy I should be honest with him. I do not mean that you always have to say everything that is on your mind. I think that it is sometimes better to wait until they ask for your opinion before giving it. But if a friend asks you a question it would be morally wrong not to answer it sincerely.

In this example, the first sentence states the view in a brief, slogan-like way. The next two sentences elaborate on it, by making it clear that it is moral wrongness that is at issue, and just what the author has in mind by "lying." The next two sentences provide a couple of examples to help show what the author has in mind. The final three sentences work to contrast the author's view with views that are pretty similar but different in important ways. It might still happen, of course, that someone misunderstands the author's view. But if the author has worked hard to make her view as clear as she can, then she will have done her duty as a critical thinker to clarify her view. Notice that in this passage the author does not provide any evidence at all for her opinion. She makes no effort to try to convince you that she is right that lying to friends is always wrong. Her goal is not to convince you that she is right, but merely to make it clear what her belief is. She is clarifying what it is that she believes, and not offering reasons for why she does or anyone else ought to believe it.

PRACTICAL STRATEGY: ASK OPEN-ENDED CLARIFICATION QUESTIONS

When discussing topics with other people, ask them open-ended questions, not questions that allow a "Yes" or "No" answer. This will reduce the risk that superficial agreement will mask interesting and deep differences. Instead of asking:

"Do you think that ... "
"Do you agree that ... "

Ask:

"Why do you think that .... "
"What do you mean by ... "
"What reasons are there for thinking that ... "

Depending on what the proposition is, you might not need to provide an example. Here is an attempt to define a belief that does not involve an example, and where it is not obvious what an example would be like.

> The Montreal Canadiens are the best team in NHL history. I do not mean that they have always won the Stanley Cup, or even always made it in to the playoffs. I know that they often struggled. I also do not mean that they have always had the best players, which they plainly have not. I mean that they have the best management, coaches, and fan support system in the entire history of the NHL. They are simply the best-run team ever.

In this example, the author does not provide an example, but she does work hard to contrast what she means by "best team" with several other things that someone might take her to mean. Notice also that she offers those contrasts right after she provides the initial slogan statement of the belief. This is very helpful in this case, since it sets her up in an elegant way to offer the elaborations of her view. The SEEC method should not be thought of as a rigid formula. It is a helpful guide for thinking about what sorts of things to include when trying to clarify your meaning.

We can also use the SEEC method to help clarify our view on what makes something a problem. Here is an example.

> I agree that illegal immigration is a real problem, but I see no problem with legal immigration. Illegal immigrants are people who live in the United States but do not have legal authorization to be here. That is what makes them illegal. I do not think that legal

immigrants are a problem. We should encourage more of them to come to work and live here. Some illegal immigrants are from Mexico, but illegal immigrants can come from all over the world and they pose a problem no matter where they come from. It is not especially Mexican immigrants that I think are a problem. Some people think that illegal immigrants are a problem because they think illegal immigrants are criminals. I am not sure about that. In my view, illegal immigration is a problem because once someone is here illegally we cannot find them to see if we can help them become legal and so help them to make a lasting contribution to our community. This is what makes it a problem.

The author starts by stating his opinion that illegal immigration is a problem, and then in the next few sentences tries to explain what he means by "illegal" and contrasts his view with other closely related ones. Again, he does not offer examples of illegal immigrants though he does in the final sentence mention one thing that he thinks makes being an illegal immigrant a problem. There is a fine line in this passage between clarifying your view and providing reasons to agree with it. Still, it is fairly clear that the author here is trying to state his position clearly as opposed to offering reasons to share it. We can imagine this passage as part of a discussion among people all of whom agree that illegal immigration is a problem. The author would not be trying to convince the other people that it is a problem, since they already agree that it is a problem, but to clarify what in her view makes it a problem.

DECIDING WHAT TO DO: CLARIFYING YOUR PROPOSALS

Clarifying and defining are just as important in deciding what to do and in evaluating a proposed course of action. Deciding what to do involves deciding both on an end to achieve and on a means for achieving it. Both the ends and the means should be clear before one decides what to do. The SEEC method can be useful here too. It is especially important to contrast the proposed end with others with which it might easily be confused. As a handy rule of thumb: if you cannot identify three contrasting ends or means then you have not made the proposed ends or means clear enough.

We have been discussing how to use the SEEC method to help us to clearly state our own views and opinions. We can also use it to state another person's views or opinions. This is a good thing to do if we are not sure just what their view is. By writing it out as if it was your own view, and then asking them whether it accurately states their view, you can make sure that you get their opinion. We also need to be able to state another person's view when we wish to raise an objection to it or to her reasons for believing it. In this case, we need to be especially careful that we accurately state her view. If we misstate her view, whether by accident or on purpose, we will have undermined our goal as critical thinkers, which is to try to get at the truth. The SEEC method can help us to avoid committing it by forcing us to think hard about how our opponent's views contrast with other closely similar ones.

EXERCISE 6

A. Using the SEEC definition method as a guide, clearly state your views on the following issues. Remember, your goal here is not to give reasons to believe that your view is correct or true, but only to state it in a way that will help others avoid confusing it with other similar views. (If you do not have a fixed opinion, just pretend that you do.)

   a. Whether Sunday is better than Saturday.

   b. Whether humans descended from other species.

   c. When abortion should be legal.

   d. What the country should do to reduce drug use.

   e. How to deal with the rising costs of college education.

   f. Whether it is sometimes OK to lie to a friend.

B. Look at the letters to the editor in a newspaper or magazine. Find two or three in which the author is stating his or her view on some issue of interest to you.

   a. Identify the perspective the author is taking on the issue.

   b. Assess how well the author does at stating that view clearly.

   c. Propose changes or additions to improve the clarity of the statement.

   d. Identify two or three contrasting views. Remember, contrasting views are not opposite views; a contrasting view is a similar view that one might easily confuse with the one being stated.

2.11   TECHNICAL DEFINITIONS

Sometimes words get defined in technical ways. This is done to avoid misunderstandings and to help resolve debates and disagreements. Sometimes this happens when researchers take a word that has an ordinary use but put it to more rigorous use in their work. This happened with words like "force" and "energy" that now have very specific and pretty clearly defined uses within physics, even though their roots are in our ordinary talk about the universe. Sometimes this can lead to even more misunderstandings.

The debate over whether nicotine is addictive provides a nice example of this. In 1964, the United States Surgeon Generals' Report stated that nicotine is not addictive. Then, in 1988, the Surgeon General's report announced that nicotine is addictive. This looks like a pretty substantial and clear cut factual disagreement, as though the US Surgeon General's office had changed its mind on a scientific topic that should have wide-ranging public policy consequences. But while there was considerable new information in 1988 on the physiological effects of nicotine and smoking tobacco, one relevant factor that changed in the 24 years between the reports was the definition of the word "addiction."

In the 1964 report, the Surgeon General offered the following: "In medical and scientific terminology the practice (smoking) should be labeled habituation to distinguish it clearly from addiction, since the biological effects of tobacco, like coffee and other caffeine-containing beverages, betel morsel chewing and the like, are not comparable to those produced by morphine, alcohol, barbiturates, and many other potent addicting drugs."[1] This definition of "addiction," which considered the production of intoxication a necessary condition for an addiction, echoes the definition that was then accepted by the World Health Organization. It seems right that, given this definition, nicotine is not addictive, since smoking a cigarette does not produce intoxication, at least certainly not like drinking alcohol or using heroin.

In 1988, though, the US Surgeon General redefined "addiction," dropped intoxication as a necessary condition, and held that for a drug to be addictive it is sufficient that it involve highly controlled or compulsive use, produce psychoactive effects, and that its use involve behavior that is reinforced by that use. Under this new definition, nicotine did count as an addictive drug. While there is no doubt that during that 24-year period a good deal more was learned about the science and medicine of drugs and nicotine, it is important when trying to understand that debate to be clear on what "addiction" means. As recently as 1998, the Tobacco Marketing Association published the following: "The definition of addiction is wide and varied. People are addicted to the Internet. Others are addicted to shopping, sex, tea, and coffee. The line I would take is that tobacco isn't addictive but habit forming."

The debate over whether nicotine is an addictive substance looks on the surface like a purely scientific and factual one, but there is actually a large terminological element to the debate. All sides in the debate—the cigarette companies, the government regulators, the independent scientists—could reach agreement on all the physiological, psychological and chemical effects, including both the long term and short term effects, of nicotine use, and on how those effects are similar to and different from the effects of short or long term alcohol or heroin use, and they might still disagree about whether nicotine is addictive, simply because they mean different things by "addictive."

In itself, this is not unusual or even very bad for researchers or ordinary people to use words in a technical way. But when people do not realize this, there is a risk that the participants will end up **talking past each other**. This mistake occurs when people in a discussion are using the same words with different meanings and are not aware of this, and so are not aware what each of them is saying. To avoid this, a good critical thinking strategy is to use the SEEC method to define our own words and those of the people we are in discussion with, in order to ensure that we all know what we mean.

2.12 MEANING IN ADVERTISEMENTS

It is wise to keep an eye out for special definitions in advertisements for goods and services. Given the recent rise in popularity of organic foods, many companies are marketing their products to tap into this popularity. Some are now being advertised

---

[1] United States Department of Health, Education, and Welfare [USDHEW]. (1964). 1964 Surgeon General's Report: Smoking and Health—Report of the Advisory Committee to the Surgeon General of the Public Health Service, p. 350. Emphasis in original.

as "all natural" or "authentic," as if this meant the same as "organic." In fact, the use of the word "organic" is highly regulated by governments around the world. The regulations were put in place mostly to help consumers avoid being tricked by producers and to protect growers whose produce really is organically grown from less scrupulous competitors. But the standards for what counts as "organic" vary from one country to the next. In particular, the United States allows products to be labeled as organic so long as they contain no more than 5% non-organic constituents.

One company even tried to market its beers as organic, even though they were made with non-organically grown hops. Apparently, since most of beer is simply water, and since the hop flavoring is so strong that very little of it is needed, many beers already fit the official definition of "organic." The government has no choice, if it is to regulate the use of a word, but to develop a strict definition including necessary and sufficient conditions. But this has the unintended effect of providing loopholes through which products that ought not to count can slip. In turn, these loopholes can confuse and deceive consumers and penalize producers who are not familiar with the technical definition, even though the original motivation for regulating the use of the word was to prevent consumer confusion and deception. Still, the benefits of regulating the use of that word are probably still higher than its costs.

In the case of the word "organic," the US government regulates both the meaning of claims used with it and also the truth of those claims. It is against the law to use that word on a product to mean something other than what the government has stipulated it is to mean and it is against the law to use on a product unless that product meets the relevant standards. But there are many words whose use in advertising the government does not regulate at all. Words used on nutritional supplements and cosmetics are a good example of this. These advertisements are required, as are all advertisements, not to be deliberately misleading. To comply, the advertisements often avoid strong claims like "will eliminate wrinkles" or "will prevent the common cold" in favor of such weak claims as "will help eliminate the appearance of fine lines" and "can support the sinus and immune system." In the case of nutritional supplements, these claims are usually accompanied by a tiny footnote that says something like: "This statement has not been evaluated by the Food & Drug Administration. This product is not intended to diagnose, treat, cure, or prevent any disease." It is hard to know what the intended meaning is of the words "support the sinus system" if it is not to mean that the product can treat, cure or prevent diseases of the sinus system. This is a case where not only is the truth of those claims not being regulated by the government; neither is the meaning. Here the general advice for thinking about claims in advertising applies: buyer-beware.

> When thinking critically about the claims in advertisements, identify the key words and phrases in the advertisement, find some contrastings ones, and ask why they were not used instead.

One strategy for thinking critically about the claims in advertisements is to identify the key words and phrases and look for contrasting ones that might have been used and to ask why they were not used. Why does the facial cream advertisement say that it can help reduce the appearance of fine lines? Why did it say, "help reduce" instead of just "reduce." Why did it mention the appearance of fine lines, instead of just fine lines? Reducing the appearance of fine lines is compatible with the continued existence of those fine lines. Is the advertisement really only claiming that the product covers up the fine lines? Then why not say that? In this way, the SEEC method, which requires us to look for closely contrasting words and concepts, can help us to think critically about claims in advertisements.

Earlier we discussed the way politicians and interest groups pick a specific framework for describing a policy in order to influence the public's attitude to the policy. Unfortunately, but not very surprisingly, they also sometimes use misleading labels to characterize or name their preferred policy proposals. (Unfortunately, there is no law against misleading advertising of public policies.) After the attack of 9/11, the congress passed a law with huge bi-partisan support that made enormous and far-reaching changes to civil rights, the rights of criminal suspects, and the power of the government to investigate and even detain citizens. This law was called the "Patriot Act," a name that had nothing to do with the substance or rationale for the bill, but which made opposing it rhetorically very difficult. Being opposed to the patriot act sounds like being opposed to patriotism itself. In a similar way, proposals to cut taxes are sometimes presented as "tax relief," even when those benefiting would be multi-millionaires, who can easily afford the taxes they are required to pay. There is, of course, a serious issue about who should pay how much tax. But this debate is stymied if one side is using misleading terms to describe the problem or their proposed solution. As good critical thinkers, we need to stay on guard for this, and the SEEC method can help by reminding us to look for contrasting ways to describe a problem or solution.

EXERCISE 7

A. Find five advertisements in your local newspaper.

    a. Identify the key claims made in the advertisement, and define them.

    b. Identify three contrasting claims that one might easily confuse for that view.

    c. Propose changes to improve the clarity of the advertisement.

B. Look for statements by local or national politicians on issues that you care about in newspaper articles, in letters written to local newspapers, or on their websites.

    a. Identify the framework within they discuss the issue.

    b. Proposes changes that would clarify their views.

    c. Identify two or three contrasting proposal or views.

C. What necessary condition is stated in each of the following?

    a. If you are going to succeed you need to think hard.

    b. The audience will love this movie, but only if the action scenes are longer.

    c. Without more water, this plant is destined to die.

    d. To make cookie dough, you need sugar, flour, butter, and an egg.

    e. If you love me, then you will set me free.

D. For the following concepts, find a condition that is necessary but not sufficient, and a set of conditions that are sufficient but not necessary.

   a. Winning the lottery.

   b. Being President of the United States.

   c. Being a doctor.

   d. Being an illness.

   e. Being beautiful.

CHAPTER SUMMARY

Thinking critically about what to believe or do usually requires reflecting on the meaning of concepts, claims, problems, and proposals. The **assertion test** can be used to figure out exactly what a concept or claim means. A useful method for constructing a definition involves providing a **slogan**; **expanding** it by explaining the relations among the slogan's key words; providing an **example** or two; and identifying some **contrasting** concepts, claims, problems, or proposals. Definitions can be evaluated by looking for **counterexamples** showing that the slogan is too broad or too narrow. Different disciplines might approach the same phenomena using different conceptual **frameworks**.

2.13   CRITICAL THINKING IN PRACTICE

2.13.1   Critical Thinking Mistakes

False Definition. It is a mistake for a definition's slogan to be too broad (by leaving out a necessary condition) or too narrow (by including a condition that is not necessary) or both. This is a mistake because it means that the definition's slogan is false. A counterexample to a definition is an example that shows that the definition is too narrow or too broad. The SEEC method can help us to avoid this mistake by requiring us to look for counterexamples and contrasting concepts.

Strawman Mistake. It is a mistake to distort or misrepresent another person's beliefs or their reasons for their beliefs. It is a mistake because it is very rude and because it prevents you and the other person from getting to the truth together. While everyone has a duty to make her beliefs and reasons clear, we all have a duty to represent each other's beliefs and reasons as clearly and charitably as we can. When in doubt, ask open-ended clarification questions to increase clarity.

Equivocation. It is a mistake to use words in different senses without realizing it. This is a mistake because it is hard to know if an assertion is true if we are not clear about what it means. One form of this mistake occurs during debates or conversations. It is a mistake for participants in a discussion not to recognize that they mean different things by the key words and phrases they use. This is a mistake because it will be very hard to agree on the truth if we mean different things by our words. This can be recognized and avoided by a careful use of the SEEC method.

2.13.2   Critical Thinking Strategies

In this chapter we have seen two practical strategies for helping us to think critically about meaning.

The Assertion Test. To tell whether a proposition is among the things a person is asserting or claiming to be true, suppose that it is false and ask whether what the speaker says could still be true. If Yes, then that proposition is not among the things asserted; if No, then it is. This test can also be used to tell whether a proposed definition is too broad or too narrow, by considering counterexamples to it.

The SEEC Method. In constructing a definition of a concept, belief, proposal, or problem, it is helpful to formulate it as a **slogan**, to **elaborate** on it by saying more about the key concepts, to offer an **example** or two, and to provide some **contrasting** concepts, beliefs, proposals, or problems. The goal of providing a definition is to prevent or remedy misunderstanding. This method can also be used to evaluate definitions.

2.13.3   From Theory to Practice: Applying What We Have Learned

2.13.3.1   Thinking Critically about Ourselves   In Chapter 1, you compiled a list of five or six character traits that you think are essential to being a morally good person, and you wrote a tentative definition of one of them. (i) Using the SEEC method for defining a concept, revise the definition including examples and contrasting concepts. (ii) Ask three or four friends how they would define the concept. Make sure you ask them open-ended questions to get them to say as much as you can. (iii) Compare and contrast the definition you developed and the ones your friends provided. What are the differences? Pay close attention to slight differences in word choice, as these often make a huge difference to the definition.

2.13.3.2   Thinking Critically in the Classroom   Thinking critically in a discipline requires knowing how to use its concepts to describe a phenomenon and to frame questions and proposals. In Chapter 1, you compiled a list of five or six of the most fundamental concepts of ideas in your field of study. (i) Using the SEEC method, try to develop a definition of the concept. Make sure that you include contrasting concepts, which need not be central to your field of study (You might show your definition to your professor to see whether she considers it too narrow or too broad.). (ii) List five or six problems or puzzles that your field of study addresses or studies. Using the concepts of your field, define them as clearly as you can, making it clear what it is that makes them a problem or a puzzle.

2.13.3.3   Thinking Critically at Work   Successfully participating in a company or organization requires being able to think about its structure, operations, and plans. Employees are regularly faced with problems that need to be solved. They can range from short-term ones that are easily solved (e.g., how to get rid of excess inventory) to longer-term problems that require thinking hard about the organization's goals and structure (e.g., responding to the lower labor costs from second world competitors). The SEEC method can be used to define the problem, thereby helping us to make sure that the solutions we employ are appropriate. It is especially helpful to now and then reframe a problem, even one we have a workable solution for. Looking at a problem from a different direction, or using a different set of concepts for describing it can reveal alternative solutions. At the very least, we will get confirmation that our existing solution is still the best one.

In Chapter 1, you compiled a list of five or six problems that you or your coworkers regularly face at work. Pick one of them and define it using the SEEC method, making sure that you make it as clear as you can why it is a problem. Now, try to reframe it by describing it in a different way or from a different perspective (e.g., from a manager's as opposed to a worker's perspective, or from a client as opposed to a manager's perspective). This is probably going to be difficult, since we usually find it difficult to think outside the box.

3

SUFFICIENT REASONS

Critical thinking is reasonable and reflective thinking aimed at deciding what to believe or what to do. As we saw in Chapter 1, part of what makes critical thinking *reasonable* is that it aims at finding or providing reasons for our decisions and beliefs. It is important to have reasons for thinking that our beliefs are true, that we have chosen the proper goals, and that our plans to reach them will be effective. If we do not have any reasons, then we will be right only by luck and relying on luck is not much of a strategy. Of course, we want more than just to have any old reasons; we want to have good ones. But what does it mean to say that a belief is *based* on or *supported by* certain evidence? And how do we know how much evidence is enough? This chapter is all about what it means to have good reasons for your beliefs and plans.

> We want our beliefs and decisions to be based on enough evidence.

3.1 CRITICAL THINKING AND ARGUMENTS

We can think critically about any subject matter and our thinking can take many different forms. But in every case, thinking critically about what to believe or do involves providing or considering reasons. As we saw in Chapter 1, critical thinking is also *reflective* thinking and this means in part that thinking critically requires thinking about our reasons *as reasons*. It requires making our reasons explicit and

A Practical Guide to Critical Thinking: Deciding What to Do and Believe, Second Edition. David A. Hunter.
© 2014 John Wiley & Sons, Inc. Published 2014 by John Wiley & Sons, Inc.

thinking about whether they provide enough evidence for the decisions we have to make.

> Whenever we are thinking critically about what to believe or do, we can formulate our reasoning in an argument that makes explicit our reasons and our belief or decision.

One technique that can help us to be reflective is to put our thinking in the form of an argument. This involves explicitly formulating the reasons we have and then assessing whether they are good reasons. The easiest way to do this is in writing. This chapter is all about analyzing and evaluating written arguments. But before we get to the details, I want to say a bit more about how arguments relate to critical thinking.

Let us start with some examples of thinking about what to believe or what to do. We look out the window to see whether it is sunny; we read a history book to learn what caused the American Civil war; we read the bathroom scale and conclude that our diet is working; we do an experiment and decide that the oxygen is causing the reaction; we conduct a survey and conclude that a majority of the population is probably opposed to capital punishment; we test different recipes to find the best way to make a pie crust; we read the newspaper to see who won last night's game; we make a scaled down model of our backyard to figure out where it makes most sense to build the new deck; we think about last night's concert to get ready to write a review for the school newspaper; we read the letters to the editor to help us decide what to think about the proposal to build a new bridge. I leave it to you to continue this list, but I trust that it is clear that it can go on for a very long time.

This very partial list gives a sense, I hope, of just how much of our ordinary, daily activity involves thinking about what to believe or what to do. What the examples have in common is that they each involve drawing a conclusion on the basis of reasons or evidence. Our belief that it is sunny out is based on what we saw when we looked out the window; the results of our tests are the evidence we use to decide how to make the perfect piecrust.

Having reasons for our decisions is essential to critical thinking. But notice that very few of the examples of thinking about what to believe or do involve reflecting on the reasons we had for our decisions. We probably do not think of what we see when we look out the window as the basis for or as evidence for our belief that it is sunny. Our thinking is not that reflective. We do not formulate the reasons *as reasons*.

I do not mean that this thinking does not involve the use of language. Reading a newspaper to find out who won the game involves using language. I mean that when we decide after reading the newspaper that our team had better start playing better defense, we probably are not (and usually do not need to be) formulating that conclusion or the reasons we have for it in words. We might be able to provide those reasons if someone asked us to. But formulating them in words is not part of the thinking itself.

When someone does offer explicitly formulated reasons in support of a claim or a proposal we say that they are offering an **argument** for the claim or proposal. We call the reasons that are being offered the argument's **premises**, and we call the claim or proposal that is being supported, the argument's **conclusion**. If Jones is arguing that we ought to build a second bridge across the river because this is the most cost-effective way to deal with the traffic congestion, then the conclusion of his argument is the proposal that *we should build a second bridge across the river* and the argument's premise is that *building a second bridge is the most cost effective way to solve the traffic congestion*. In this sense, an argument is just a collection of assertions some of which, which we will call the premises, are meant to support one of the others, which we will call the conclusion. Thinking of an argument in this way can help us to see how reasons are related to conclusions and will help us to find some strategies for telling when we have good reasons and when we do not.

> The reasons offered in support of a belief or decision are the **premises**. The belief or decision is the **conclusion**.

Sometimes arguments are written down, as in a letter to the editor of the local newspaper where the author offers reasons for thinking that more money should be spent on welfare programs. Books and articles can also contain arguments. Some history books, for instance, contain arguments about the origins of the American Civil War, pulling together evidence of different kinds and from different sources to support the author's conclusion. We can find arguments in the editorials published in the college newspaper. Argument can be spoken out loud, as when a politician offers her reasons for supporting a new bylaw prohibiting smoking in public places. So long as she is doing more than just expressing her support for the bylaw and is actually saying why she thinks the bylaw is a good one, then she is giving an argument for it. In these cases, someone is explicitly offering reasons in support of a position or belief, trying to persuade others to agree.

This use of the word "argument" is a bit unusual, since ordinarily by an argument we mean an emotionally heated dispute or disagreement. There is no doubt that discussions about what to believe or what to do can be emotional, and we are often, as we saw in Chapter 1, emotionally attached to our own beliefs, opinions, and traditions. But we also saw that emotional reasons are not reasons to believe that something is true or that some practice is good or effective. We also saw that emotion can get in the way of thinking critically. The fact that my believing something brings me a good deal of comfort does not show that the belief is true. Our focus in this book is on epistemic reasons, reasons to think that something is true or that our proposals are the best ones. So we can stick with this somewhat unusual sense of the word "argument" because it will help us to think about how good reasons are related to our beliefs and proposals.

> What makes reasons good is the same for all subject matters. So if you know how to think critically about one topic, you know how to think critically about them all.

Letters to the editor, books, and speeches may contain an author's reasoning about what to believe or what to do. But usually they contain other things too. Sometimes, a person will write a letter to the editor simply to express her opinion on a subject, and will not include her reasons. Her goal is not to try to convince anyone to agree with her, but merely to make sure that her voice is heard. This is fine, though it would of course be better if we were still undecided or if we were considering a change of mind to know her reasons. Likewise, some speeches are intended to encourage emotions or team spirit and not to provide reasons to believe something. There is no sure-fire way to know when a piece of text or a speech does contain reasoning about what to believe or what to. We do know that it does if, but only if, the author is offering reasons in support of some conclusion.

The difference between thinking that relies on explicitly stated premises and conclusions and reasoning that does not has nothing to do with what the reasoning is about. Take the case of trying to decide what to believe about the local team's performance. One could conclude that they are in last place simply by reading the standings published in the paper; or one could reach that same conclusion by reasoning that involved explicit words with premises and conclusions. One could draw the conclusion that the compound is responsible for the chemical reaction from seeing the results of the experiments, or from reading the published report that lays out the experimental procedures and results. What is common to all cases of reasoning about what to believe or what to do, at least when that reasoning is done well, is that evidence of some sort is being offered in support of some conclusion, and this has nothing to do with whether the premises and conclusions have been explicitly formulated or not. No matter what we are thinking about, if we are trying to decide what to believe or do, then we can put our thinking in the form of explicitly stated reasons and conclusions.

There is a real advantage to putting our thinking in the form of an argument, an advantage that ties arguments very closely to critical thinking. Critical thinking is not just reasonable thinking, it is also *reflective* thinking. Part of what this means is that thinking critically requires paying careful attention to the acceptability and strength of the reasons one is considering. It is true that for a lot of our reasoning we do not reflect very much on whether the evidence is acceptable or strong enough. I look at the bathroom scale and draw conclusions about my weight without reflecting on just what the evidence is that I am relying on, or about under what conditions that evidence is trustworthy. I read the newspaper and draw conclusions about the local politics without thinking very much about what makes that a reliable or reasonable way to form beliefs.

> Putting our reasoning in the form of an argument helps identify our reasons, assess whether they are true, and determine whether they support our conclusion.

But unless we are able to think about these questions our thinking will not be critical thinking. We will be engaged in thinking that we do not fully understand, trusting somewhat blindly, not fully in control of our beliefs and decisions. By reflecting on how reading the newspaper can be a source of evidence, we can take greater control of our beliefs. Instead of letting our beliefs be formed on their own, we will become responsible for them in knowing what their grounds are. By thinking about how standing on a scale can give me evidence for my weight I can become more sensitive to the conditions when that method will provide unacceptable or insufficient evidence. Not only will this help me avoid mistakes about my weight, which is always a good thing, but these lessons may even be transferred to other domains, helping me to develop better and more reliable methods.

Thankfully, we will not always need to formulate our reasons and conclusions in words in order to be thinking critically. But there is almost no harm in doing it periodically and much to be gained from knowing how to do it. The form that our thinking takes and the questions we will need to ask about whether the reasons are acceptable and sufficient may vary from one subject to another. In later chapters we will consider some of this variation in more detail. In this chapter I want to stay focused on what all cases of reasoning about what to believe and what to do have in common: that they involve offering reasons in support of a conclusion.

EXERCISE 1

Comprehension Questions. (When you answer these questions, pretend that you are explaining or teaching the answer to a friend who is not in the class. Doing that will force you to put in LOTS more background information than you would if you were trying to answer them for your instructor.)

  a. What is an argument?
  b. What is the difference between a premise and a conclusion?
  c. Could an argument have more than one premise? If so, give an example.
  d. Could an argument have more than one conclusion? If so, give an example.

3.2 IDENTIFYING PREMISES AND CONCLUSIONS

We have seen that critical thinking is *reflective* in part because it involves thinking about one's reason as reasons, and considering whether they are **acceptable** and whether they provide **sufficient** support for one's beliefs and decisions. But distinguishing reasons from the conclusions they are meant to support is difficult. In this section we will look at how to analyze very simple arguments into premises and conclusions.

Unfortunately, there is no foolproof, sure-fire method for doing this. People who write editorials may give reasons without saying that they are reasons, or might state their conclusion without saying that it is the conclusion. Sometimes, they even leave their conclusions or reasons unstated and leave it up to the reader to figure out what they are. (Perhaps they do this because they have not themselves reflected enough on the nature of their reasons.) Knowing how to figure out what the reasons are and what the conclusion is supposed to be is one of those skills that is acquired mostly through careful training and repeated practice. There are lots of examples throughout this chapter to help you practice. But let us look at some examples to bring out some helpful bits of advice.

Consider the following bit of reasoning.

> The city should build a second bridge to cross the river, for this is the cheapest solution to the traffic congestion and we should adopt whatever is cheapest.

The first step in analyzing an argument is to **identify all of the assertions it contains**.

It might already seem pretty obvious what the conclusion is here. But let us approach the analysis of the text very slowly and methodically, in order to be as reflective as we can. The first thing to keep in mind in analyzing an argument is that reasons and conclusions are always **asserted** in the text. (Well, almost always. Sometimes conclusions or premises are left out altogether. But we will ignore that for now.) So it is helpful to begin the analysis of an argument by identifying all of the assertions it contains. (It might help to look back at the assertion test, discussed in Chapter 2.) In the text above, we can identify three assertions. The first one is expressed in the very first sentence of the text.

Remember to always analyze conjunctions into their conjuncts. Each conjunct is a separate assertion.

1. The city should build a second bridge to cross the river.

The next sentence in the text is a **conjunction**, and you will remember from Chapter 2 that a conjunction makes at least two assertions. So we ought to break this sentence into two. (Our goal at this stage in the analysis is to identify all the assertions that are made. Later we can decide which assertion is the conclusion and which are the premises.)

2. Building a second bridge across the river is the cheapest solution to the traffic congestion.
3. We should adopt whatever solution is the cheapest.

There are several things to notice.

When analyzing an argument, replace pronouns like "it," "he," and "she" with what they are pronouns for.

First, I left the word "For" out of the second assertion. That word is not really part of the assertion. Rather, it plays a special role that I will return to in a moment. Second, notice that I replaced the word "It" with the phrase "Building a second bridge across the river." I did this because I want each assertion that I identify to be as complete as possible. Even though I know what the word "it" refers to in that sentence, it will be helpful later on if we replace pronouns like "it," "he," "she," etc. with appropriate names or descriptions. I also left off the word "and" from the third assertion, because it simply forms a conjunction, and is not really part of the assertion.

> To identify an argument's premises and conclusion, look for premise and conclusion indicator words.

Now that we have analyzed that text into three assertions, we can ask which one is the conclusion. Look back to the word "For," which I left out of the second assertion. The author used the word "For" to let us know that what comes next is a reason for accepting or agreeing with the point that came first, namely that the city should build a second bridge. The word "For" is a **premise indicator**, because it indicates that something is a premise. More specifically, it tells us that the next thing asserted is going to be a premise. But it also tells us that we just got a conclusion. So the presence of that word in that part of the text tells us a lot about the identity of the conclusion and the premises. We know that the first assertion is the conclusion, and the next one is a premise. As it turns out, the third one is a premise too. Eventually we will want to know how those premises are related to each other, but that can wait.

Here is a second text.

A second bridge should not be built, since building one will only encourage more people to drive across the bridge than already do now. What is more, if we build two bridges, then we will end up with traffic congestion troubles on two bridges instead of just one.

We can apply what we just learned to this text. The very first sentence has two parts, separated by the word "since." We can pretty easily identify two assertions; so let us separate them.

1. A second bridge should not be built.
2. Building a second bridge will only encourage more people to drive across the river than already do now.

Like the word "for," the word "since" is a **premise indicator**. It tells us that we are about to get a premise. When the word "since" occurs, as it does in this case, in the middle of a text, it also tells us that a conclusion was just asserted. So we know that the first assertion is a conclusion and the second one is a premise. Sometimes the word "since" occurs at the very beginning of an argument. There are examples of this in the chapter exercises. In that case, it tells us that what comes next is a premise, but it does not tell us what the conclusion is.

Look now at the final sentence. How many assertions does it contain? (Hint: it is a conditional, and we discussed what they assert in Chapter 2.) There is only one. Neither the sentence after the "if" (which we call the antecedent), not the sentence after the "then" (which we call the consequent) is asserted. So we must not separate them into two. This is REALLY important, for reasons that we will see later.

3. If we build two bridges, then we will end up with traffic congestion troubles on two bridges instead of just one.

Once again, I left out the words "what is more," since they are used to indicate the presence of a premise. Using them is like saying "here is another reason to believe me."

> When analyzing a text into assertions, never analyze a conditional into its parts. For neither the antecedent nor the consequent is asserted.

Now that we have analyzed the text into its assertions, we can ask which are the premises and which is the conclusion. We have in fact already answered that. Once again, the very first assertion is the conclusion, while the next two are premises.

Here is one last example.

It would be too expensive to replace the bridge with a tunnel and tearing the current bridge down will harm all the businesses that rely on cross-border traffic. We should simply build a second span across the river.

Once again, the very first sentence is a conjunction and so should be separated into two assertions. The final sentence is an assertion on its own. So we have three assertions.

1. It would be too expensive to replace the bridge with a tunnel.
2. Tearing the current bridge down will harm all the businesses that rely on cross-border traffic.
3. We should simply build a second span across the river.

Notice that in this case there are no indicator words. There are no words to tell us what the premises are or what the conclusion is. We need to figure it out some other way. The only way left is to use our own judgment. There are different approaches to try. You might start by pretending that you were the author, and asking yourself: If I had written this, which of the assertions would I be trying to convince someone to believe? Which would I want a reader to consider the big take-home message?

Another strategy is to insert an indicator word in between the assertions and see which makes most sense. For this strategy to succeed, it is important to have on hand indicator words that you feel very comfortable with. My own favorite indicator word is "therefore," which I know tells me that I was just given reasons and am about to given a conclusion. Consider the following.

It would be too expensive to replace the bridge with a tunnel; therefore, we should simply build a second span across the river.

We should simply build a second span across the river; therefore, it would be too expensive to replace the bridge with a tunnel.

To identify the premises and conclusion in an argument without indicator words, try inserting one between the assertions. This can help reveal what the author intended.

When I consider these it seems clear to me that the first one makes much more sense than the second. This suggests that the first assertion on our list is a reason to accept the third assertion. If we tried the same experiment using the second and third assertions we would get the same result. All of this suggests, what might have already seemed a bit obvious, that the third assertion in this text is the conclusion. I call this strategy for identifying premises and conclusions, the *Therefore Test*.

PREMISE INDICATORS

Premise indicators show which assertions are the premises in an argument. Here is a partial list of premise indicators:

Since, because, for, after all, for the reasons that, given that.

CONCLUSION INDICATORS

Conclusion indicators show which assertion is the conclusion in an argument. Here is a partial list of conclusion indicators:

Therefore, so, it follows that, this shows that, in conclusion, this proves that.

It is a good idea to find one premise indicator and one conclusion indicator that you feel really comfortable with, in the sense that you know exactly how to use it to indicate to someone when you are about to give them a reason or a conclusion. Having them on hand will help when we are analyzing a text that does not contain them. It will also prove helpful when we try to figure out the relations among multiple premises.

PRACTICAL STRATEGY: HOW TO IDENTIFY PREMISES AND CONCLUSION

(i) Identify all the assertions.

–Analyze conjunctions into their conjuncts.

–DO NOT analyze conditionals, disjunctions, or sentences with non-asserted noun clauses.

(ii) Look for indicator words.

(iii) If there are no indicator words, use your own judgment or the *Therefore Test*.

The word "because" is a tricky indicator word. It can be used to give a reason for doing or believing something, as in the following.

We should build a bridge rather than dig a tunnel, because bridges are cheaper.

Jones must be the murderer, because he was at the scene of the crime and owns a gun just like the one used to kill the victim.

In these cases, the word "because" works in the same way as the word "since." It indicates that what comes next will be a reason to believe or do what was mentioned first. So the word "because" can be a premise indicator.

But the word "because" can also be used to indicate that one event caused or helped to cause another. Consider the following.

The window broke because the ball hit it.

This sentence contains two assertions: that the window broke and that the ball hit the window. In this way, this sentence is like a conjunction, with the word "because" linking two assertions. But this sentence asserts more than just that two things happened. It also asserts that one caused the other. It asserts that the ball's hitting the window caused the window to break. A sentence like this is not formulating an argument. We know this because it has no premise or conclusion and nor is it trying to convince us to believe that the window broke or that the ball hit the window. Rather, this sentence formulates a **causal assertion**. A causal assertion is just an assertion that one thing caused another. We will return to causal assertions in Chapter 5. We will have more to say about what they mean and about how to tell when they are true. But for now, the point is simply that we need to be a little careful when we see the word "because," for it can be used in two ways: to indicate a premise in an argument, and to indicate a cause in a causal assertion.

> The word "because" is used in two ways: sometimes to indicate a premise in an argument; sometimes to indicate a cause in a causal assertion. Causal assertions are not arguments.

EXERCISE 2

A. Comprehension Questions.

    a. What is a premise indicator word?

    b. What is a conclusion indicator?

    c. Why do not we want to analyze a conditional into two assertions when we analyze an argument?

    d. Why is a word like "since" not really part of an assertion? What roles does it play?

B. Compose an argument with two premises using "therefore" as a conclusion indicator.

C. Compose an argument with two premises using "since" as a premise indicator.

D. Compose an argument with two premises using no indicators.

E. In the following texts, identify all of the assertions made and then identify the premises and conclusion.

    a. The infection is getting worse, for the fever is staying high.

    b. Dinosaurs were animals and they roamed the earth before humans did. This shows that humans were not the first animals.

    c. The leaves are drooping and the petals are falling off. This means that the flower is dying.

    d. The dress is too short and the color is all wrong. So, you should not buy it.

    e. Jones was at the party last night. Jane said so.

    f. The traffic on the highway is really terrible. So we should take a side road.

    g. Voting makes no difference. Politicians always do whatever they want and one vote can never make a difference.

    h. That plant will die. It never gets any light and it is bone dry.

    i. Inflation is rising and so are interest rates. A recession is approaching.

    j. The American Civil War was good for the United States. It clarified the powers of the states in relation to each other and to the Federal Government, and it highlighted the importance of the constitution's bill of rights.

    k. 85% of students we surveyed are in favor of some legal limitations on gun ownership. Therefore, most people are in favor of gun control.

    l. Cars are nothing but a money sink. I have owned three cars in the last six months and all of them required really costly repairs.

    m. If we eat the bananas, then we will not have any fruit left. And if we have no fruit then we have to go to the store. So, if we eat the bananas we have to go to the store.

    n. Either we drive to Florida or we fly. But flying is now really expensive and is also bad for the environment. So, we had better drive.

    o. Investing in the stock market is like throwing money down the toilet. And we can all agree that that is a bad thing. So investing in the market is bad too.

    p. The acting was wooden, the scenery was cheap and the dialogue was empty. That was a terrible movie.

    q. If you save your money in a bank account you will gain interest. If you gain interest you will become richer. So, saving money in your bank account can make you richer.

    r. We have to fire that worker. He is incompetent, always in a bad mood, and he just left early.

F. Using the following sentence as a conclusion, "Tofu is very delicious," compose three arguments with different premise. Use premise and conclusion indicators. (Note: the arguments do not need to be persuasive, and do not worry about making sure that the premises are true. The argument could be crazy, if you like. So long as they are arguments.)

3.3 DEPENDENT AND INDEPENDENT PREMISES

Thinking critically about what to believe or do requires having or finding reasons for the decisions we make. Sometimes, we have more than one reason when we make a decision. And sometimes, the reasons we have work together in complicated ways to support our decision. In this section we will study the different ways that reasons can work to support a belief or an action.

When I decided to write this textbook, I thought that the challenge of writing a book would be fun and rewarding. I also thought that I could say things in a helpful and clear way. Oh, and I was hoping to retire early on the enormous profits I would make. (It has been fun and rewarding. One out of three is not bad!) In this case, the reasons were independent of one another, in the sense that each of them would have been a reason to write the book even in the absence of the other two. Looking forward to the challenge would have been a reason to write it even if I was pretty sure that I could not say things clearly and would not be able to retire on the proceeds. In analyzing an argument it is important to figure out whether the premises are independent of one another in this way.

Here is another set of arguments.

Sam robbed the bank, and robbing a bank is a criminal act, so Sam is a criminal.

Sam robbed a bank, and he sells illegal drugs, so Sam is a criminal.

Both arguments have two premises. But the relation between the premises in the first argument is very different than the relation between the premises in the second argument. In the first argument, the premises are working together—each needs the other to support the conclusion. In the second argument, the premises are independent of one another. Each supports the conclusion all on its own. This difference, the difference between dependent and independent premises, is the topic of this section.

3.3.1 The Words Test

The first strategy I call the *words test*.

THE WORDS TEST

To tell whether premises are dependent or independent, see whether some of the conclusion's key words occur only in one premise and other key words only in another. If so, then those premises are probably dependent.

To see how it works, consider the following argument.

John should not become a doctor. After all, he really hates to be around sick people, and doctors spend their whole day around sick people.

> The premises in an argument are dependent on each other if none of them would be a reason to accept the conclusion if the others were false.

We can analyze it into three assertions.

1. John should not become a doctor.
2. John really hates to be around sick people.
3. Doctors spend their whole day around sick people.

(Notice that I replaced the pronoun "he" from the second assertion with the name "John." The words test works properly only if we always do that.) We know from what we learned in the previous section that the first assertion is the conclusion. The words "After all" are used here as **premise indicators**. So we know that the second and third assertions are supposed to provide reasons to accept the conclusion. What we now want to know is whether they are dependent on each other, or whether they provide independent support for that conclusion.

We can see that the conclusion contains two key words: "John" and "doctor." But the word "John" only occurs in the second assertion and the word "doctor" only occurs in the third assertion. This suggests pretty strongly that those two assertions are working together—that is, dependently—to support the conclusion.

The idea behind the **words test** is this: *there should not be more information in the conclusion than there is in the premises.* If an argument's conclusion does contain more information than there is in the premises, then this means that a logical leap is needed to get from the premises to the conclusion. In other words, the conclusion does not really follow logically from the premises. (We will look more closely at just what that means in a little while, but for now we can stick with a pretty intuitive grasp of that idea.) One way to see whether there is more information in the conclusion is to compare the key words used in formulating it with the words in the premises. That is why the *words test* works pretty well for figuring out whether premises are dependent or not.

3.3.2   The False Premise Test

But the words test cannot always help us. Here is an argument where the words test will not help.

Sam robbed the bank. And he sells illegal drugs. So he is a criminal.

We can analyze it into three assertions:

1. Sam robbed the bank.
2. Sam sells illegal drugs.
3. Sam is a criminal.

We know that the first and second assertions are premises and the third one is the conclusion. Are those premises independent of one another? The **words test** is not going to help us here, since one of the key words in the conclusion, "Sam," occurs in both premises and the other one, "criminal," occurs in neither one. In this kind of case, it is better to use a somewhat more complicated, but much more reliable test.

THE FALSE PREMISE TEST

To test whether premises are dependent or independent, suppose that one were false, and ask whether the other one would still provide some support for the conclusion. If it would, then the premises are independent. If not, then they are dependent.

To use this test, we need to suppose for the sake of the test that one of the premises is false. So let us suppose that Sam did not rob the bank, but that he does sell illegal drugs. Just to help us suppose this, let us imagine that his friend Michael robbed the bank. Now we ask: would the fact that Sam sells illegal drugs still be some reason to accept the conclusion that Sam is a criminal? Clearly it would. Selling illegal drugs makes someone a criminal, even if he never robbed a bank.

Let us do the test on the other premise. Let us suppose that Sam does not sell illegal drugs, but that he did rob the bank. Would the fact that Sam robbed the bank be some reason to accept the conclusion that Sam is a criminal? Again, the answer is clearly yes. What this shows is that those two premises do not depend on each other to be a reason to accept the conclusion. Each is on its own a reason to accept that conclusion. In other words, they are independent premises.

Let us use the **false premise test** on the argument for the conclusion that John should not go to medical school. Let us suppose that John *does not* hate being around sick people, but that it is true that doctors spend a lot of time around sick people. Would the fact that doctors spend a lot of time around sick people be a reason to think that John should not go to medical school? No. It is a reason to think that *only if* it is also true that John does not like being around sick people. Try it the other way. Suppose that it is not true that doctors spend a lot of time around sick people, but that John hates being around sick people. Would that fact about John be a reason for him not to go to medical school? Again, no. It would be a reason for him to avoid becoming a doctor only if doctors spent a lot of time around sick people. So this shows that these premises are dependent on each other: neither premise would be a reason to accept the conclusion if the other premise were false. So we get the same result using the false premise test as we got using the words test.

The false premise test is trickier than the words test. The words test is almost mechanical: we just need to compare words in the conclusion and the premises. But it will not work for all arguments. The false premise test will always give us the right answer. But it is trickier to use, for it requires us to assume that one thing is false and then ask whether something else could be true. (Flashback: you might remember that this is the very same bit of mental gymnastics needed for the Assertion Test! Did I not tell you we would use that gymnastics move again? We will use it one more time before the Chapter is done.) And this is especially difficult to use when the premise we have to assume is false is one that we already know for a fact is true. Using the false premise test can sometimes require a vivid imagination. But the words test will not always work, whereas the false premise test will always work.

Let us consider one more case.

Capital punishment should be banned. It is often cruel and cruelty should be banned. Moreover, our justice system sometimes makes mistakes and it would be horrific to execute an innocent person.

We can analyze this into five assertions:

1. Capital punishment should be banned.
2. Capital punishment is often cruel.
3. Cruelty should be banned.
4. Our justice system sometimes makes mistakes.
5. It would be horrific to execute an innocent person.

We know that the first assertion is the conclusion. This leaves us with four premises. Reading them through carefully, we can see that there are two main ideas in the premises. One has to do with whether capital punishment is cruel and the other has to do with whether our justice system might make mistakes. Using the words test, we can see that the second and third assertions work together to support the conclusion and that the third and fourth work together to support the conclusion. We can also see, using the false premise test, that these pairs of premises are independent one from the other. Even if the justice system never made mistakes, if it is true that capital punishment is cruel and that cruelty is wrong, then this would be some reason to accept the conclusion. Likewise, even if capital punishment was not cruel, if our system sometimes makes mistakes and if it would be wrong to execute innocent people, then this would be some reason to accept the conclusion. So here we have two independent sets of dependent premises!

PRACTICAL STRATEGY: DIAGRAMMING ARGUMENTS

It can be helpful to construct a diagram to make the structure of an argument clear.

Give each assertion in the argument a number. Place the number for the conclusion at the bottom of the diagram and the numbers for the premises above. If the premises are dependent, connect with a "+" and then draw an arrow from it to the number of the conclusion. If the premises are independent, connect each of them directly to the conclusion with an arrow.

Deciding what to do: clearly distinguish reasons for the ends and reasons for the means

Deciding what to do involves deciding on an end to try to achieve and deciding on a means to achieve it. So two kinds of reasons are important in deciding what to do. For we need to have good reasons both for the ends we are trying to achieve and for the means we are choosing to use. In constructing an argument to represent our reasoning about what to do, we should make sure that we separate out these kinds of reasons. When we analyze someone else's reasons for acting we should also be careful to distinguish the reasons to achieve that end from the reasons to choose those means.

SECTION SUMMARY

We often have different reasons for our beliefs and decisions. Reasons are independent of one another when each would be a reason even if the other was not. If we explicitly formulate our reasons as an argument with premises and conclusions, then we can ask whether some of the premises work together to support the conclusion. We can use the **words test** or the **false premise test** to determine whether they are dependent or independent.

EXERCISE 3

A. After section 2, the final exercise asked you to compose an argument. Were the premises dependent or independent? Compose two new arguments, one with dependent premises and one with independent premises.

B. In the following arguments, identify the premises and conclusions and determine whether the premises are independent or dependent. (Do not worry about whether the premises or conclusion are true.)

   a. The math class is worth taking because it is easy and the teacher is really nice.

   b. North Korea is a dangerous country, because it is a dictatorship and all dictatorships are dangerous.

   c. Jones will probably win the race. He is the fastest skater and the fastest skater usually wins.

   d. Wind power is the way of the future. It is really inexpensive; it does not pollute; and there will always be wind.

   e. The plant is dying. The leaves are turning brown, and this is a sign of plant death.

   f. Raccoons are digging up the grass again, and every time they do this it is because there are grubs. So, the grass has grubs again.

g. This camping site already has wood and it has a nice western exposure so we will get a nice sunset. This is a good site.

h. The new car has higher fuel efficiency and better suspension. We should buy it. Oh, it also comes in five cool colors.

C. For the following conclusions, construct two arguments, one with two dependent premises and one with two independent premises (or two independent sets of dependent premises).

a. The team lost the game last night.

b. The liquid contains salt.

c. Harvard University is in Cambridge.

d. The car is out of gas.

e. The rent is due tomorrow.

f. Honesty is the best policy.

D. You probably have reasons in your own life for your beliefs or decisions. Here is a list of topics that are of importance. If you have an opinion, try to formulate it as clearly as you can (It might help to look back to our discussion in Chapter 2 on how to define a view or position.). Then formulate your reasons, and see whether you have multiple reasons for them. Finally, put the while together in the form of an argument.

a. The morality of capital punishment.

b. The morality of abortion.

c. Your decision to go to college.

d. Whether marijuana should be legalized.

e. Whether creationism should be taught in schools.

f. Whether it is sometimes morally OK to lie to your friends.

3.4 SUB-ARGUMENTS

Consider the following argument.

John and Peter are the only skaters left in the competition. But Peter will not win, for her just broke his ankle. So John is going to win.

We can identify the following assertions:

1. John and Peter are the only skaters left in the competition.
2. Peter will not win the competition.
3. Peter just broke his ankle.
4. John will win.

A **sub-argument** is an argument supporting a premise.

We have two indicator words to work with. The word "for" is a premise indicator and it connects assertion 3 to assertion 2. So assertion 3 is a premise for assertion 2. So, assertion 2 is a conclusion. But there is also another indicator word. The word "so" occurs right before the final assertion. That indicates that the final assertion is a conclusion. So this argument has two conclusions! Actually, it is not unusual for an argument to contain two conclusions. In the case of this argument, one of the conclusions occurs as part of a sub-argument. A sub-argument is a conclusion for a premise. In this section we will learn how to identify sub-arguments.

To identify sub-arguments in texts, we can use the very same methods we studied in the previous two sections. Consider the following text.

> The restaurant was not very good. The salad was too salty and the cake was very dry. Worst of all, the service was terrible, for the waiter was slow and the hostess was rude.

Here we find the following assertions.

1. The restaurant was not very good.
2. The salad was too salty.
3. The cake was very dry.
4. The service was terrible.
5. The waiter was slow.
6. The hostess was rude.

The first assertion is the conclusion. Assertions 2, 3, and 4 are independent premises supporting that conclusion. But what about assertions 5 and 6? The presence of the premise indicator "for" tells us that they are premises. And it tells us that we just got a conclusion. This means that assertions 5 and 6 are meant to provide support for assertion 4, which in turn supports the conclusion. (Assertion 4 is thus both a premise for a conclusion and a conclusion.) If we use the false premise test, we can see that assertions 5 and 6 each provides independent support for 4.

DIAGRAMMING SUB-ARGUMENTS

Sub-arguments can be diagrammed using the "+" and arrow symbols we have already seen. The argument we have been considering would look like this:

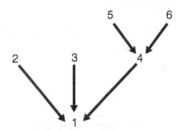

Here is one final case to consider.

Brian is going to lose his job. He keeps showing up late. And he stole money from the cash register. I saw him take it.

Here we have four assertions.

1. Brian is going to lose his job.
2. Brian keeps showing up late.
3. Brian stole money from the cash register.
4. I saw Brian steal the money from the cash register.

The first assertion is the argument's conclusion. Assertions 2 and 3 are independent premises supporting that conclusion. But what about assertion 4? What is it doing in the argument? It is a premise for assertion 3: its role is to provide reason to believe that Brian stole money from the cash register. So, in this argument, the author is offering his own eye-witness testimony in support of one of the premises.

Searching for sub-arguments is tedious. Here is a good rule of thumb. *Unless there is a premise or conclusion indicator that clearly indicates a sub-argument, assume that there is not one.* Analyzing texts into component assertions, identifying the main conclusion, and determining whether the premises are dependent or independent is already a lot of hard work. It is pretty rare, in my experience, for authors of typical arguments—the kinds we find in letters to the editor or even opinion columns in newspapers—to provide a lot of help by using clear indicator words. Perhaps this is because most authors have not thought as much as we have about how to organize their reasons.

SECTION SUMMARY

A sub-argument is an argument for a premise. A sub-argument can consist of dependent or independent premises. We can use the same methods for identifying these sub-premises and for determining whether they are dependent or independent as we used for arguments.

EXERCISE 4

A. In the following texts, identify the conclusions, premises and any sub-arguments.
   a. Coke is better than Pepsi. It has more flavor and it is more popular. Survey after survey show that most Americans prefer Coke.
   b. Joan is definitely pregnant. She missed her period, and the urine test was positive. She told me about the test herself.

c. Slavery is odious. It prevents the slaves from becoming fully autonomous. It also prevents the slave owner from achieving this full humanity, since no one can own slaves and feel good about themselves.

d. If we execute Steven for his crimes, then we will set a bad precedent. And setting bad precedents is not good. For it usually leads to unintended consequences down the road. So, we should not execute Steven.

e. Building a new bridge is very expensive. The labor will cost a lot, and so will the steel. Moreover, because the trucking industry will have to bypass the city while the construction is going on, the city will lose that source of revenue. We cannot afford these costs. So we should not build a new bridge.

f. Downloading music from friends is wrong. It is like stealing from a store, and we all know that stealing is wrong. What is more, downloading music from friends is effectively robbing from the musician, and we need to support them not rob from them because they are poor and struggling.

g. If evolutionary theory is correct, then we would expect to see similar bone structures in different species. And we have found this. Dogs and cats have similar bone structures in their arms and paws as birds have in their wings. So, evolutionary theory is correct.

h. Abstinence before marriage is a good thing. It promotes more respectful relationships after marriage and before marriage. It helps prevent unwanted pregnancies, which are bad because they make it difficult for mothers and fathers to achieve their life and career goals.

i. Abstinence before marriage is a bad thing. It is important for partners to know whether they are sexually compatible before they marry. What is more, abstinence is just like prohibition on alcohol and that only made the urges even stronger.

j. The map says that the park is over the right. But the map was wrong about the museum's location. It said it was on Elm Street when in fact it is on Green Street. So I am not sure that we should trust the map.

B. One of the exercises at the end of the previous section asked you to identify some of your reasons for your beliefs or decisions. Look back at those, and add some sub-arguments to them.

3.5 EVALUATING LOGICAL SUPPORT

Let us quickly recap what we have done so far in this chapter. We started by noting that critical thinking is **reasonable** thinking in part because it requires us to have reasons for our beliefs and decisions. But we do not just want to have any old reasons; we want to have good reasons. We saw that to evaluate whether our reasons are good ones, it is helpful to put them in the form of an argument. And we have seen that arguments can take several different forms, with dependent and independent premises and even with sub-arguments.

Now that we know how to identify premises and conclusions, how to distinguish dependent from independent premises, and how to find sub-arguments, we are ready to look at how to evaluate what makes reasons good. We will study a relatively simple and straightforward test to tell when an argument's premises provide the best possible kind of logical support.

But first, we need to draw some important distinctions.

> There are really only two questions to ask when evaluating an argument. Are its premises true? Is the argument valid? These questions are independent of each other.

Ideally, an argument should have two features. It should have true premises and its premises should support its conclusion. Here is one of the most important lessons of the entire book: whether the premises in an argument are true has **nothing** to do with whether they support its conclusion. This may seem pretty counter-intuitive, but it is true and it really is extremely important.

To see this, consider the following argument.

(1) Jon Stewart is the Prime Minister of Canada, and (2) all Prime Ministers of Canada are Martians, so (3) Jon Stewart is a Martian.

We know that assertion (3) is the conclusion and that assertions (1) and (2) are dependent on one another, as the words test or the false premise test would show. We also know that all three assertions are false. (If you do not know about Jon Stewart or Martians, or Canada, then just take my word for it that these assertions are all false!)

But suppose that the premises were true. What would that mean for the truth of the conclusion? That is, suppose that Jon Stewart really were the Prime Minister of Canada. (He is not; he is an American comedian and TV show host. But just suppose that he were the PM of Canada.) And suppose that as a matter of fact all PMs of Canada were Martians (they are not, even if some of them behave rather strangely.) That would mean that the conclusion would have to be true. If Jon Stewart **were** the PM of Canada, and if all PMs **were** Martians, then he would have to be a Martian too. So, if that argument's premises were true its conclusion would have to be true too.

> An argument is **valid** when it is not possible for its premises to be true and its conclusion false. If its premises were true, its conclusion would have to be true too.

We have a special word for this: an argument is **valid** when it is impossible for the premises to be true and for the conclusion to be false. It is relatively easy to tell whether an argument is valid, just by thinking about it. We can use the **validity test**. As you can probably tell, the validity test is a lot like the Assertion test and the false premise test. All three involve the same sort of mental gymnastics. We have to suppose that one thing is true (or false) and then consider what this would mean for the truth of something else. The test can be tricky to use, especially when the thing we are supposing to be false is something we already know is true, or vice-versa. But this sort of mental manoeuver is at the heart of critical thinking. And like any skill, the more you do it, the better you get at it, and the easier it becomes.

TESTING FOR VALIDITY

To test an argument for validity, first suppose that the premises were true. Then ask: could the conclusion still be false? If Yes, then the argument is not valid. If no, then the argument is valid.

Our argument about Jon Stewart shows that an argument can be valid and still have false premises and a false conclusion. A valid argument can also have false premises but a true conclusion.

> Jon Stewart is a Martian and every Martian hosts a TV show, so Jon Stewart hosts a TV show.

In this argument, the premises are false, though the conclusion is true. If we use the validity test, we can see that just as before the argument is valid. If it were true that Jon Stewart was a Martian and that every Martian hosts a TV show, then it would have to also be true that he hosts a TV show. So this argument is valid too. This shows that a valid argument can have false premises and a true conclusion.

A valid argument can also have true premises and a true conclusion. Here is an example.

> Jon Stewart is human and all humans have parents, so Jon Stewart has parents.

There is only one possibility that validity forbids: no valid argument can have true premises and a false conclusion. This simply follows from the very definition of validity. Validity means that it is not possible for the premises to be true and the conclusion false. So, if you are evaluating an argument and you know that the premises are in fact true and the conclusion is false, then you can safely conclude that the argument is not valid.

> Jon Stewart is a man, and all men are humans, so Jon Stewart is the Prime Minister of Canada.

This is a silly argument, one that no one would take seriously. But it does illustrate the point that an argument with true premises and a false conclusion cannot be valid.

Whether an argument is valid has nothing to do with whether its premises are in fact true.

Keeping these points about validity is mind is more than a little tricky. I suggest that you find examples of each combination we discussed that you feel totally comfortable with, and which you can compare to other arguments in order to see whether those other arguments are valid or not. The examples I have given might do the trick. But if they do not, then you should come up with your own.

> When an argument is valid and its premises are true, then it is a **sound** argument. A sound argument is perfect.

DECIDING WHAT TO DO: EVALUATING REASONS

Evaluating reasoning about what to do requires independently evaluating both the reasons for pursuing the end in question and the reasons for adopting the proposed means. Reasons to pursue some goal or end are reasons to believe that the end or goal is a good one. Reasons to adopt some means to achieving that end are reasons to believe that those means will be effective in bringing about that end. We can make these reasons explicit in the form of an argument.

Here is how Jones might reason about becoming a lawyer.

I want a career that will bring me money and responsibility and also be fulfilling. So, I should become a lawyer or a doctor. But I do not like to see blood, so I should not become a doctor. So, I should become a lawyer.

Here is how Jones might reason about the appropriate means to achieve that objective.

The best way to become a lawyer is to get accepted at the best law school I can afford. If I study hard for the LSATs, do lots of extra-curricular activities, and volunteer on the weekends, I will have a good chance of getting into the University's law school. So, I should do that.

These arguments can be assessed as valid or not.

EXERCISE 5

A. Comprehension Questions
  a. What does the word "valid" mean?
  b. If an argument is valid, must its premises be true? Using the concepts discussed in this chapter, explain your answer. Give an example.
  c. If an argument has false premises, must it be invalid? If not, give an example?

B. Using the following proposition as a conclusion, "Tofu is delicious," construct two arguments:
  a. One that is valid and has two false premises
  b. One that is invalid with two true premises

C. Using the validity test, assess whether each of these arguments is valid.

    a. Cats are warm-blooded and warm-blooded animals are mammals, so cats are mammals.

    b. The table is blue, so it is colored.

    c. The War of Independence was a revolution, and revolutions are morally wrong, so the War of Independence was morally wrong.

    d. If a plant dries out it will die. This plant is all dried out. So it will die.

    e. I should make dinner. It is my turn and my wife and I take turns.

    f. The cat is asleep. Cats always dream when they are asleep, so he is dreaming now.

    g. $2 + 2 = 4$ and $4 + 4 = 8$, so $2 + 2 + 4 = 8$.

    h. Lying to someone is like robbing them of the truth, and robbing is wrong, so lying is wrong too.

    i. The movie was terrible. It was too long and the theatre was way too overcrowded.

    j. Running helps to build cardiovascular strength and can extend your life. Anything that has these effects is good for you, so running is good for you.

D. For each of the following, find a conclusion that follows validly and one that does not.

    a. The table is made of wood and wood always dries out.

    b. Cats are warm-blooded, and warm-blooded animals eat meat.

    c. Jones is a bachelor.

    d. Frank murdered Henry.

3.6 MISSING PREMISES

As we have seen, there are two questions to ask when evaluating an argument: are the premises true and is the argument valid? If an argument is not valid, then it is not a good argument. But sometimes, a person will give an argument but leave out a crucial premise. The argument, as they wrote it, is not valid. But, by adding a premise, it can be turned into a valid argument. We can call it a missing premise. It is important when thinking critically about another person's reasons to look for missing premises when evaluating their arguments.

Here are some examples.

Miranda really wants her plants to thrive, so it will probably rain today.

It has not rained in many days; so it will probably rain today.

The bridge is too expensive. We should not build it.

The validity test makes clear that these arguments are not valid. It is not that hard to imagine a world where even though Miranda really wants her plants to thrive it still will not rain, or where even though it has not rained in many days it still will not rain today, or where even though the bridge is too expensive it still gets built. So with these arguments it is possible for the premises to be true and the conclusion to be false.

PRACTICAL STRATEGY: BE CHARITABLE

When evaluating someone's argument, try to turn it into a valid argument. That way, you can focus on whether the premises (including the one that you added) are true, as opposed to whether the premises support the conclusion. As we know, it is easy to add a premise to make an argument valid. So be charitable by helping the other person find a valid argument for their conclusion.

There is a trick for turning any invalid argument into a valid one. Simply add to the argument as a new premise a conditional whose antecedent is the existing premise and whose consequent is the conclusion. Using our previous examples, we get the following valid arguments.

Miranda really wants her plants to thrive, and *if she really wants her plants to thrive, then it will rain today*, so it will rain today.

It has not rained in many days, and *if it has not rained in many days, then it will rain today*, so it will rain today.

The bridge is too expensive, and if it is too expensive, then we should not build it; so, we should not build the bridge.

These arguments are now valid, as an application of the **validity test** will confirm. In evaluating them, there is now no question of whether the premises logically support the conclusion: they provide the strongest possible kind of support.

But remember that an argument is good only if its premises support the conclusion **and its premises are true**. Transforming an invalid argument into a valid one will not necessarily make it into a good argument. For the premises might still be false. Indeed, it might be that the only premise that we could add to make it valid would be a false premise. In that case, the argument is hopeless. Still, by focusing our attention on the truth of the premises, rather than on the question of support, we can get clearer on the factual questions at issue, and this is (I think) always a good thing.

EXERCISE 6

A. Using the SEEC definition method from Chapter 2, construct a definition of validity that would help someone who had never studied critical thinking understand it.

B. Using the concepts you have learned in this chapter, explain why it is better for an argument to be valid than for it not to be valid.

C. In Chapter 1, we saw that emotional reasons are not epistemic ones. Using the concepts from this chapter, explain why this is so.

D. If an argument has a false premise, might it still be valid? Using the concepts from this chapter, explain your answer, and give an example.

E. Using the SEEC definition method from Chapter 2, define the following:

(i) Premise indicator

(ii) Independent premise

(iii) Sub-argument

F. The following arguments are not valid. Add a premise to make each of them valid. Assess whether the missing premise you added is true.

a. (i) The glass is full of water. I can see it with my own eyes.

(ii) The glass is full of water. Joan told me so.

b. (i) The car is really low on gas. We have to stop.

(ii) The car has a flat tire. We have to stop.

c. (i) The sun will rise tomorrow. After all, it has risen every day for the past million years.

(ii) The sun will rise tomorrow. For the Earth continues to spin on its axis.

3.7 PILING ON INDEPENDENT PREMISES

One final point is worth noting here. Sometimes in arguments where there are lots of apparently independent premises, the premises are actually meant to be working together producing a kind of "piling-on" effect. Here is an example.

Let's not go to the movie tonight. I am tired, and we still have all those dishes to do. Plus, we need to save some money for lunch tomorrow and anyway we can watch a movie on TV. Let's just stay home.

When we analyze this into assertions we find the following.

1. We should not go to the movie tonight.
2. I am tired.
3. We still have to do the dishes.
4. We need to save money for lunch tomorrow.
5. We can watch a movie on TV.

The first assertion is the conclusion and the rest are premises. If we used the false premise test, we would get the result that each premise constitutes an independent reason to accept the conclusion. This might have been the author's intent. Maybe she thought that each on its own was sufficient reason not to go to the movie. But if so, she would have been mistaken. Each of them is some reason, but surely not a sufficient reason.

Sometimes, a large number of independent premises are actually meant to work together, with a missing premise, to support the conclusion.

But maybe she instead meant that, although none of the reasons is sufficient on its own, when you consider them all together they do constitute a good reason not to go. Maybe she thought that if the dishes did not need doing and if they did not need to save the money for tomorrow's lunch, then the fact that she was tired would not be good reason to miss the movie, but that when all of those considerations are put together, *when you pile them all in together*, then they do make up a good case. If this is what she is thinking, then there would have to be a missing premise, something like this.

Given all of these considerations, we should stay home.

This "piling on" effect is common in criminal cases, where the prosecution presents a lot of little bits of evidence of guilt, none of which is in itself conclusive, but which, when considered all together, strongly suggest guilt.

John is the robber. He was in the bank at the time of the crime. He owns a weapon of the very same kind as the one used during the crime. He has no alibi for where he was during the crime. And the money from the robbery was found in his building.

Perhaps none of this evidence on its own is conclusive. None of it on its own removes every possible reasonable doubt as to whether John is guilty. But when put together, it does make a pretty strong case. The missing premise here is something like this: If John was at the bank and owns the weapon that was used, and has no alibi, then he is the robber. This makes the argument much stronger, for reasons that we saw when we studied how to identify missing premises.

CHAPTER SUMMARY

Thinking critically about what to believe and what to do requires having reasons. We can make these reasons explicit in the form of an argument, with the reasons as premises and the belief or action as the conclusion. An argument is valid if it is not possible for the premises to be true and the conclusion false. Sometimes we have reasons that depend on each other and sometimes they are independent reasons. Sometimes, we even have reasons for our reasons, and we can make them explicit in a sub-argument. Sometimes, reasons for believing or doing something are left unsaid or implicit. Indicator words are useful in constructing and analyzing arguments.

3.8   CRITICAL THINKING IN PRACTICE

3.8.1   Critical Thinking Strategies

We discussed two strategies for deciding whether an argument's premises are dependent or independent.

The Words Test. To tell whether premises are dependent or independent, see whether some of the conclusion's key words occur only in one premise and other key words only in another. If so, then those premises are probably dependent.

False Premise Test. To test whether premises are dependent or independent, suppose that one were false, and ask whether the other one would still provide some support for the conclusion. If it would, then the premises are independent. If not, then they are dependent.

We discussed a test for deciding how much logical support an argument's premises provide.

Validity Test. To test an argument for validity, first suppose that the premises were true. Then ask: could the conclusion still be false? If Yes, then the argument is not valid. If no, then the argument is valid.

3.8.2   From Theory to Practice: Applying What We Have Learned

3.8.2.1   Thinking Critically about Ourselves   In Chapter 1, you identified some character traits that you think are essential to being a morally good person. You picked one of them and wrote out some reasons for thinking that it really is essential. In Chapter 2, you then provided a definition of the trait. Now that we have studied the nature of arguments and the structure of reasons, do the following:

   a. Construct two arguments for the conclusion that character trait is really essential to being a morally good person. Make sure that you rely on the definition you developed in Chapter 2. Make sure that the arguments are valid.
   b. Construct an argument for the view that it is not really essential. That is, the conclusion of this argument should be that one can be a morally good person even though you lack that trait. Make sure that the argument is valid. Try to make this argument as strong as you can, by using premises that are reasonable.

3.8.2.2   Thinking Critically in the Classroom   In Chapter 1, you developed a list of the five or six most important concepts in your chosen field of study. (If you do not have a chosen field of study yet, then just pick your favorite course.) Look for arguments in the texts you use in that course. Find five arguments. Analyze them into their component assertions. Identify the premises and conclusions. Identify any sub-arguments. Rewrite them in such a way that their logical structure if perfectly clear. Make sure that the argument is valid.

3.8.2.3   Thinking Critically at Work   Studies show that employers value an ability to think critically more than just about any other trait in an employee. They want their workers to be able to think critically about both day-to-day problems as well as about broader organizational performance and plans. In Chapter 1, you listed several tasks that you do at work. Pick one of them, and do the following.

a. State what its goal is.
b. Identify three reasons for thinking that that goal is valuable for your organization, and formulate those reasons into a valid argument.
c. Identify reasons for thinking that the task you chose will in fact succeed at attaining that goal, or is an essential part of what it will take to attain that goal. Formulate those reasons into a valid argument. (These are challenging; do your best, and do not worry too much about accuracy here. The goal of the exercise is to get you to think critically about what you did at work.)

4

ACCEPTABLE REASONS

Critical thinking is reasonable and reflective thinking aimed at deciding what to believe and what to do. It is reasonable in part because it requires us to have reasons for our beliefs and decisions—reasons to think that our beliefs are true or that our decisions are the right ones. Critical thinking is reflective in part because it requires us to think about whether our reasons are good enough, and this means that to think critically we need to think about our reasons as reasons.

> When evaluating an argument there are only two questions to ask: Are its premises true? Is it valid?

We saw in Chapter 3 that a person's reasons for believing or doing something can be put in to the form of an argument, with the reasons as premises and the belief or action as the conclusion. And we saw that there are really only two questions to ask when thinking critically about an argument. First, are the premises true? Second, is the argument valid? And we saw that these questions are wholly independent of each other. An argument might be valid even when its premises are false. And an argument's premises might be true even if they do not support its conclusion. So when we think critically about an argument, we always need to ask these two questions. In Chapter 3 we studied the question about validity. In this Chapter we look at the question of truth.

A Practical Guide to Critical Thinking: Deciding What to Do and Believe, Second Edition. David A. Hunter.
© 2014 John Wiley & Sons, Inc. Published 2014 by John Wiley & Sons, Inc.

When considering whether an argument's premise is true, we need to consider whether its source is reliable. If it is not, then it would be unreasonable to accept the premise.

You might have noticed, though, that this Chapter is not entitled "Truth." It is entitled "Acceptability." There is a good reason for this. Sometimes, we might already know whether the premises in an argument are true or not. Maybe we are already an expert on the topic, or the argument will concern matters we are quite familiar with. But often we will not already know whether the premises are true. In that case, it is important to consider the source of the information in the premise. Some sources of evidence are very trustworthy, and others are not. If the source of the evidence is not trustworthy, then the evidence will not be acceptable. This Chapter is about how to think critically about when evidence is acceptable.

To start, imagine that you are on a jury and that Jones has been charged with murder. Suppose that Smith testifies that Jones was at the murder scene. We can think of this testimony as a premise in an argument for the conclusion that Jones is the murderer. The prosecutor is offering that testimony as a reason to believe that Jones is guilty. As a member of the jury, you need to assess that argument. As we have seen, there are really only two questions you need to answer. First, does the testimony prove that Jones is guilty? To answer this question you would use the strategies we discussed in Chapter 3. Second, is the testimony true? To answer this second question, you need to consider whether Smith is trustworthy. Should you take him at his word? Is he lying, or misinformed? Was he confused about who he saw that night? These are questions about whether the evidence Smith provided is acceptable.

Observation, measurement, and testimony are among our most reliable sources of evidence.

The aim of this Chapter is to study when evidence is acceptable. Smith is a source of evidence in that trial. In this case it is testimonial evidence. But there are many different sources of evidence including observation and various kinds of measurement. To decide what the weather is or will be, we collect evidence by looking out the window and by measuring the air's temperature and pressure. To decide whether our diet is working, we collect evidence by looking at our waist, and by measuring our weight on a bathroom scales. When trying to predict the future of the local economy, we collect evidence by reading the newspaper, by measuring unemployment rates, by studying business starts and stops. In all these cases, we rely on a source of evidence to supply us with reasons for our beliefs and actions. Observation, measurement, and testimony are among our most valuable sources of evidence. Without them, we probably would not have much if any knowledge at all.

In this chapter we will focus on these three sources of evidence. These sources differ from one another in important ways, and this means that there are special questions we need to ask and terminology we need to use when thinking critically about each of them. We will study these questions and cover this terminology. But first, it will be helpful to begin at a somewhat more abstract level. For no matter what source of evidence we consider, the fundamental question to ask is the same: Is the source of evidence reliable in this particular case? Let us take a closer look at what this question means, and how we can answer it in a particular case.

4.1   RELIABLE SOURCES

A source of evidence is **reliable** when it provides correct evidence more often than not. Three points are important to note. First, reliability is a matter of degree: some sources are more reliable than others. Second, reliability can depend on the surrounding conditions: a source of evidence may be more reliable in certain conditions than in others. Third, reliability depends on topic: a source may be reliable on evidence for one topic but not for another topic. Let us look at each of these in turn.

We can illustrate the idea of a reliable source of evidence with a somewhat silly example. Suppose that we want to know whether it is currently raining in Washington DC. Here are two sources of evidence. We might use the coin-flip method which tells us the following: flip a coin and if the coin lands heads, believe that it is raining; if the coin lands tails, believe that it is not raining. We might instead use the phone-call method: phone our friends who live in DC and ask them whether it is raining. If they say that it is, then believe that it is raining; if they say that it is not, then believe that it is not raining. It is pretty obvious that the phone-call method is better than the coin-flip method. But why is it better? Why is a friend who lives in DC a better source of evidence than the result of randomly flipping a coin? Part of the answer, surely, is that the phone-call method is far more likely than the coin-flip method to provide us with accurate evidence about the weather in Washington DC.

> The reliability of a source of evidence is always a matter of degree, and some sources are more reliable than others.

The coin-flip method might give us the right answer on this particular case. But this would only be by sheer luck. And the chance that it would give us the right answer next time is not very high. In fact, the chance that it would give us the right answer is probably no better than 50%. By contrast, the chance that the phone-call method would give us the right answer is much, much higher, maybe even as high as 95%.

So part of what makes the phone-call method a better source of evidence than the coin-flip method is that the phone-call method is far more likely to give us the right answer. This is part of what makes the phone-call method a better source of evidence than the coin-flip method, at least concerning the weather in Washington DC. This silly example nicely illustrates how the acceptability of evidence depends on whether it comes from a reliable source. Because the phone call method is more likely to give us the right answer means that it is more **reliable** than the coin-flip method. The more often a source of evidence gives the correct answer, the more reliable it is.

The coin-flipping story illustrates the important fact that the reliability of a source of evidence is a **matter of degree**. Some sources of evidence are more reliable than others. It is hard to imagine a source that could be 100% reliable, since every source we know about can malfunction. So we should not demand that level of reliability. But it is reasonable to think that there is a minimum level of reliability needed for the evidence provided by a source to be acceptable. And it seems right that the coin-flip method will never yield acceptable evidence simply because it is not nearly reliable enough.

The reliability of a source of evidence depends on whether it is operating under optimal conditions.

A second important point is that the reliability of a source of evidence depends on whether it is operating in **optimal conditions**. My friend in DC might be a better judge of the weather in the morning on his way to work than in the afternoon when he is sitting in his office cubicle. This means that as a source of evidence on the DC weather he is more reliable in the morning than in the afternoon. The bathroom scale is reliable only when it is on a flat and level surface. Our eyesight is reliable only when the lighting is right. Optimality conditions can vary from one source of evidence to another. In asking whether a source of evidence is reliable we need to keep in mind whether the conditions are optimal. This means that we cannot judge whether a source of evidence is reliable unless we know whether it is operating in optimal conditions, and this means knowing what those conditions are. The more we understand about how our sources of evidence work to provide us with evidence, the more reflective we can be in our thinking.

A source of evidence may be reliable on some topics but not on others.

The third point to keep in mind is that reliability is **topic relative**. My DC friend might be a reliable source of evidence on the weather in DC, but not on which wines to have with fresh fish. Maybe he can tell when it is raining, but not whether it is better to have a German or a French white wine with grilled ocean salmon. The bathroom scale is a good source of evidence on my weight, but not on my mood or cholesterol levels. This means that when we judge whether to accept some evidence we need to ask whether the source is an appropriate source on this topic. Just because the source is reliable for one topic does not mean that it is reliable for others.

SUMMARY: RELIABILITY

A source of evidence is reliable when it provides accurate information most of the time. The reliability of a source of evidence is always a matter of degree, depends on optimal conditions, and is topic relative.

4.2   UNDERMINING AND OVERRIDING EVIDENCE

In Chapter 1 we saw that pieces of evidence can conflict in two ways. First, one piece of evidence **directly** conflicts with another when it supports an opposite conclusion. Second, one piece of evidence **indirectly** conflicts with another, when it indicates that the second piece of evidence is from an unreliable or untrustworthy source. This is a good time to look again at these different kinds of conflicts.

One piece of evidence directly conflicts with another when it supports an opposite conclusion. Sometimes when one piece of evidence directly conflicts with another, one of the pieces of evidence will be stronger than the other. In that case, the stronger evidence **overrides** the weaker evidence. Overridden evidence is not acceptable. This means that it would be unreasonable to rely on overridden evidence when deciding what to believe or do.

> When two pieces of evidence directly conflict, if one is stronger than the other, then the stronger evidence overrides the weaker evidence. It is unreasonable to accept overridden evidence.

For example, Smith's testimony that Jones was at the hotel the night of the murder directly conflicts with Sam's testimony that Jones was at home the night of the murder. Those two bits of testimony directly conflict. And suppose that Smith's testimony is stronger than Sam's evidence and so overrides it. Sam's evidence is thus not acceptable. This means that it would be unreasonable for the members of the jury to rely on Sam's evidence.

It is not always easy to tell which piece of evidence is stronger than another. Where we have directly conflicting evidence we have to be extremely cautious. It will not always be obvious which source of evidence is at fault. We can formulate some general rules of thumb. A piece of evidence is overridden if:

- it conflicts with evidence from a known reliable source; or
- it conflicts with expert opinion; or
- it conflicts with what we already have good reason to believe.

In cases of conflict, we need to make a judgment. Do we reject the new evidence; do we reject the evidence it conflicts with; or do we reject both? It will not always be obvious which piece of evidence is most accurate. Maybe the source we thought was reliable has made a mistake. Maybe the expert opinion is wrong in this case. Maybe the proper response to the new evidence is to make a relatively large revision to our standing beliefs. If we want to avoid making a mistake, we should withhold judgment altogether, and collect more evidence before we make a judgment. We need to decide which source of evidence is most reliable. Until we make that decision, the best or at least the most prudent course is to withhold judgment as long as possible.

One piece of evidence indirectly conflicts with another when it indicates that it is from an untrustworthy or unreliable source.

Evidence can conflict in a second way. One piece of evidence **indirectly** conflicts with another when it indicates that it is from a source that is not reliable or trustworthy. If the first piece of evidence is stronger than the second, then the first **undermines** the second. Undermined evidence is not acceptable. This means that it would be unreasonable to rely on undermined evidence when deciding what to believe or do.

When one piece of evidence indirectly conflicts with another, if the first is stronger than the second, then the first piece of evidence **undermines** the second piece of evidence. It is unreasonable to accept undermined evidence.

Suppose, for example, that Ayesha testifies that Smith hates Jones and would lie on the stand to harm him. Ayesha's testimony indirectly conflicts with Smith's, because it suggests that Smith is not trustworthy. Let us suppose that Ayesha's testimony is stronger than Smith's and so undermines it. Smith's testimony, then, is not acceptable. This means that it would be unreasonable for the members of the jury to rely on Smith's testimony when deciding whether Jones is guilty.

Undermined evidence can still be true.

There is an extremely important point to keep in mind. Undermined evidence may still be true. Consider again Ayesha's testimony. Her testimony was stronger than Smith's and so undermined it. This means that Smith's testimony is not acceptable, and that the member of the jury should not rely on it when deciding whether Jones is guilty. But none of this means that Smith's testimony is false. He might have been telling the truth, even if he hated Jones and was willing to lie on the stand to harm him. Even liars sometimes tell the truth. So when the members of the jury decide that Smith's testimony is not acceptable, this does not mean that they can then also decide that Smith's testimony is false. All they can reasonably decide is that Smith is not trustworthy—his testimony is not acceptable. They should remain agnostic, and withhold judgment about where Jones was the night of the murder until more of the evidence is in.

Consider another case. Suppose that my kids have been playing with the bathroom scale again and that I know that the last time they did this, the scale broke and gave crazy readings. I now have reason to think that they have once again broken the scale's internal mechanisms. In this case, I should not trust what it tells me when I step on it. Of course, the reading I get from it might be accurate, but still I should withhold judgment until I can make sure that it is not broken.

**CRITICAL THINKING MISTAKES: APPEAL
TO IGNORANCE**

It is a mistake to believe something just because you do not have evidence that it is false. This is a mistake because a bit of investigation might show that it is false, and thinking critically requires looking for evidence when one can. One form of this mistake is to accept a piece of evidence just because you do not know of any overriding or undermining evidence. Critical thinkers should look for overriding and undermining evidence, before accepting a piece of evidence.

We have seen that evidence is acceptable if it comes from a reliable source and it is neither (ii) undermined nor (iii) overridden by other evidence we have. We usually do not need to know that a source is reliable in order to be justified in relying on it. But if we have reason to think the source is not reliable or to think that the evidence is inaccurate, then we are not justified in relying on it. These general points about when we can trust evidence from a source apply to every source of evidence. They are general enough that we can keep them in mind whether we are relying on observation, testimony, or measurement. This will help us as we move forward. Still, there are important differences between these three sources of evidence, and seeing them will help us identify some additional questions to ask.

**SUMMARY: UNDERMINING AND OVERRIDING
EVIDENCE**

When two pieces of evidence directly conflict, if one is stronger than the other, then the stronger evidence overrides the weaker evidence. Overridden evidence is not acceptable.

When one piece of evidence indirectly conflicts with another, if the first is stronger than the second, then the first piece of evidence **undermines** the second piece of evidence. Undermined evidence is not acceptable.

EXERCISE 1

A. Comprehension Questions

    a. What does it mean for a source of evidence to be reliable?

    b. Why is reliability a matter of degree?

    c. Explain why reliability is topic relative? Could there be a source of evidence whose reliability is not topic relative? Explain.

    d. What is the difference between overriding and undermining evidence?

    e. Construct an example of a case in which some evidence is overridden but not undermined.

f. Could a source that is highly reliable nonetheless provide false evidence? Describe an example other than the ones discussed in the text.

g. Suppose that you had evidence that undermined the evidence provided by some source of evidence, S. Could it still be that S is highly reliable? Explain, and use examples to illustrate.

h. Suppose that the evidence provided from one source always conflicted with the evidence provided by another source. Should we continue to trust those sources? Which one should we doubt?

i. Some people think that fortune telling is a good source of evidence. What do you think? Why?

j. Suppose that we wanted to determine whether perceptual observation is a reliable source of evidence about the colors of medium-sized objects. How could we do this?

4.3   OBSERVATION

The English philosopher John Locke (1632–1704) claimed that without perceptual observation we would have no ideas or thoughts and so no knowledge at all. It is very difficult to disagree with this claim. From the moment we wake up in the morning, we rely on our observations of our surroundings to get around—to find out where we are and what we have to do to get our breakfast. We know that—blind people still have beliefs and knowledge, as do deaf people and people like Helen Keller who lack several senses. But it is hard to imagine how a person who had no sense organs at all could possibly have any knowledge of anything at all. Perceptual observation certainly seems essential to knowledge, or at least to human knowledge. At the same time, we know that observation is not infallible—it can and sometimes does make mistakes. Sometimes, things are not quite as they seem to be. So while we have little choice but to rely on our observations, we need to do so reflectively. In this section, we will study the conditions under which we are justified in relying on perceptual observation.

By perceptual observation we can include the ordinary five senses—taste, touch, smell, hearing, and sight. But we can also include our capacity to tell such things as when we are hungry or thirsty and to tell the relative position of our body parts, such as where our arms are in relation to each other—a capacity called "proprioception" by philosophers and psychologists. Each of these sources of evidence about the world and ourselves is reliable, but only under certain conditions. Sight, for example, only works properly when the external conditions are right. The light has to be bright enough, but not too bright. Changing the color of the light can affect the visual appearance of things. There are also internal conditions that must be right. Vision is not reliable after the optometrist has put dilating drops in—everything looks fuzzy and shadowy. The internal and external optimality conditions are already pretty familiar to us, and we do not need to go into a lot of detail about them here.

Perceptual observation is reliable on some topics but not others. We can often tell by looking what colors things are and where a thing is in relation to other things.

We can tell whether the toaster is on the counter or in the cupboard. We can tell by hearing whether the radio is on. We can tell by smell whether the stew is burning. We also know that different senses are reliable on different topics. We can tell by looking, but not by smell, whether the TV is still on. We can tell by smell, but not by hearing, whether the milk has gone sour. We can tell by touch, but not by sight, whether the water is cool enough for swimming. It is obviously important to make sure that we are using the proper sense for a given topic. It is also familiar that there are lots of things we cannot tell with any of our sense organs. We cannot tell by observation whether a person has AIDS—we need to run complex tests for this. Nor can we tell by observation alone whether the economy is improving—we need to make some complex measurements for this. Running the tests and making these observations would be impossible without observation—but the evidence they yield is not observational evidence.

Observation improves as we mature and with training. Anyone who has tried to teach little kids to swing a baseball bat knows that it can be frustrating. It seems to take little kids a long time to learn how to time the bat's swing—something that seems so easy for adults. It is as if the kids cannot even see the ball. Recent studies on the development of the visual system seem to suggest that this is exactly what is going on! The capacity to tell how quickly things are moving requires a relatively advanced level of brain development. On reflection, this is not that surprising. Our perceptual systems are after all just part of our body and we know that our bodies mature and change. In fact, it would be surprising if our perceptual systems did not become more reliable as we grew up. We also know that we can increase the reliability of our perceptual systems with training. Trained musicians can hear rhythms and melodic progressions and patterns in musical performances that others cannot hear. Skilled gardeners can tell by looking whether plants need watering or fertilizer. Doctors learn to identify various skin conditions just by sight. Experts on wine can taste things in wine that most of the rest of us cannot. These improvements are not just the result of maturation—they result from training and practice.

Perceptual capacities are also subject to illusions. This is especially familiar in the case of vision. Some visual illusions are **optical**—that means that their explanation has to do with the way light works. For instance, a straight stick in a glass of water looks bent because the light reflected off the part of the stick in the water is slowed down as it travels through the water causing it to change directions slightly, producing the illusion. But other visual illusions are **cognitive**—they have to do with the way our visual system is structured or the way it works. The illusion that parallel railroad tracks meet has to do with the distance between our eyes. The same is true of the Müller-Lyer illusion, we saw in Chapter 1. Others are harder to classify. For instance, it is a familiar experience that a full moon seen close to the horizon looks a lot bigger than a full moon seen high in the sky. At first, people thought it was an optical illusion, caused by the fact that light reflected off the moon has to travel through much more atmosphere when it is on the horizon than when it is in the high sky. But if this was so, then one would expect the image on the eyeballs to be of different sizes. But the images are the same size whether the moon is on the horizon or in the high sky. It is now thought that the illusion is produced as the brain "interprets" or processes the information. One possibility is that it has to do with the fact that the moon on the horizon is seen as close to other objects. But this illusion is not yet fully understood.

4.4 MEMORY

We often rely on our memories to ground or sustain our beliefs. But memory's role in the justification of beliefs is a special one. For memory is not a source of evidence; rather; it is a repository of evidence. Whereas observations are bits of evidence, memories are not. Memory stores evidence. This means that when we rely on our memory, our evidence is no more acceptable than the acceptability of the evidence we remember.

But we also know that memory can be unreliable: it is as if in the storage process the evidence gets modified or changed. The US National Transportation Safety Board (NTSB) provides an especially striking example of this. After a plane crash, the agents of the NTSB collects as much evidence as they can in the hopes of trying to recreate the sequence of events that led to the crash. Among the evidence they collect are reports from eyewitnesses on the ground. But over time, they have found that eyewitness reports are highly variable. In the case of the crash of American Flight 587 in 2001, the NTSB interviewed 394 eyewitnesses. They found that:

> ... 52 percent said they saw a fire while the plane was in the air. The largest number (22 percent) said the fire was in the fuselage, but a majority cited other locations, including the left engine, the right engine, the left wing, the right wing, or an unspecified engine or wing. Nearly one of five witnesses said they saw the plane make a right turn; an equal number said it was a left turn. Nearly 60 percent said they saw something fall off the plane; of these, 13 percent said it was a wing. (In fact, it was the vertical portion of the tail.)[1]

Why are eyewitnesses so unreliable? It might be that their visual observations of the event are unreliable. But it is hard to see how so many people could have had such different visual experiences, especially when they were all looking at the very same event, and maybe even standing right next to one another. More likely, their visual experiences were somehow distorted as they got put into memory, while they stayed in storage, or while they were being retrieved from storage. Whether the distortion happened before the storage, during the storage, or during the retrieval process, their memories are distorted. The NTSB still collects eyewitness reports, but they do this as for largely public relations reasons. They no longer rely on these reports when trying to figure out what happened. Admittedly, memories of horrific visual scenes such as the crash of an airplane are the exception, and the fact that such experiences

[1] Wald, M. For air crash detectives, seeing isn't believing. *The New York Times* (June 23, 2002), Section 4, p. 3.

are misremembered does not by itself show that memory is not in general reliable. But it does illustrate once again the reason for the following maxim: trust, but verify.

CRITICAL THINKING IN PSYCHOLOGY

Researchers have found that a person's memory can be manipulated in different ways.[1] In one study, subjects were shown a fake advertisement of Disneyland featuring Bugs Bunny standing next to the Magic Castle. The ad looked just like a real ad for Disneyland. After studying the ad, subjects were asked to describe their own experience as children visiting Disneyland. Sixteen percent of them said that they remembered meeting Bugs Bunny at Disneyland. The greater the number of exposures to the fake ads, the higher the percent who claimed to remember personally meeting Bugs in Florida. Some even claimed to remember specific details, such as hugging him and touching his ears. But since Bugs Bunny is not a Disney character, these supposed memories are all false, somehow implanted or encouraged by the false advertisements. Researchers have even been able to instill false memories of quite unusual and memorable events. In one study, a subject's parents were enlisted to tell the subject that she had poured a slimy substance onto the head of her Grade 1 teacher. The story was the very same for each subject, aside from names and places, and was full of detail. They were even provided with fake photos of the event to show to the subject. Remarkably, 65% of the subjects later reported to researchers that they remembered the event in vivid detail, and expressed shock and surprise when told the entire event was fictional.

EXERCISE 2

A. List five conditions under which visual perception is not reliable. Do the same for our sense of touch.

B. We learned that our senses are reliable for some topics but not others. List some topics for which vision but not touch is reliable. List some for which hearing and sight are both reliable. List some on which no sense is ever reliable.

C. Sometimes, our different senses provide us with conflicting evidence. Describe such a case. Which sense should we trust in a case like that? If you can, think of a general rule or principle that can be used to always decide which sense to trust when senses conflict.

4.5   TESTIMONY

It is difficult to exaggerate the importance that testimony plays as a source of evidence for us. Without it we would have almost no knowledge. But it is also a very complex source of evidence, one that critical thinkers need to be very cautious about. In this section we will study why.

Imagine that you only relied on your own, personal observations. How much knowledge would you be able to acquire? Not very much, probably. Just think of how little you can actually see and feel at any one time. Even if our perceptual faculties are as highly reliable as we hope, they are also extremely limited. But we all know (or at least think that we know) a lot about things we have never seen or touched. We know about the history of the US constitution, about the battles of the two world wars. We may have seen the 9/11 attacks with our own eyes, but we need more than our own eyes to figure out the causes of the attack or what structural causes made the towers fall down. We know about distant places and times, beyond our observation. Most of our knowledge, in fact, would be out of reach if we did not rely for information on other people, whether it be our parents, friends, teachers, authors we read in the news or see on TV shows, or even just people we overhear in the local coffee shop or bar. (Hopefully you have learned a thing or two from me in reading this book.)

Evidence that consists in what other people tell us is **testimonial evidence**. It may sound a bit fancy to call the information we get from newspapers, teachers, and parents, "testimony." It sounds a bit odd to say that our best friend is testifying when he tells us that the fridge is full of beer. But the analogy between these ordinary cases of believing what people tell us and the role of witnesses in a trial is very strong. In all of these cases we are treating other people as sources of evidence. We are taking them at their word; trusting their say-so. This raises the question: when is testimonial evidence acceptable?

SUMMARY: TESTIMONIAL EVIDENCE

Testimonial evidence is acceptable only if

   (i) it is on an appropriate topic; and
  (ii) the witness is properly trained; and
 (iii) the witness is properly informed; and
 (iv) the witness is unbiased.

The first three conditions are already familiar, though we will see that there are some special factors to keep in mind. But the fourth condition is a new one. It is needed because whenever we are deciding whether to trust what someone is telling us, we need to think about whether that person is biased or prejudiced. Let us look at each of these conditions in more detail.

4.5.1   Appropriate Testimony

First, testimonial evidence is acceptable only if the topic is **appropriate**. As we saw above, a source of evidence might be reliable on some topics but not others. The same is true for people. When a person is a reliable source of evidence on some topic, we can think of her as an expert on it. Some people are experts on sports, while others are experts on the chemistry of cells. A person can be an expert on several very different topics. But there are some topics where there simply are no experts.

A familiar example is any topic where there are no real objective facts, but just matters of taste. For example, I doubt whether there are facts about whether one popular musician is better than another. There are, of course, people who know a lot about pop music, about the different performers and their histories and musical capacities. There are experts about who can carry a tune and play the guitar. But is there really such a thing as being an expert on whether Madonna's music is better than Bruce Springsteen's? I have always liked Bob Dylan's singing, though many people find it (and my musical preferences) horrifying. But is there anything more to this disagreement than just a difference in taste? I doubt it. I am inclined to think that it is inappropriate to appeal to experts to settle disputes about which pop musician is better.

But it is not just in matters of taste that there are no experts. Sometimes, when a new field of study is very young and just getting established, there will not yet be experts either. This is the case at cutting edge fields in natural science. When the scientists working at that cutting edge disagree among themselves about the field, and especially when they disagree about which methods are best for measuring or describing the phenomena, then there are probably no real experts yet. In cases where the best-placed people in the field cannot agree, then we as nonexperts should probably withhold judgment too. This was the case at some time in almost every branch of science. It was the case for the science of global warming until about 20 years ago. But now there is no doubt that there are experts on global warming, and that it is perfectly appropriate to rely on what they say when we decide what to believe about global warming.

4.5.2   Trained Testimony

Second, testimonial evidence is acceptable only if the witness is properly trained. This is just a way of asking whether the witness is reliable, whether there is a high likelihood that his testimony will be true.

What it takes to be properly trained depends of course on the topic. Trials provide lots of good examples. Only in special kinds of cases will an eye witness to a crime have to show that her eyes were working properly the afternoon of the crime, though if she ordinarily wears glasses that will be relevant to whether she really did see what happened. But it is much more common for a witness on a specialized scientific topic to have to demonstrate to the court that she has the proper training. Expert witnesses on DNA testing or finger printing need to show they have the training and certification needed for their testimony to be acceptable. Usually, the fact that a witness has been certified by the relevant organization is good reason to think she has the proper training to count as an expert witness on that topic.

These examples are from court trials. But the same issues arise in more mundane cases too. I would trust my highly trained electrician over my 9-year-old daughter to tell me whether the wiring in the panel is adequate. I would turn to the pharmacist and not the grocery clerk for advice on which antihistamine to buy, though I might trust the grocery clerk over the pharmacist on which streetcar will get me downtown fastest. In this last case, it is not the training but the experience that matters.

4.5.3   Informed Testimony

The difference between being properly trained and being properly informed is an important one. A person might be an expert at fingerprint identification, but if she has not actually studied the fingerprints given during the trial, then she is not properly informed. The following analogy might help: a thermometer is really good at telling the temperature of the water in a glass. But it will not get the reading right unless it is in the water. This is like the difference between being trained and being informed.

Sometimes, people who are considered experts find it difficult to admit that they do not know an answer to some question. This is understandable. But it is also an obstacle to critical thinking. We should prefer for them to keep quiet or admit to ignorance than say something that is ill informed. In general, we should not accept what a witness says if we have reason to think she is not sufficiently informed on the issue at hand, even if we think she is an expert on the general topic.

4.5.4   Unbiased Testimony

Finally, testimonial evidence is acceptable only if the witness is **unbiased**. The reason for this condition is pretty straightforward: sometimes witnesses are motivated in different ways to lie about the facts.

The example of the murder trial illustrates one possible source of bias. The defense attorneys claimed that the witness was biased because he was being paid by the prosecution to give his testimony. The implication was that the witness might not have given the same testimony had he been paid by the defense attorneys, or by no one. Of course, the fact that the witness was being paid for his testimony does not prove that he was lying or overstating or understating anything. But it might, and for some of the jury it did, raise the possibility that he was biased against the defendant and so was not to be trusted. Desire for financial gain is one source of bias, but it is not the only one. Just about anything can be a source of bias. People are moved to lie by jealousy and by love, by pride and by humility, out of loyalty and out of revenge, by a desire for fame and by a desire for anonymity. If we know that someone is biased, then obviously we should not accept what they say. Their testimony is acceptable only if there is no reason to suspect that they are biased.

CRITICAL THINKING MISTAKES: UNACCEPTABLE TESTIMONY

It is a mistake to accept testimony from a witness if the topic is inappropriate, the witness is not properly trained, or not properly informed, or if the witness is biased. It is a mistake because such evidence is not acceptable. Testimony is appropriate only on topics for which there are recognized experts. An expert must be properly trained and properly informed. And a witness must not be motivated to lie about or exaggerate the facts.

Judgments about witness bias can be tricky and can require balancing different facts about the witness. Suppose that the lead scientist for a well-known environmental group testifies before Congress that the water levels in the Great Lakes are dangerously low and that expensive conservation steps must be taken to reduce water usage in the cities and farms that depend on the water from the Lakes. What are her motivations? We know that she is paid by the environmental group to champion its environmental policies. If there were no environmental problems to report on, she would be out of a job. She probably also wants to keep her high-profile position, and might enjoy being in the spotlight before Congress. She might think that advocating an extreme position might, given the political realities involved in passing complex regulatory legislation, be the best strategic move. All of these considerations suggest that she might be motivated to exaggerate or even lie about the real findings.

CRITICAL THINKING MISTAKES: AD HOMINEM

It is a mistake to believe that a piece of testimony is false just because the witness is unreliable or biased. It is a mistake because it confuses undermining and overriding evidence. Testimony can be true even if it is from an unreliable or biased source.

This mistake is traditionally called "ad hominem" because it involves criticizing testimony by criticizing the witness (the "hominem"). But we need to be a bit careful here in identifying this mistake. For it is not always a mistake to conclude that a witness is unreliable or biased. There can be very good reason to believe this. But it is always a mistake to conclude that *a witness's testimony is false* just because they are unreliable or biased.

On the other hand, it is often hard to get away with a lie, and the reputation of her organization will suffer if it becomes public that its lead scientist has been lying. She also has a professional reputation as a scientist that she probably wants to maintain and even enhance. Lying or exaggerating will surely hurt her image among other scientists. And she probably has a personal sense of honor that forbids lying or exaggerating, except perhaps in extreme cases, which this surely is not. These considerations suggest that she is highly motivated to speak the truth, at least as she sees it. What should we conclude about her testimony? Since we are not experts, we are in a difficult spot.

CRITICAL THINKING AND LEGAL HISTORY

In a famous American trial from the 1990s, the defendant was accused of having viciously murdered his wife and her friend. The prosecution's case was built on forensic evidence that seemed to connect the defendant to blood samples found at the scene of the crime, in the defendant's home and on a bloody glove of a kind once owned by the defendant. To many outside observers, the case seemed quite strong. But the defense attorneys did a remarkable job of undermining the prosecution's star witness, a forensic scientist who testified that the blood samples matched the defendant's blood type. First, the defense lawyers argued that this testimony was inappropriate because the science of blood sampling was too young and not yet fully established. Second, they argued that the scientist was not properly trained to use the equipment involved in the sophisticated analysis of the blood. Third, they argued that the scientist was not properly informed about the facts at hand, because the police had mixed up the blood samples they had collected and there was no sure way to tell which samples were found in which place. Finally, they argued that the scientist was biased because he was being paid by the prosecution to give his testimony. Point by point, the defense attorneys had done a masterful job of undermining the witness. In the end, the jury decided that the scientist's evidence was not acceptable.

4.6 ADVERTISING

Advertisements are a special case of testimonial evidence. Advertisements can serve many purposes, but generating sales of the advertised product or service is surely one of the most important. Advertisements can try to achieve this in different ways. Some appeal to emotions, as in the wonderful ads for Apple's IPod music player that involve nothing but a person dancing to the music they're listening to on their IPod. That ad works not by informing us of the product, but by trying to establish an emotional connection between the product and a desirable lifestyle. But many ads do aim to produce sales by informing potential customers about the product or service. Such ads can be thought of as involving testimonial evidence. (Indeed, some even involve "testimonials" by famous people describing their experience with the product or service.) We should evaluate claims made in such ads in the very same ways that we evaluate any other case of testimonial evidence.

We should first ask whether testimonial evidence is appropriate on that topic. Advertisements for food sometimes include claims about great taste. But are there really experts on taste? Recently, drug companies have been permitted to advertise their products. These ads are highly regulated and the drug companies are required to provide quite detailed information about potential side effects. But there is an underlying concern about the appropriateness of these claims, given that for many medicines so little is known about potential long term effects, both positive and negative ones. This is especially true for claims about the health benefits of diet supplements, since many of those products are neither tested nor regulated by the government, though advertisements of them are subject to the regulations that govern all advertisements against being misleading. In general, the acceptability of claims in advertisements about the health effects or benefits of products is questionable simply on the grounds that such claims are inappropriate.

When famous people promote things in advertisements we should ask ourselves whether they are properly trained and properly informed. Is a famous movie star really an expert on which phone plan is best for me? (Set aside for now the fact that the actor is being paid to say that it is.) Is the CEO of an automotive company really an expert on the performance of his company's cars relative to the competition? Should we trust what students in college ads say about the benefits of their college compared to the competition? Unless the ad involves a recognized expert, there is good reason to not accept the claims made in the advertisement.

Finally, though, given that the advertisement is aimed at producing sales, the risk of bias is inevitable and serious. Advertisers know this and sometimes include favorable evaluations from independent organizations. An ad for a car might refer to the results of crash tests performed by an independent safety group, or might cite awards the car received in independent performance tests. (Of course, claims by outside organizations are themselves just more testimonial evidence and need to be evaluated on their own.)

There are also governmental rules regulating commercial speech, designed to prevent false or misleading ads. But these regulations are difficult to enforce. One recent study, reported in The New Yorker, suggests that more than 50% of advertisements for nutritional supplements involved false or misleading claims.[2] The history of advertising also offers little reason to trust claims made in advertisements. It is perhaps best to approach claims made in advertisements with an initial and healthy skepticism: given the high risk of bias, best not to accept the advertised claims.

We have been discussing the conditions under which testimonial evidence is acceptable. We have seen that it is acceptable if, but only if, (i) the testimony is on an appropriate topic; (ii) the witness is properly trained; (iii) the witness is properly informed; and (iii) the witness is not biased in any way. If any one of these conditions is not met, then the testimony is not acceptable. Of course, testimonial evidence that is not acceptable might still be true. A nonexpert might be right about the facts. A biased person might still be speaking the truth. Deciding that testimonial evidence is not acceptable is not itself reason to believe that it is false. In cases where our only evidence is testimonial evidence and we have determined that the testimony is not acceptable, the reasonable thing to do is to withhold belief.

4.7 NEWS REPORTS

The news media is a further special case of testimonial evidence. News reports, whether in newspapers, magazines, on TV or on the Internet, all involve a reporter making claims about some topic or other. The reporter might be writing about what happened yesterday on Capitol Hill or in a refugee camp in the Middle East or Africa. Or maybe the report is on economic conditions in Asia or in our local region. Whatever the topic, we should treat what we read or hear on the news in the way we treat other forms of testimonial evidence and we should be ready to ask the same questions. Is the report on an appropriate topic (one on which there are experts)? Is the reporter an expert? Is the reporter biased in any way? Let us look at each question in turn.

---

[2] Specter, M. (2004). Miracle in a bottle. *The New Yorker* (February 2, 2004), pp. 64–75.

Testimonial evidence is **inappropriate** if it is on a topic where there are no experts. This can happen where the facts are so complex that no one counts as an expert. Sometimes, news reports will make claims about the nature of causes of events where it is questionable whether anyone really knows what is going on. It is, of course, not always obvious to us when a topic is that complex. But in some kinds of cases, it is perhaps better to err on the side of caution. Here are two examples. The first concerns reports on the stock market. Reporters who cover the stock market not only report on changes in the value of various stocks as the day goes on, they sometimes offer explanations of why the markets as a whole are moving in one direction or another. The sharp drop was caused by fear that interest rates will go up; or the rise in stocks was a reaction to the morning news that the unemployment rate has once again crept up. These kinds of claims are almost never trustworthy. No doubt there is some explanation of the change in stocks values. But surely that explanation is enormously complex. The same is true, I think, when reporters offer explanations of complex international events, and this is especially clear in the case of wars. During the war in Iraq, it was regularly reported that the violence in Baghdad was getting worse in the middle of 2007, even as the Americans sent in more troops. These reports were difficult to assess. It is hard to know how to evaluate violence in terms of worse and better—if there are fewer attacks but each attack is more deadly, does that mean the violence is worsening? And because there were so many attacks every day, and because Baghdad is a huge city, it is hard to know everything that is going on. The complexity involved in measuring and defining the level of violence is so high that it might be best to treat claims like that made by reporters as inappropriate.

In general, testimonial evidence is acceptable only if the source is an **expert** on the topic. But this is almost never the case with news reports. Many reporters are trained in journalism schools. This means that they are trained in how to collect information and how to present it in various media. But it does not mean that they are trained in or well informed on the topics on which they report. Indeed, most reporters are not experts on what they are reporting on. This is why they rely on experts in the field when preparing their reports. They present the expert's testimony. In a way, this makes our task as critical thinkers even harder. For not only do we need to assess whether we should accept the reporter's account of the expert testimony, we have also to assess whether that expert testimony is itself acceptable. Cases when reporters rely on expert testimony are like double testimony! Just to make matters worse, reporters sometimes rely on witnesses who insist on remaining anonymous. The witnesses might have legitimate reasons to insist on this—perhaps their career or health depends on it. But this makes our task next to impossible: how can we assess whether the witness is properly trained, informed, and unbiased if we do not even know who it is? To some extent, perhaps, we can trust the reporter to tell whether the expert she has interviewed is competent and unbiased. But this is less than ideal.

If you think that some piece of testimony is not acceptable, then you need to say which of the four conditions was violated.

A news report is acceptable only if the reporter is well informed. It is not always easy to tell how hard the reporter worked to collect the information she used in her report. **Passive reporting** occurs when a reporter merely accepts testimonial or other evidence without doing background checks and without questioning the acceptability of the evidence. We know that most news reports are produced very quickly, and have to be quite short. Articles in the newspaper and stories on the evening news are unlikely to be as well informed as full-length documentaries. The time pressures are too great. But this means that we, as critical thinkers, have to decide whether the report is based on acceptable information. There are some things to look for in deciding whether a report is well informed: (i) Number and variety of sources. Did the reporter rely on one source or on many? In general, it is better if the reporter asked for many expert opinions. Did the reporter rely on a variety of experts? If all the experts are from a single organization, then there might not be enough variety in their testimony. (ii) Background and fact checking. Did the reporter do any background investigation of her own, or did she solely rely on sources? Without some background work, it can be difficult to know what questions to ask the experts or how to follow up on their answers. Did the reporter check whether factual claims made by her sources are correct? Or is she simply uncritically reporting what the source told her? The more reason there is to think the reporter relied on a large number and variety of sources and did some background and fact checking, the more acceptable the report will be.

Like any testimonial evidence, a news report is acceptable only if it is **unbiased**. In the case of news reports, bias is a potential factor at several different levels, starting with **reporter bias**. Reporters are under pressure to produce, just like anyone else. And we all know that salacious and juicy stories are more fun to read than dry and factual stories, even if the factual ones are intrinsically more important or newsworthy. "If it bleeds, it leads." Reporters are under pressure not just to report the news, but also to report what they think their audience wants to read or hear about. Very rarely, reporters even react to this pressure by making up the news, or by focusing their report on what they think will be most interesting or catchy.

Corporate bias is also possible. Newspapers and news stations are businesses and this means that they are in the business of making money. They do this by reporting on what their audience is interested in. Inevitably, this means that they leave some stories completely unreported. The latest celebrity arrest for drunken driving is covered in more detail than the thousands of children who die every day in refugee camps around the world. The fact that news organizations are in the business of making money also means that they are reluctant to report stories that would make their audience feel uncomfortable. A newspaper that published every day the names of all the children who die of hunger would not be very successful. News organizations are also careful not to offend the patriotism of their audience. News reports that focus on war crimes sometimes face criticism.

Finally, news reports are subject to **cultural biases**. This affects not just what stories are told but how they are told. We find stories about local events more interesting than stories about events in distant parts of the world. It is not easy to detect bias. Respectable news organizations work hard to draw a sharp line between news reporting and editorializing, and some have ombudsmen whose job it is to keep an eye on and even report on the extent to which the organization is succeeding at being unbiased. Finally, it is always good advice not to rely on only one source for news. Reading different reports on the same event is the best way to avoid falling prey to biased reporting.

EXERCISE 3

A. Comprehension Questions

    a. Under what conditions is testimonial evidence acceptable?

    b. What is the difference between being trained and being informed? Illustrate your answer with an example.

    c. If a witness is biased, does this make their testimony false? Give an example to illustrate.

    d. If a witness is testifying about his own personal observations, what are the critical thinking questions that we should ask before accepting his evidence?

    e. Under what conditions is testimonial evidence overridden and undermined? Use examples to illustrate your answer.

    f. What are some sources of media bias?

    g. What is passive reporting? Is it a form of bias? Why or why not?

    h. When are claims made in advertisements acceptable?

B. The following passages involve appeals to testimonial evidence. Determine whether the evidence is acceptable. If not, then identify which of the conditions is violated. Be as detailed as you can.

    a. One of Thomas Jefferson's most trusted advisors said that the United States should not trade with tyrants. We should take that advice and cut off all economic relations with tyrannical regimes around the world.

    b. There is milk in the fridge. I just called home and Joan told me that there is.

    c. I am failing this class. My teacher just told me so.

    d. The cookbook says to boil the eggs for 12 minutes to make them hard, so this is what I am doing.

    e. The newspaper just reported that the stock market will drop tomorrow, so I am selling all of my stocks now.

    f. The bank president says that there is no risk that his bank will go out of business, so I have decided to keep my money in it for now.

    g. The man at the garden supply store told me that this plant will thrive best in a shady spot, so I am going to put it underneath that tree.

    h. The man at the garden supply store told me that this hose will not leach lead poisoning into the soil. That is why I bought it.

    i. I think that you will really like this band. The girl at the music store said that they are the best all boy band since 'N Sync.

C. The following passages involve attempts to undermine a witness' testimony. Using the concepts we have discussed in this chapter, explain whether the attempt is successful. If not, explain why it fails. Be as detailed as you can.

    a. The man at the garden supply store said that the plant thrives in shade, but he just stocks the shelves there. I do not trust him.

    b. Our local politician says that we should revise campaign finance legislation to make it harder for politicians to be influenced. But he is just trying to raise funds from the "little guy." Do not trust him.

    c. The regional coordinator of that environmental group gets paid to recruit new members, so we cannot trust what he says about the effects of global warming. He is just trying to get us to contribute.

    d. The newspaper article says that the new highway is very dangerous. But I do not think the reporter has any background in that field. He cites a lot of expert reports, but he has no training for himself. We should not trust him.

    e. The witness claims that Jones robbed the bank, and that she saw him leaving with the bag of money. But there were so many people coming and going that day that there is no way the witness could be reliable on this. No one could remember every face they ever saw.

    f. The cookbook says that it is best to add fresh anchovies to the dressing, rather than canned ones. But the cookbook author owns a chain of fresh food stores, so she is probably just trying to increase sales.

D. Look at a newspaper article. Using the concepts discussed in this chapter, assess whether the reporter is guilty of passive reporting. Be as specific as you can in your criticisms, and make sure to support them carefully.

E. Look in the newspaper or on TV for five examples of testimonials. Assess whether the testimonial evidence is acceptable. Be as specific as you can, and be sure to support your conclusions with reasons.

F. Look at today's newspaper and find a report on some international incident. Then go to the library or go online and find news articles from different continents on the very same incident. Compare the reports looking for significant differences.

4.8 MEASUREMENT

When we try to decide what to believe or what to do, we often rely on evidence from measurement. After all, one way to collect information on some subject or phenomena is to measure it. We have a huge number and variety of measuring instruments and tools at our disposal. We measure our own mass using a bathroom scale and that of objects in deep space using highly sophisticated instruments; we measure public opinion using surveys and questionnaires; we measure the intelligence of our children using IQ tests; meteorologists measure the speed and direction of traveling storms; we measure student performance using final exams. (What, in your view, do final grades actually measure?) Businesses use personality tests to find out about their employees and to build better teams. It would not be much of an exaggeration to say that measurement plays as important and prevalent a role as observation or testimony in our reasoning about what to believe and do. Thinking critically about the acceptability of measurements involves asking some of the very same questions we asked about observation and testimony.

> We need to use an appropriate scale when we measure something.

Here is an initial question: what is it, exactly, to **measure** something? Measuring usually involves assigning a number. But not always: Doctors sometimes ask children with sore throats to indicate the level of soreness using a chart of face drawings, ranging from a happy smiling one to one that is crying. The kids are using this chart to measure their pain, even though no number are involved. And assigning a number to something is not always measuring it. Counting, for instance, involves assigning a number. We count and find that there are five donuts on the table. Have we measured the donuts? We have not measured their size or mass. Have we measured their number? This sounds odd. We do, though, measure the size of crowds.

Calculating averages also illustrates the difference between measuring a phenomena and merely assigning it a number. As you may know, there are many different kinds of averages. Suppose that 100 students wrote a final exam and that each was assigned a grade from 0 to 100. The **mean** grade is the result of adding the 100 grades and dividing by 100. The **median** grade is that grade such that half of the grades are above it. The **mode** grade is the most common grade. These three averages vary independently of one another—changing any one of them might not change the other two. Which kind of grade measures average student performance depends on what question we are asking. More students might be in the B-range, even if the mean is C- and the median is a C+. The moral is clear: simply assigning a number to a phenomenon is not the same as measuring it.

When we measure something we assign a number and relate that number to a standardized scale of some kind. We say, not just that my weight is now 175, but that it is 175 **pounds**. The concert lasted not just 30, but 30 minutes. The restaurant review gives the new Indian restaurant not just five, but five stars. Understanding a measurement requires knowing which scale is being used. The acceptability of a measurement depends on the scale too. Some scales are appropriate for measuring some aspects of a phenomenon but not for measuring others. We can measure a liquid's temperature but not its mass using degrees Celsius. We can measure a car's velocity, but not its acceleration, using meters per second. In some cases, there is more than one appropriate scale, as in the case of temperature, which we can measure using either the Celsius, the Kelvin or the Fahrenheit scale. So, one question we need to ask in deciding whether some measurement is acceptable is whether the measurement employs an **appropriate scale**.

We measure something using a measuring instrument of some kind. We measure our mass using a bathroom scale; temperature using a thermometer; student performance using a final exam; voltage using a voltmeter; public opinion using a questionnaire. Whether a measurement is acceptable depends on whether the instrument used in the measurement tends to yield accurate measurements. A measuring instrument is **reliable** only if it tends to accurately measure what it is supposed to measure. If a test is designed to measure a person's latent hostility, then it is a reliable instrument only if it does in fact provide accurate measurement of the latent hostility of people who take the test. A procedure for measuring the size of crowds at rallies and demonstrations is reliable only if it provides an accurate (or accurate enough for the purposes at hand) measure of the crowd size.

> Measurements are acceptable only if they are made using a reliable instrument.

It is sometimes difficult to know for sure whether an instrument is reliable. Just because something is called an intelligence test does not guarantee that it really is a reliable instrument for measuring intelligence. Likewise, just because something is called a public opinion survey, this does not mean that it reliably measures public opinion. There is a deep and difficult methodological problem involved in determining whether a measuring instrument is reliable.

The only way to know for sure whether a measuring instrument is reliable is to compare its readings with those of a device that is known to be reliable. This is called "calibrating" the instrument. I can check to make sure that my meat thermometer is reliable by comparing its readings to one I know is reliable. But what if we do not know whether that second one is reliable? Do we need to compare its reading with those of a third instrument? Where would this regress end? Or what if we do not have another instrument for measuring the phenomena? If we have independent access to the phenomena being measured, then this is not a serious problem. Measuring the length of wooden boards is such a case, since we can more or less confirm by looking whether the tape measure is giving us the right reading. But with tests used to measure human intelligence or student performance, this is a serious problem, since we often have no independent way to measure the phenomena. We have no independent way to check to make sure that it really is the students' intelligence, as opposed to some other trait, that is being measured.

Thankfully, we do not need to sort out this difficult problem here. It is enough for us to be aware of the methodological problems facing measurement, and to be armed with the concepts needed to think critically about them. But in deciding whether a measuring instrument is reliable, there are two very important points to keep in mind here.

4.8.1   Measurement Consistency

First, consistency is not a guarantee of reliability. An instrument is consistent if it gives the same readings on repeated uses. Whether a reliable measuring instrument must be consistent depends on the nature of the phenomena being measured. If it is a phenomenon that can change quickly between measurements, such as levels of sugar in a person's blood or the electricity usage of a building, then a reliable instrument might not need to be consistent, since its readings would have to change to keep track of the changes in the phenomena. An instrument that always gave the same reading of a person's blood sugar levels throughout the day would be very consistent, but that might actually be a reason to think that it is not reliable, since a reliable instrument for measuring blood sugar should give different readings at different times of the day. On the other hand, if the phenomenon does not change rapidly between measurements, then a reliable instrument would have to be consistent. If my bathroom scale gives five different readings within a few minutes then this is good reason to think it is no longer reliable. If a drugstore pregnancy test gave different readings every 5 minutes, then we would have good reason to question its reliability. So, whether consistency is a virtue in measurement depends on what it is that we are measuring. An inconsistent instrument might be reliable, and a consistent instrument might be unreliable.

> A measurement instrument is consistent if it gives the same measurement on repeated uses. Consistency is not a guarantee of reliability.

If we know that the phenomenon we wish to measure does not change very quickly, then a measuring instrument would have to be consistent in order to be reliable. The easiest way to tell whether an instrument is consistent would be to use it to measure the same case several times. I can test the consistency of my new food scale by repeatedly putting the same bag of potatoes on it to see whether it always gives the same reading, which it would if it was consistent. But just to make matters a bit more complicated, in certain kinds of cases, an instrument designed to measure a very stable phenomenon might nonetheless not be consistent. This is the case for instruments designed to measure human intelligence or knowledge, like the SAT test or standardized tests in grade school. A subject who has written a standardized test once knows all the questions and so it is likely that she would do better the second time around. It is not that taking the test has by itself made her smarter or more knowledgeable (although she does know more about the SAT test); if we did repeat the test, we would expect different outcomes. But this need not be a reason to think that the test is not reliable. The relations between instrument reliability and instrument consistency are obviously quite complex.

4.8.2 Measurement Precision

Second, precision is not a guarantee of reliability. The precision of an instrument is a matter of how finely graded its readings are. A scale that measures only in pounds is less precise than one that measures in ounces. But precision is no guarantee of reliability. If the more precise scale is off by more than 2 pounds, then the less precise one may be more reliable. Still, precision is alluring. Sometimes, the results of public opinion polls involve decimal points, such as that 56.3% of the population is opposed to some policy. This precision seems to suggest that the instrument they used to measure public opinion must be very accurate. But this is a mistake. Precision is neither necessary nor sufficient for reliability.

DECIDING WHAT TO DO: MEASURING COSTS AND BENEFITS

Deciding what to do requires comparing the anticipated costs and benefits of competing proposals. But this comparison is often very difficult. Here are two of the main reasons for this.

Incomplete Information. Sometimes, it is just not possible to know what the anticipated costs and benefits of a given proposal are. Unfortunately, global warming is a good example. The nature of the Earth's climate is so complex and its dynamics so subtle that it is very difficult to know which of the many proposals for counteracting its effects will be most efficacious.

Incommensurability. Sometimes, the costs and benefits of a proposal are difficult to measure, and so difficult to compare and balance. Decisions that affect quality of life are like that. There is no easy way to measure, compare, and contrast pains and pleasures.

Inevitably, we sometimes must decide on a course of action in the absence of complete information or in the presence of incommensurability. In such cases, it is good to make the ignorance or incommensurability as clear as possible. If one must act in the face of ignorance and incommensurability, it is better to do so knowingly than blindly.

CONFUSING THE LIKELIHOOD OF SOMETHING WITH ITS VALUE

We need to be careful not to confuse how good or bad some consequence would be with how likely it is. Winning the lottery would be terrifically good, but it is extremely unlikely. So when comparing the costs and benefits of alternative proposals, you need to factor in the likelihood of those costs and benefits, as well as their value. A course of action that promises very high value but at very low probability (e.g., spending your money on the lottery), might not be as good as one that promises a high probability of moderate value (investing cautiously for the long run). This distinction between the likelihood and the value of a cost or benefit is especially important to keep in mind when assessing risk. Being killed in a plane crash would be far worse than getting a flat tire on the highway, but the odds of the flat are much higher than those of the crash. Flat-tire insurance may be a better investment than crash insurance.

CRITICAL THINKING MISTAKES: APPEAL TO IGNORANCE

It is a mistake to believe something just because you do not have evidence that it is false. This is a mistake because a bit of investigation might show that it is false, and thinking critically requires looking for evidence when one can. One form of this mistake is to discount or ignore potential costs or benefits of a proposal just because you do not know how to measure or compare them. It is important for critical thinkers to do what they can to discover these costs or benefits.

4.9   SURVEYS

Opinion surveys are a very familiar form of measurement. Pollsters and researchers ask people for their opinions on everything from politics, to sexuality, to sports, to food, to history.

SUMMARY: ACCEPTABLE SURVEY EVIDENCE

Evidence from a survey is acceptable just in case:

(i)   The survey questions are not ambiguous, biased, loaded, or otherwise bad; and

(ii)   Those surveyed are properly trained and informed on the topic of the survey; and

(iii)   There is no researcher or subject bias.

Researchers even use questionnaires to learn more about the nature of happiness, as we will see in a moment. Often, the researchers are interested in measuring the opinion of a large population—perhaps all Americans—and administer their survey to a sample of the general population. In Chapter 6, we will consider when reasoning using samples is valid, but here we will stay focused on the question of when the results of a survey are themselves acceptable.

It pretty much goes without saying that happiness is a prime motivator in our life. Everybody wants to be happy and most of us want to help make others happy too. Companies and governments want people to be happy with the products and services they provide. Economic theory assumes that we are all "happiness maximizers," that we can be expected to act in ways that we think will make us the happiest. If we choose the burger over the green salad, then that shows that we believed that we would derive more happiness from the burger. In moral theory, Utilitarians hold that the moral value of an action, practice, or policy is a matter of how much overall happiness that action, practice, or policy would produce as compared to alternatives. Public discussions about whether to implement one kind of government program or another often turn on questions about which program would have the best results, where this is usually a matter of how much happiness it would produce. Building a new bridge will make truckers and commuters happier, but it will make those living near the waterfront less happy. Deciding whether to build the bridge requires thinking hard about happiness. Given the central role that happiness plays in our thinking about our own lives and in our thinking about public policy, it might come as a bit of a surprise that we actually have little idea how to measure it.

Suppose that we were trying to measure happiness by asking people a simple question like this: On a range of 1–10, how happy would you say that you are? The question is simple enough that most people would be able to answer it. It includes a numerical range so we can get a number to deal with. If we asked enough people, we could even calculate an average of some kind (a mean or a mode or a median?), and figure out how happy the average person is. We could do the same for people under 30 and college kids and grandparents, and thereby learn quite a lot about how happiness varies from one group to another. But in fact there are good reasons for doubting whether this simple instrument is really a valid instrument for measuring human happiness.

One difficulty is that the question is a **bad question**. There are (at least) two problems with the way it is worded. First, it is **ambiguous**. Opinions about what it is to be happy vary quite widely. It is not just that people find that different things in their life make them happy. Some people find that a career-centered life makes them happy, while others derive happiness from their hobbies or from a vibrant community of family and friends. Variation from one person to another—and from one culture or time period to another—in views on the essential elements of a "good life" is not at all surprising. But people who agree on the elements of a happy life might still disagree about what it means to be happy. Is happiness, as John Stuart Mill thought, a kind of feeling, like an emotion or a sensation? If being happy is the same as feeling pleasure, then maximizing happiness is a matter of maximizing the amount of pleasure in the world. Or is happiness, as Aristotle thought, a matter of achieving and sustaining a kind of balance in one's life, independently of one's actual feelings? In that case, maximizing happiness would require organizing the elements of one's life—work, family, friendship, love, sport, pleasure, etc.—in a special way. Of course, people who agree on this view of the nature of happiness might also differ over just what elements are required and how to properly balance them. Disagreements over the nature of happiness are, as we know from Chapter 2, disagreements over the meaning of the word "happiness." So, the question is bad because it is ambiguous.

The other reason to think the question is badly framed concerns the point we saw earlier that measuring something is not the same as simply assigning it a number. Measuring requires both a number and a scale. But what is the scale in our proposed question? What are the units? Happiness units? But what are they? Moreover, what is the relation between the numbers on the scale? Is it like the relation between numbers on a scale for measuring mass, where something that weighs 6 lbs is twice as heavy as something that weighs only 3 lbs? Is a person who is 3 on the happiness scale half as happy as one who is a 6? Or is the relation between the numbers on the happiness scale like the relations between numbers on a temperature scale, where 20°C is not twice as hot as 10°C? Because we do not know the answers to these kinds of questions, we do not know what the question is asking us. This is a second reason to think that our proposed survey question is a **bad question**.

> Survey evidence is acceptable only if the survey is reliable at measuring opinion.

There are other ways that a survey question can be bad. A question is bad if it uses **charged** or **slanted** words. If we want to know a person's opinions about the morality of abortion, it will not do to ask whether they are in favor of the deliberate killing of unborn humans. A question is bad if it presupposes something such that no matter how one answers it, one will be saying or implying something controversial. The classic case of "Have you stopped cheating on your exams?" nicely illustrates the problems with a loaded question. Answering "Yes" implies that you once did cheat; answering "No" implies that you still are cheating. Lawyers questioning a witness in a trial have to be very careful that their questions do not presuppose anything controversial. The goal is always to get as good a handle as possible on the truth, and badly framed questions are an obstacle to the pursuit of truth.

But even if we could agree up front on the nature of happiness and on the scale for measuring it, there are other reasons for doubting the validity of that simple survey question as a measure of human happiness. Because the survey asks people to report on their own level of happiness, it is a measuring instrument that relies on testimonial evidence. As we have seen, testimonial evidence is not acceptable if we have reason to think the witness is **incompetent** or **biased**. So the instrument is reliable only if people are pretty good at telling whether they are happy and only if they are not motivated to exaggerate or lie about their levels of happiness. As it turns out, we have some reason to think that people are not very good at detecting their own levels of happiness. We are all familiar with the way that people live in denial. People sometimes lie to themselves about their true feelings, fabricating stories about themselves and their lives to paper over the problems that lie just beneath the surface. And if happiness is a matter of having a well-balanced life, it is likely that some people will not be good at telling when their life is well balanced. Researchers have found that people's reports on their happiness are not very consistent and can be influenced by irrelevant factors. In one study, researchers found that subjects tended to report a higher degree of happiness if the sun was shining or if they had just found a bit of money (left on purpose by the researcher.) Subjects also focus on the best events and ignore or fail to remember the negative events in their daily life. All of this suggests that some amount of error and ignorance about one's own happiness is inevitable. If so, then we have some reason to doubt whether people are good at telling whether they are happy, and this is some reason to doubt the validity of the proposed measuring instrument.

> Evidence from an opinion survey is acceptable only if those surveyed are properly trained, properly informed, and unbiased.

Surveys of popular opinion on policy matters also raise questions about whether the people being surveyed are properly trained and informed. It is one thing to have an opinion, but quite another to have an educated or justified opinion. Consider a poll asking for opinions on a certain plan for the changing the health-care system. Most people pay very little attention to the details of government proposals. And most of those proposals are so complex, and most of the problems they are nominally intended to remedy are so multidimensional that it is not very likely that most people will have an educated opinion on the matter. Even if the survey accurately reports people's opinions, these opinions are themselves of only little value since they are probably not educated opinions.

CRITICAL THINKING ABOUT HUMAN HAPPINESS

Researchers on human happiness have proposed a different series of questions to measure a person's happiness. Instead of asking something like our proposed question, some have used what is called a "day reconstruction method", where the subject is asked to describe the sequence of events in their day and report on the emotions they felt during each event. These researchers hope that this method will lead to a more accurate report from the person about just how happy they are with their day-to-day life. So there may be ways to formulate surveys that will enable more accurate reports from subjects. (For a discussion, see "The not so dismal science: how economists measure happiness," Tim Harford, *Slate*, http://www.slate.com.)

CRITICAL THINKING MISTAKES: BAD QUESTION

It is a mistake to ask a question that is ambiguous, contains charged or slanted words, or that hides a controversial presupposition. It is a mistake because it makes it harder to know what the person answering the question really believes.

But suppose that people were in fact quite good at telling whether they are happy. Their testimonial reports would still be unacceptable if we had good reason to think that they are **biased**. The possibility that they are biased would be a case of what in critical thinking we call **subject bias**. It is probably not right to suspect that most people would lie about how happy they are. We do know that people tend to exaggerate what economic class they are in, so that people well in the working class tend to report that they are in fact in the middle class. So it is probably right that we should expect that some people will be motivated to overstate their happiness, either out of shame or in order to impress. There is also in the case of this kind of survey, the possibility of **researcher bias**. The researchers asking the questions might themselves introduce a bias into the reports, either in the way they ask the questions or in other subtle features of their interactions with the subjects.

The best way to eliminate the risk of subject or researcher bias is to make the test **double blind**. A study is double blind if both the subjects that are being studied and the researchers doing the studying are ignorant of key facts about the study. In the case of drug trials, researchers ensure that they study is double blind by ensuring that neither the research subject nor the researcher knows who got the placebo and who got the trial drug. One way to reduce the risk of bias in a survey is to add a lot of questions on irrelevant topics. That way, neither the subject answering the questions nor the person hired to ask the questions knows what the researchers are really trying to find out about. This ignorance reduces the risk that bias will distort the results.

EXERCISE 4

A. Comprehension Questions
   a. What is the difference between mode, median, and mean? Use examples to illustrate when each would be valuable.
   b. What is the difference between measurement validity, measurement consistency, and measurement precision? Use examples to illustrate your answer.
   c. Suppose that you had a watch that was designed only to tell the hour and another designed to tell the time to the closest second. Which is most consistent? Which is most valid? Which is more precise?

B. Make a list of 10 measuring instruments you use every day. Order them from the most valid to the least valid. Order them from the most precise to the least precise. Order them from the most consistent to the least consistent.

C. Make a list of 5 phenomena that you do not currently know how to measure, but which you think should be measureable. Pick one of them and think of a way to measure it.

D. Look through the newspaper and find 5 articles that make measurement claims. Using the concepts we discussed in this section, identify some questions that need to be considered in deciding the measurements are acceptable.

E. In the following passages, identify the premises and conclusion(s). Then identify whether the argument relies on evidence from observation, testimony, or measurement. Finally, using the concepts we have discussed in this chapter, identify some questions that need to be considered in deciding whether the argument's premises are acceptable. Be as specific as you can.
   a. The roast is probably done. I just took out the thermometer and it read 150 degrees Fahrenheit, and the cookbooks says that a roast is done when it reaches 145 degrees Fahrenheit. It also smells like it is starting to burn.
   b. It is safe to go into the water. The city tested the water yesterday and the level of potentially infectious chemicals was very low.
   c. The new standardized math test is really accurate. We used it on several students from grade three and they all got the same score.
   d. You have heard the witness testify that she saw the defendant enter the bank on the time of the crime. And you have been presented with ballistics evidence

proving that the defendant's gun was used in the shooting. You have no choice but to find the defendant guilty.

   e. Our new American Motors sedan is the safest car in America. It scored a record 98.79 overall safety rating in our crash tests, the highest of any car we have ever manufactured. Just watch what happens in this video of a head-on car crash. See how the airbags inflate in time to prevent serious injury. This shows that the car is as safe as can be.

   f. Beauty Derm skin lotion removes 87.95% of wrinkles. Our clinical tests show it.

   g. South Park High School is the best school in the city. Its students recently scored higher than every other student in the city on the new standardized tests.

F. For each of the arguments in the previous question, decide whether the premises provide sufficient support for the conclusions. If not, suggest ways the argument might be strengthened.

G. Look in the newspaper for articles reporting on surveys. Find the questions that were asked, and assess whether they are ambiguous, loaded, biased, charged, or otherwise bad. Be as specific as you can, and do not charge a survey with asking a bad question unless you can support your claim.

CHAPTER SUMMARY

Reasons to believe or do something have to be acceptable. They are acceptable if they are from a **reliable** source and there is no **undermining** or **overriding** evidence. A source of evidence is reliable if it tends to provide true or accurate information most of the time. Observation, testimony, and measurement can be reliable sources of reasons.

4.10   CRITICAL THINKING IN PRACTICE

4.10.1   Critical Thinking Mistakes

Appeal to Ignorance. It is a mistake to believe something just because you have no evidence that it is false. This is a mistake because a bit of investigation might show that it is false, and thinking critically requires looking for evidence when one can.

   One form of this mistake is to accept some evidence just because you do not know of any overriding or undermining evidence. Critical thinkers should look for overriding and undermining evidence, before relying on some evidence.

   Another form of this mistake is to discount or ignore potential costs or benefits of a proposal just because you do not know how to measure or compare them. It is important for critical thinkers to do what they can to discover these costs or benefits.

Unacceptable Testimony. It is a mistake to accept testimony from a witness if the topic is inappropriate, the witness is not properly trained, or not properly informed, or if the witness is biased. It is a mistake because such evidence is not acceptable. Testimony is appropriate only on topics for which there are recognized experts. An expert must be properly trained and properly informed. And a witness must not be motivated to lie about or exaggerate the facts.

Bad Question. It is a mistake to ask a question that is ambiguous, contains charged or slanted words, or that hides a controversial presupposition. It is a mistake because it makes it harder to know what the person answering the question really believes.

4.10.2   Critical Thinking Strategies

Trust, But (Be Prepared to) Verify. Most critical thinking theorists agree that evidence can be acceptable even if we have not proven that its source is reliable. Instead, they recommend the following: evidence from some source is acceptable *unless one has strong reason to think the source is not reliable.* Trusting our sources is a default right, as it were. But we should not let ourselves get carried away. For we know that some apparent sources are not reliable at all, and others even ones that are reliable can still yield mistaken evidence. To borrow Ronald Reagan's remark about the proper attitude to take to enemy superpowers: trust, but be prepared to verify.

Measure Twice, Decide Once. The goal of critical thinking is knowledge, and this means that it places a premium on getting the right answer. To this end, it is better (to paraphrase a familiar wood-working lesson) to measure twice and decide once. This applies just as much to observation and testimony as it does to measurements. It is, all things considered, more prudent to collect more evidence than less evidence, and evidence from different sources is best of all. Finally, it is just as important to consider possible undermining evidence as it is to consider possible overriding evidence. For part of what makes critical thinking reflective is that it requires us to think about what makes a source of evidence reliable.

4.10.3   From Theory to Practice: Applying What We Have Learned

4.10.3.1   Thinking Critically about Ourselves   This exercise is designed to help you reflect on your strengths as a witness. In Chapter 1, you compiled a list of five or six character traits that you think are essential to being a morally good person. Being a trustworthy person might not have been on that list, but I think that most of us would agree that we strive to be someone others can trust. We have seen that testimonial evidence is acceptable only when (i) it is appropriate; (ii) the witness is properly trained and informed; and (iii) the witness is not biased in any way. This exercise is designed to have you reflect on the extent to which you meet these criteria. As always, the more sincere effort you put into it, the more you will get out.

For 2 days, observe yourself as you answer people's questions or give them information, or tell them your beliefs. As you do this, be willing to think critically about whether you are meeting the standards for being an acceptable witness. Do you ever offer an opinion as if it were the truth on a subject where there may not be experts? Do you ever offer a firm opinion on a subject where you are not really fully trained or fully informed? Do you ever let biases creep into your responses?

One way to do this exercise is to keep a journal for 2 days, pausing at noon and before bed, to reflect and describe a few events from the day. Use the Testimonial Rubric we discussed in the text.

4.10.3.2   Thinking Critically in the Classroom   This exercise is designed to help you identify the different sources of evidence that you rely on in studying or engaging in your chosen discipline. Some disciplines rely on one source of evidence much more than others. (Philosophy involves virtually no measurement at all, and little direct observation.) In Chapter 1, you compiled a list of five or six of the tasks that you are required to do in your chosen discipline that require critical thinking. That list might have included such things as performing measurements, collecting observational data, and doing factual research. Make a list of the kinds of evidence that you rely on in studying or that someone actively engaged in your chosen discipline would regularly rely on.

(i) Direct observation
(ii) Reliance on testimony
(iii) Measurement

4.10.3.3   Thinking Critically at Work   This exercise is designed to help you think critically about the sources of information you or the organization you work for rely on for success. All organizations rely on testimonial evidence and measurement in order both to achieve their organizational goals and to make adjustments to their internal operations. In Chapter 1, you compiled a list of tasks that you regularly perform at work that require critical thinking. Look over that list and identify those tasks that require you to collect or rely on testimonial evidence or measurement. Pick one of each kind, and do the following:

1. Assess how reliable those sources typically are.
2. Think of some ways to improve their reliability.
3. What other testimonial sources or measuring instruments would help you with your task?

5

REASONING ABOUT ALTERNATIVES AND NECESSARY AND SUFFICIENT CONDITIONS

Critical thinking is reasonable and reflective thinking aimed at deciding what to believe or what to do. In Chapter 1, we saw that thinking critically requires having good reasons for the decisions we make and the beliefs we form, and we saw that reasons are good if they are both acceptable and sufficient. Since critical thinking is aimed at knowledge, the kinds of reasons it requires are epistemic reasons, which are more commonly called "evidence." In Chapter 2, we learned how to think critically about the meaning of claims, plans, and proposals. In Chapter 3, we studied what it is for our evidence to be **sufficient** and we saw that a valid argument provides the ideal amount of logical support. In Chapter 4, we saw that our evidence is **acceptable** when it comes from a reliable source that we have no good reason to doubt, or when it is itself sufficiently supported by acceptable evidence. If we rely only on sufficient and acceptable evidence for beliefs and plans that are as clear as we can make them, then we have pretty much done our duty as critical thinkers. Though our beliefs might still be mistaken and though our plans may yet fail, we will have done the most we can in advance to avoid this. We will have pretty much fulfilled our intellectual obligations as critical thinkers.

But it would be nice to have easier ways to tell when our reasons are sufficient. In Chapter 3, we studied the notion of validity, which is the ideal level of support. An argument is **valid** just in case it is not possible for the evidence contained in the premises to be true and yet for the conclusion to be false. That means that the evidence provides the very best kind of support—it leaves no room for error, at

A Practical Guide to Critical Thinking: Deciding What to Do and Believe, Second Edition. David A. Hunter.
© 2014 John Wiley & Sons, Inc. Published 2014 by John Wiley & Sons, Inc.

least in the sense that if the evidence contained in the premises is true, then the conclusion is guaranteed to be true too. We learned a method for testing whether an argument is valid: suppose that its premises are true, and then ask whether there is any conceivable way that its conclusion might nonetheless be false. If the answer is NO, then the argument is valid. But we also saw that this method is tricky to use. It requires a healthy imagination to suppose that the premises are true and then to consider whether there is any conceivable way for the conclusion yet to be false. Thankfully, there are some forms of argument that are guaranteed to be valid and, for this reason, are very commonly used in deciding what to believe or what to do.

PRACTICAL STRATEGY: TESTING FOR VALIDITY

To test an argument for validity, first suppose that the premises were true. Then ask: could the conclusion still be false? If yes, then the argument is not valid. If no, then the argument is valid.

In this chapter and the next, we will study three very familiar and very useful forms of reasoning, methods for drawing conclusions from the evidence that we can rely on when thinking critically about what to believe and what to do. In this chapter we will look first at reasoning about alternatives and then study reasoning about necessary and sufficient conditions. In the next chapter, we will examine reasoning using analogies. As you will see, you have probably already relied on these forms of reasoning in your own thinking. Indeed, you are probably already pretty good at that kind of reasoning. Still, by studying their different natures and by identifying some of the more common mistakes that can be made, you can help make your reasoning more reflective. Being reflective in one's reasoning is a core element in being a critical thinker.

5.1 REASONING ABOUT ALTERNATIVES

Often when we try to decide what to believe or what to do we are faced with several alternative possibilities from among which we have to choose and we reason to a conclusion by trying to rule some of them out. I do not remember where my watch is, but I do know that it is either in the bathroom or in my backpack. The city can either build a new bridge or renovate the one it has, and has to find a way to decide between these options. The patient's symptoms are consistent with both a simple viral infection and a more severe early form of cancer, and the medical team needs to figure out which it is. Jones can continue his education by going to either law school or medical school, or he can follow his bliss by pursuing an acting career. Sherlock knows that either the Maid did it or the Butler did it or the Chauffeur did it, but he is not sure who. Before he reaches a conclusion about who the murderer is, he needs to rule out some of the possibilities. Reasoning about possibilities is one of the most common forms of reasoning, and it is important to do it well. In this section, we will study the nature of this kind of reasoning and identify some mistakes to avoid.

5.2   THE MEANING OF DISJUNCTIONS

When we reason about alternatives, we usually formulate them using a **disjunction**. As we saw in Chapter 3, a disjunction is just a statement containing the word "or." (It might be worth taking a moment to review that section before reading on.) Here are some examples of disjunctions.

Jones can go to Law School or to Medical School.

The patient either has a viral infection or an early form of cancer.

Either the sickly plant needs more water or else it has been overwatered and needs to dry out.

The defendant either lied before the grand jury or else she told the truth.

Using the Assertion Test, we can see that in asserting a disjunction one does not assert either disjunct. In claiming that the patient has either a viral infection or a form of cancer, the doctor is not claiming that the patient does have cancer and nor is she claiming that the patient does have a viral infection. All she is claiming is that an infection and cancer are the only two possible causes of the patient's symptoms. Perhaps she has already decided which of the two she thinks is most likely. But in asserting that disjunction she has not yet said that.

As we saw in Chapter 2, a disjunction is true just in case at least one of the disjuncts is true. This means that the doctor's assertion is true just in case one of the two possibilities she described is the real cause. A disjunction can be true if both disjuncts are true, as the following examples illustrate.

Either Jones is a student or Jones is a teacher.

Either Susan has a nephew or she has a niece.

A disjunction is **inclusive** if all of its disjuncts can be true at once.

Jones might be a student and a teacher, and Susan might have both a nephew and a niece. The disjunction is inclusive. If we can keep in mind these facts about what is asserted in a disjunction, and about the conditions under which a disjunction is true, then reasoning about alternatives is pretty straightforward.

5.3   REASONING BY DENYING A DISJUNCT

Let us study this kind of reasoning by starting with a simple example. To find the murderer, Sherlock Holmes starts by listing the possibilities and then through his investigations he rules them out one by one until only one possibility remains. His reasoning is something like this:

> I know that the Maid, the Butler, or the Chauffeur is the murderer. But I now have a good reason to believe that the Maid was in town buying meat at the time of the murder and that the Chauffeur was driving to the train station to pick up the General's daughter. This leaves the Butler as the only remaining possibility. So he must be the murderer.

If we wanted to formulate this reasoning in abstract terms, we could rewrite it as follows.

> Either P or Q or R is the case.
>
> But it is not the case the P.
>
> And it is not the case that R.
>
> So, it must be the case that Q.

Because the second and third premise involve ruling out a possibility, we can call this form of reasoning about alternatives, **denying a disjunct**. This kind of reasoning starts by listing a series of possibilities in the form of a disjunction, and then denying one or more of the disjuncts, concluding that the remaining disjunct must be true. Using the False Premise Test we studied in Chapter 3, we can see that these premises are dependent: they work together to support the conclusion. If any of the premises were false, the remaining ones would not provide any support for the conclusion. In reasoning about alternatives by denying a disjunct, the premises are always dependent. Using the tests we studied in Chapter 3, we can also see that denying a disjunct is a valid form of reasoning: if the premises are true, the conclusion has got to be true too. If Sherlock is right that one of those three did it, and if he is right that neither the Maid nor the Chauffeur did it, then he must also be right in concluding that the Butler did it. There is no other possibility. If the doctor is right that patient either has a viral infection or cancer, but is able to rule out cancer, then it must be that the patient has a viral infection. Denying a disjunct is thus a powerful way to reason about alternatives because it is relatively easy to use and is always valid.

SUMMARY: DENYING A DISJUNCT

Denying a disjunct is reasoning by ruling out a possibility and concluding that the remaining possibility must be the case. It is always valid.
It has the following symbolic form:

1. A or B (1) + (2)
2. It is not the case that A
3. So, it must be the case that B (3)

5.4   FALSE DISJUNCTIONS

Unfortunately, there are several ways that reasoning about alternatives can go wrong. As we know, we always want more from our reasoning than just validity. Not only do we want our reasons to support our conclusion, which is what validity guarantees, we also want our reasons to be **acceptable**. In the case of reasoning about alternatives, this means that we also want our disjunctions and our claims denying a disjunct to be true.

An argument that has a false disjunction as a premise makes the mistake that we call the **Mistake of the False Disjunction** (sometimes also called False Alternative or False Dilemma). The risk of a false disjunction poses a special problem for reasoning about alternatives. You may recall that, in general, a valid argument with false premises might still have a true conclusion; one can get the right answer even if one's evidence is inaccurate or misleading. But in the case of denying a disjunct, which is always valid, this general rule fails. If the disjunction is false—that is, if neither disjunct is true—then reasoning by denying the disjunct will inevitably yield a false conclusion. Here is an example.

> The car will not start. Either its battery is dead or it is out of gas. I just checked and there is plenty of gas. So, the battery must be dead.

This reasoning is valid and the disjunction is the proposition that either the battery is dead or the car is out of gas. Let us suppose that this disjunction is false, that is to say that the battery is fine and the car has lots of gas. This means that the argument's conclusion—that the battery is dead—is also false. The reason the car will not start, let us suppose, is that the spark plugs have been removed. Reasoning by denying a disjunct will yield a false conclusion when the disjunction itself is false. Consider a more serious example. Suppose that the doctor is mistaken that one of those two conditions is the cause of the patient's symptoms. Perhaps the symptoms are caused by a bacterial infection. In that case, when she rules out cancer and concludes that it is a viral infection, her conclusion is mistaken, even though her reasoning was valid. So we want to make sure that our reasoning about alternatives does not involve the mistake of false disjunction. We want to make sure that our disjunctions are true. Making sure that our disjunctive premises are true when denying a disjunct is important not just because having true premises is always important to having a good argument, but because if the disjunction is false, then the conclusion of our reasoning will be false too.

MISTAKE TO AVOID: FALSE DISJUNCTION

It is a mistake to reason with a false disjunction. It is a mistake because an argument with a false premise is not sound. Moreover, in the case of reasoning by Denying a Disjunct, if the disjunction is false, then the conclusion will be false too.

5.5 WHEN ARE DISJUNCTIONS ACCEPTABLE?

We know that a disjunction is true if we know which of its disjuncts is true. But if we knew this, then we would not need to reason about alternatives, since we would already know which alternative was the truth. If we already knew that the spark plugs had been removed, then we would know that the disjunction was false. But then there would be no need to reason about alternatives. The reason the doctor considers different possibilities is that she does not know which of the several possible causes, the actual one is.

> A disjunction is **exhaustive** when it includes all the possibilities that have not yet been ruled out.

One way to make sure that our disjunctions are true, even when we do not know a disjunct is true, is to make sure that they are **exhaustive**. A disjunction is exhaustive when it includes all the possibilities that have not yet been ruled out. If we make sure that our reasoning about alternatives includes all the possible alternatives, then we will be guaranteed to have a true disjunction. Exhaustive disjunctions help us to avoid the Mistake of the False Disjunction.

Making sure that we have an exhaustive disjunction can also help us to avoid a second and related mistake. Suppose that the doctor ignored or overlooked other possible conditions that could cause the very same symptoms. Suppose those conditions could have been caused by a bacterial infection, by a bladder condition, and by a vitamin deficiency, and that she overlooked or ignored these possibilities. But suppose that as a matter of fact it is a viral infection causing the patient's symptoms. If we later found out that the Doctor had overlooked or ignored these possibilities, then we would be very disappointed. We would feel that she ought to have been more careful to rule out all the relevant possibilities. She should have ordered more tests than she did. We would say that she did not really **know** that the patient had a viral infection; she just got lucky. She was lucky that the disjunction she relied on in her reasoning about the possibilities just happened to be true. She should have done a more exhaustive study; she should have relied on an exhaustive disjunction. So exhaustive disjunctions are preferable not just because they are guaranteed to be true (and so help us to avoid the mistake of the False Disjunction), but they are also preferable because they eliminate the need to rely on luck in our reasoning.

But how can we be sure that a disjunction is exhaustive? How can we be sure that we know what the relevant possibilities are? This is very difficult. Sometimes, even the experts in a field are not sure just what they are. It can take years of study to discover all the possible causes of some set of symptoms. It can require a highly trained and flexible imagination—the kind that scientific geniuses like Galileo, Newton, and Einstein and artistic geniuses like Picasso and Pollock are reported to have had—to conceive of new possibilities, to think "outside the box." Because it is so difficult to know when we have identified all the possibilities, part of our duty as critical thinkers is to keep an open mind about what is possible.

More specifically, we have to keep in mind that just because we do not know of (or even cannot conceive of) other possibilities this does not mean that there are no other possibilities. Believing that there are no other possibilities on the grounds that one does not know or cannot think of any more is to commit a special version of the **Mistake of Appeal to Ignorance:** it is a mistake to believe that something just because you do not have evidence that it is false. This mistake can occur in reasoning about any topic at all, but is especially common in reasoning about alternatives. Here is an example.

> James must have spilled the milk. Either he did it or the cat did it. What other possibility could there be? And there is no way the cat did it, since she would be covered in milk if she had. So this is why I am sure that James spilled it.

It might be that those are the only two possibilities. But the fact that the author could not think of others is not sufficient reason to believe that those are the only two possibilities. Making sure that our reasoning about alternatives involves exhaustive disjunctions can be exhausting—but that is no reason not to try. And it is certainly no reason to ignore the possibility that we have overlooked some possibilities.

CRITICAL THINKING MISTAKES: APPEAL TO IGNORANCE

It is a mistake to believe something just because you do not have evidence that it is false. This is a mistake because a little bit of investigation might reveal that it is false. One form of this mistake is to believe that a disjunction is true just because you cannot think of any other possibilities. Thinking critically about alternatives requires making sure that we have done what we can to make our disjunctions exhaustive.

5.6   EXCLUSIVE DISJUNCTIONS

We have been discussing the idea of an exhaustive disjunction. An exhaustive disjunction is the one that includes all the possibilities that have not been ruled out. A disjunction can also be **exclusive**. A disjunction is exclusive if its disjuncts cannot all be true at once. The following are examples.

The soccer team won, tied or lost.

The symptoms are either caused by cancer or by something else.

A disjunction is **exclusive** if its disjuncts cannot all be true at once.

Sometimes when we know that a set of possibilities is exclusive we still use a disjunction to state the alternatives. But this is a bit misleading, since in asserting a disjunction we are sometimes allowing that more than one of the disjuncts is true. If we know that at the most one is true, we should say this explicitly. Usually we do not have to because we know that our listeners also know that the disjunction is an exclusive one. But it is even more important to make this explicit when we reason using disjunctions that we know are exclusive. To see why, consider the following argument.

> Either the Maid did it or the Butler did it. The Butler just confessed. So the Maid is innocent.

Affirming a disjunct is valid only when the disjunction is exclusive.

In this argument, instead of denying a disjunct, Sherlock asserts that one of the disjuncts is true and then concludes that the other one is not true. This form of reasoning is called **affirming a disjunct**. Unlike denying a disjunct, which is always valid, affirming a disjunct is valid only when the disjunction is exclusive. Only if one and only one of the disjuncts is true does it follow from the fact that one is true that the other is false. We can rule out the other possibilities only when we know that the possibilities are incompatible. To make matters even more complicated, it is possible for a disjunction to be partly exclusive: only some of the disjuncts are incompatible one with another. For example:

> To balance the books, the government has several possibilities: it can raise income tax rates; or cut spending; or borrow money; or it can cut income tax rates and hope that stimulates the economy enough to raise the needed revenues.

A government could both raise taxes and cut spending in order to balance the books, but it cannot raise and lower the income taxes at the same time. So a disjunction can be partly exclusive or wholly exclusive. This makes reasoning with them more complicated than denying a disjunct. What is more, just as it is often hard to know whether a disjunction is exhaustive, it is also hard to know whether a disjunction is exclusive. This often takes specialized knowledge. Moreover, if we know that the disjunction we are reasoning with is exclusive, then this bit of knowledge is in effect a premise that we are relying on when we reason by affirming a disjunct, and we should make this premise an explicit part of our reasoning. If Sherlock knows that the murderer acted alone, then he should make this clear.

> Either the Maid did it or the Butler did it. *And I know that the murderer worked alone.* And the Butler just confessed. So, the Maid is innocent, after all.

In this bit of reasoning, the premises are dependent just as with denying a disjunct. And it is clear that here the reasoning is valid. If we were to write it out in symbolic form, it would look something like this:

Either P or Q is the case.

But only one of them can be the case.

P is the case.

So Q is not the case.

This form of reasoning is always valid, just as is denying a disjunct, which is a good thing. Even better, the argument makes explicit all the evidence the author was relying on in drawing the conclusion. Reasoning using disjunctions that we know are exclusive is more complicated than reasoning about alternatives by denying a disjunct. This does not mean that we should avoid affirming a disjunct, but only that when we do we should make this explicit so that we can make it a question whether the disjunction really is exclusive.

CRITICAL THINKING MISTAKES: AFFIRMING A DISJUNCT

It is a mistake to conclude that one disjunct is false just because the other one is true. This reasoning is valid *only if the disjunction is an exclusive disjunction*. But if one knows that the disjunction is exclusive, then one should add this piece of information as an additional premise in one's reasoning.

5.7   HOW TO CRITICIZE REASONING ABOUT ALTERNATIVES

We have been discussing reasoning about alternatives, and we have seen that there are several ways that this kind of reasoning can go wrong. We need to keep them in mind when we reason about alternatives. We also need to keep them in mind when we assess someone else's reasoning. If we read an argument in the newspaper or in a book where the author reasons about some alternatives we should ask ourselves whether the author is committing any of the mistakes we have identified here. Is her disjunction true? Is it exhaustive? Is she claiming the disjunction is true just because she cannot think of any other possibilities? Is she affirming a disjunct even though her disjunction is not exclusive?

If we decide that the author has committed one or more of these mistakes, then we should be able to say exactly which mistake it is and we should be ready to back this up with evidence. If we claim that someone has ignored or overlooked some possibilities, and so charge them with using a disjunction that is not exhaustive, then we have to be ready to make good on this claim either by pointing out some specific possibilities that have been overlooked or ignored or else by providing some other reason to think the disjunction is not exhaustive.

If we claim that someone is reasoning with a false disjunction, then we should be ready to say what alternative she has overlooked.

We also have to be careful not to ridicule the author's view by noting possibilities that are extremely unlikely or unreasonable. Usually, there are many possibilities that are simply out of the question—so far from what might actually happen—that they are ruled out without argument. They are not, we might say, "live options." Perhaps, building a land bridge across the river might be an alternative to either building a new bridge or renovating the existing one. But, depending on the discussion, it might be that it is simply not a live possibility. In that case, it would be unreasonable—a form of the Red Herring—to charge an author with relying on a nonexhaustive disjunction if this was the only possibility one could mention. This would be a case of the **Red Herring Fallacy** since one would be introducing an irrelevant possibility simply in order to criticize the author's position.

DECIDING WHAT TO DO: IDENTIFY ALTERNATIVES

Thinking critically about what to do invariably requires thinking about alternatives. For, usually, one has to decide from among several competing ends, and there are almost always several different means for achieving any given end. As a general rule of thumb, one has not thought carefully enough about what to do unless one has identified three possible courses of action.

CRITICAL THINKING MISTAKES: RED HERRING

It is a mistake to raise irrelevant matters when criticizing someone's beliefs or reasons to raise irrelevant matters. This is a mistake because it is rude and because it makes it harder to find the truth together. One form of this mistake is to criticize a disjunction in someone's argument by raising possibilities that are ridiculous or that have already been ruled out.

EXERCISE 1

A. Comprehension Questions
  a. What does a disjunction assert?
  b. What is the difference between an exclusive and a nonexclusive disjunction? Construct three examples of each kind.
  c. Why must the conclusion of an argument that denies a disjunct be false if the disjunction is false too? Use examples to illustrate your answer.
  d. When is affirming a disjunct valid? Give an example.
  e. What is the symbolic form of denying a disjunct?
  f. Are the premises in denying a disjunct dependent or independent? Explain, using an example.
  g. What is an appeal to ignorance, and why is it a critical thinking mistake?
  h. What is the red herring fallacy, and why is it a critical thinking mistake?
  i. What is an exhaustive disjunction? Give two examples.

B. Construct five disjunctions that are true and exclusive but that a reasonable person would think are not exhaustive.

C. In the following arguments, identify the premises and conclusions and then determine whether the argument is valid. If it is not valid, identify the error.

   a. The city can either build a new bridge or else renovate the new one. But building a new bridge is so expensive that it cannot be afforded. We will have to live with a renovated one.

   b. A father to his child: The restaurant's menu says that you can have cake or apple pie for desert. You have already ordered the cake, so you cannot have the pie too.

   c. I have to do the dishes or the laundry. I just finished the dishes, so I do not have to do the laundry.

   d. Either humans evolved from other species or else God created us. But I am sure that God created all life. So humans did not evolve from other species.

   e. I cannot walk and chew gum at the same time, and I am walking now. So I had better not chew gum.

   f. To fight global warming, we can either raise taxes on fossil fuels or else find alternatives sources of energy right now. Since there is no chance of finding alternative sources of energy now, we must raise taxes.

   g. According to the computer models, either the economy will grow by 2% in the next quarter or else unemployment will continue to rise. Since unemployment cannot rise any higher than it is, the economy is probably going to grow.

D. Look through the letters to the editor in your local newspaper or magazine and find five examples of reasoning about alternatives. Analyze them by identifying their premises and conclusions. In your judgment, are they examples of good reasoning? Do they commit any of the mistakes that we have discussed?

5.8 REASONING ABOUT NECESSARY AND SUFFICIENT CONDITIONS

Sometimes, when we reason about what to believe or what to do, we reason about necessary and sufficient conditions. Here are some examples.

   If the city decides to build a new bridge, then it will have to raise taxes to pay for the construction, and raising taxes will negatively affect the business climate, so the city should not build a new bridge.

   If the patient's symptoms had been accompanied by a fever that had lasted for more than 3 days, then it would have been caused by a bacterium rather than by a virus; but it was not; so the illness is probably viral.

   The restaurant claims to provide excellent service, but this requires careful attention to detail, which the waiters completely lack, so it is simply not true that the restaurant provides excellent service.

I want to keep my grass green, and I learned from the gardening book that grass needs regular watering to thrive. So I plan to water it regularly.

I need to pass this course, and studying hard for it is the only way to guarantee that I will pass. So my plan is to study really hard.

If we leave Iraq now, a civil war will break out and the neighboring countries will probably enter in, leading to a vast and bloody conflict far worse than what will happen if we stay. So we must stay come what may.

These are all cases of reasoning about what is necessary for what or about what is sufficient for what. The fact that they differ so much from one another shows that this kind of reasoning occurs in a wide variety of disciplines. And as these cases illustrate, we commonly reason about necessary and sufficient conditions using conditional sentences, sentences with an "if" and a "then." In this section, we will study the nature of this kind of reasoning and identify some of the mistakes that can arise.

5.9 THE MEANING OF CONDITIONALS

We saw that we can make our reasoning about alternatives more reflective if we keep in mind what we learned in Chapter 2 about the meaning of disjunctions. The same is true for reasoning about necessary and sufficient conditions. If we keep in mind what a conditional sentence is used to say, and under what conditions that kind of sentence says something true, then this will make it easier to understand reasoning about necessary and sufficient conditions. It will help us to identify, and so avoid, some of the possible mistakes. So let us start by reviewing some of what we know about the meaning of "if, then" assertions.

Here are some examples of conditionals.

If Stephen is the Prime Minister of Canada, then Stephen is a politician.

If you want the lawn to be green, then you have to water it.

If a restaurant has excellent service, then its waiters pay careful attention to every detail.

The part of the conditional that follows the "if," we call the **antecedent** and the part that follows the "then," we call the **consequent**. In making an assertion using a conditional, we do not assert either the antecedent or the consequent. That is, someone who claims that if Stephen Harper is the PM of Canada, then Stephen Harper is a politician is not thereby claiming that Stephen Harper **is** the PM of Canada or that Stephen Harper **is** a politician. She might well believe these things, and she may even be willing to assert them. But she is not asserting them in using that conditional to make an assertion. Instead, she is asserting that there is a relation of a certain kind between the antecedent and the consequent. Let us look more closely at this.

> In asserting a conditional, neither the antecedent nor the consequent is asserted. Rather, what is asserted is that the truth of the antecedent is sufficient for the truth of the consequent.

When a person uses a conditional sentence to make an assertion, she is asserting that if the antecedent is true, then so is the consequent. It is helpful to state this relation using the notions of necessary and sufficient conditions. In asserting a conditional, one is asserting two things. First, one is asserting that the truth of the antecedent is **sufficient** for the truth of the consequent. Second, one is asserting that the truth of the consequent is **necessary** for the truth of the antecedent. Let us look at each of these points in turn.

First, if a conditional is true, then the truth of the antecedent is **sufficient** for the truth of the consequent. We are already familiar with the logical idea of sufficiency. It is the idea behind the notion of validity. To say that the truth of the antecedent is sufficient for the truth of the consequent just means that all that it would take for the consequent to be true is for the antecedent to be true. The truth of the antecedent would be enough for the truth of the consequent.

> If a conditional is true, then the antecedent is sufficient for the consequent.

One way for Stephen Harper to be a politician is for him to be the PM of Canada. Being a PM is sufficient for, or guarantees, that one is a politician. One way to become a millionaire is to win the lottery. Winning the lottery is sufficient for becoming a millionaire. If you win the lottery, you will become a millionaire. One way to pass this course is to get an A. If you get an A, then you will pass. Getting an A is sufficient for passing this course.

These examples also can help us to see another important point. Something can be sufficient for something without being necessary for it. Winning the lottery is one way to become a millionaire; but it is not the only way. Inheriting from a rich uncle may also make you a millionaire. Working hard and saving money is another way to become a millionaire. Robbing a casino may make one a millionaire (if only for a few moments). Any of these conditions is sufficient for becoming a millionaire, but none is necessary. Likewise, getting a C in this class—or even a D—is also sufficient for passing it. There are often, as the saying goes, many ways to skin a cat.

> A condition can be sufficient for something without being necessary for it.

The second point is that if a conditional is true, then the truth of the consequent is **necessary** for the truth of the antecedent. In other words, if the conditional is true, then there is no way that the antecedent could be true if the consequent were false. If you are not a millionaire, then you did not win the lottery. If you did not pass this course, then you did not get an A. Just as there can be many sufficient conditions for something, so there can be many necessary conditions for it too. Having a healthy lawn requires more than just lots of water; it also requires lots of sunshine, fertilizer, and an absence of grubs. Becoming a millionaire requires having more than $100, and it also requires having more than $200. It also requires a system of property law to establish ownership and a stable currency system to make money possible. To bake cookies you need more than just butter and flour, you also need some sugar and vanilla and chocolate chips (these are needed if you want the cookies to be any good, anyway). Usually, there are lots and lots of necessary conditions for something.

If a conditional is true, then the consequent is necessary for the antecedent.

A condition can be necessary for something without being sufficient for it.

We have seen that a condition that is necessary for something can also be sufficient for it. Jones' being an unmarried male is necessary for his being a bachelor, but it is also sufficient. To be a bachelor, you must be a male and unmarried. Those two conditions are each necessary, though neither one is sufficient on its own for being a bachelor. But together, they are sufficient. We can put this by saying that those conditions are **individually necessary** and **jointly sufficient**. Sugar, butter, and flour are each necessary for having cookie dough, and they are jointly sufficient. All you need to have some cookie dough is sugar, flour, and butter. We can state the fact that certain conditions are individually necessary and jointly sufficient using a conjunction of conditionals.

If Jones is a bachelor, then he is an unmarried man **and** if he is an unmarried man, then he is a bachelor.

But it is usually easier just to join the conditionals with what we call a "biconditional", as follows:

Jones is a bachelor **if and only if** Jones is an unmarried man.

A biconditional asserts that the antecedent is both necessary and sufficient for the consequent.

We use biconditionals to say that certain conditions are both necessary and sufficient for something.

As is already clear from our discussion, there are many ways in English to state a necessary or sufficient condition. It is worth spending a bit of time noting some of them. We can state a sufficient condition using the "If . . . , then." form of a conditional as follows:

If Stephen is the PM of Canada, then Stephen is a politician.

If Jones is a bachelor, then Jones is a man.

If the lawn grows, then it has been watered.

If you are a millionaire, then you have more than $200.

In these sentences, the focus is on stating a sufficient condition for the consequent. We can also put the focus on the necessary condition using the "only if" form of conditional, as follows:

Stephen is the PM of Canada only if Stephen is a politician.

Jones is a bachelor only if Jones is a man.

The lawn will grow only if it is watered.

You are a millionaire only if you have more than $200.

Because of the intimate relation we have noted between necessary and sufficient conditions, these are (for most intents and purposes, anyway) just two ways of saying the very same thing. In general, the following are just two ways of saying the same thing.

If P, then Q;

P only if Q.

Sometimes, we reverse the order of the two parts of the conditional, as follows:

I will go to the party, if Jones goes too.

If Jones goes to the party, then I will go too.

Only if Jones is a man can Jones be a bachelor.

Jones is bachelor only if Jones is a man.

The first and second sentences identify Jones' attendance at the party as a sufficient condition for the speaker's going to the party. The third and fourth sentences identify Jones' being a man as a necessary condition for his being a bachelor. The word "unless" is also used to state a necessary condition.

Jones is married, unless he is a bachelor.

If Jones is married, then he is not a bachelor.

If Jones is a bachelor, then he is not married.

These are just three ways of saying the same thing: that being unmarried is a necessary condition for being a bachelor. The important thing to keep in mind as one reads a conditional sentence that is not in the nice and neat "if, then" form is to ask what is being said to be necessary or sufficient for what. One strategy is to begin by identifying the two conditions, and then asking which the author is saying is sufficient for which. This is sometimes difficult to do if, as does happen, the antecedent and consequent in the conditional are not complete sentences. Sometimes, the author leaves out some of the implicit information, just for ease and because her audience can figure it out. When analyzing a bit of reasoning, it is always best to rewrite the conditional inserting that missing information.

CONDITIONALS WITH FALSE ANTECEDENTS

A conditional is used to assert that the truth of the antecedent is sufficient for the truth of the consequent. This means that a conditional is false if the antecedent is true but the consequent is false. But what if the conditional's antecedent is false, as in the following?

1. If Obama is a bachelor, then he is unmarried.

Is it true, or is it false?

Ordinarily, when we reason with a conditional we assume that the antecedent is either true or at least an open possibility. It is very difficult to understand what someone would be saying if they asserted (1), while knowing full well that Obama is not a bachelor. Maybe they have in mind something more like (2).

2. If Obama *were* a bachelor, then he *would* be unmarried.

(2) is a subjunctive conditional, and it is true, since being a bachelor is sufficient for being unmarried. It would be more reasonable for someone who knew that Obama is not a bachelor to assert (2) rather than (1).

But what about (1)? Is it true or not? In mathematical logic, all conditionals with a false antecedent like (1) are said to be "trivially" true. This is harmless, since it does not affect the validity or soundness of any actual argument. But it is also a little paradoxical, since it means that (3) should be treated as true!

3. If the sky is green, then Obama is a bachelor.

Thankfully, we do not need to decide whether conditionals like (1) and (3) are true or false, or neither.

EXERCISE 2

A. Comprehension Questions

  a. What does a conditional assert? Use the SEEC definition method discussed in Chapter 2 to answer this question, and use examples to illustrate your answer.

  b. Could a conditional be true if its consequent is false? Use an example to illustrate.

c. What is the difference between a necessary and a sufficient condition? Use the SEEC definition method discussed in Chapter 2 to make your answer clear. Use examples.

d. Give an example of something that is necessary but not sufficient for something else.

e. Give an example of something that is both necessary and sufficient for something else.

f. Give an example of something that is a necessary part of a sufficient, but not necessary, condition for something.

B. For each of the following, find five things that are necessary but not sufficient for it.

a. Being a father

b. Being happy

c. Being a good movie

d. Murder

e. Love

f. Being President

g. Passing this class

C. For each of the following, find something for which it is sufficient but not necessary.

a. Having 25 dollars

b. Getting an A in this course

c. Being the President of the United States

d. Being the spouse of a supermodel

D. For the following conditionals, find a conditional of the "If, then" form that means the very same thing.

a. Jones will go to work only if Jones gets paid today.

b. I would have retired if someone had asked me to.

c. The economy will rebound only if taxes are cut.

d. The economy will not rebound unless taxes are cut.

e. The economy will not rebound if taxes are not cut.

f. The movie will not be entertaining unless it is a musical.

g. The movie will be entertaining unless it is a musical.

h. The grass will not grow unless you water it.

i. To make grass grow you need to water it.

j. Eating lots of vegetables is essential to a healthy diet.

k. To be good at critical thinking you need to trust but verify.

l. The burger is adequately cooked when its internal temperature is 150 degrees Fahrenheit.

E. In the following arguments, identify the premises and conclusion. Rewrite any conditionals in an "If, then" form that means the same thing. If a conditional premise is implicit (or missing) insert it.

a. If someone had asked to resign, I would have. But no one ever asked me to, so that is why I did not.

b. If I had gone to the party, Jones would have seen me. If he had seen me, he would have been pretty angry. So I did not go.

c. The grass is growing very well. I guess that someone watered it.

d. If humans were alive when the dinosaurs roamed the earth, there would be evidence of this in the fossil record. But there is no such evidence. So I think humans were not alive then.

e. Success requires hard work, and I am working hard; so I will succeed.

f. The recipe says that the cake is done when it starts to pull away from the sides of the pan, and this is exactly what is happening; so the cake is done.

g. The chain on my bike is very rusty; so it is about to break.

h. Vitamin C helps to avoid colds, and Emily is very sick; so she has not been taking Vitamin C.

5.10   VALID REASONING ABOUT NECESSARY AND SUFFICIENT CONDITIONS

Now that we have studied necessary and sufficient conditions and how we can use conditional sentences to formulate them, we can study how to reason about them. Just as with reasoning about alternatives, reasoning about necessary and sufficient conditions is very common and relatively straightforward. However, just as with reasoning about alternatives, there are some ways to go wrong that we should be aware of.

Let us begin our discussion with a famous example of an argument.

Aristotle is man. If Aristotle is a man, then Aristotle is mortal. So, Aristotle is mortal.

As always, before we assess an argument we should analyze it into premises and conclusion. In this case, the presence of the indicator word "so" tells us that the final assertion is the conclusion. The first two assertions are thus premises.

Using the False Premise Test, we can see that in this case the premises work together; they are dependent. If either were false, the other would provide no support at all for the conclusion. To see this, suppose that it were not true that Aristotle is human. In that case, the fact that that if he was human then he would be mortal would provide no reason at all to think that Aristotle is mortal. Likewise, suppose that being human were not sufficient for being mortal. In that case, the fact that Aristotle is human would provide no reason to think that he is mortal. So the premises are supposed to work together.

Now that we have analyzed the argument, we can assess it. As always, there are two questions to ask: do the premises support the conclusion and are they true? Let us start by considering whether the premises support the conclusion. If we keep in mind what we learned about necessary and sufficient conditions, figuring out whether the premises support the conclusion in a case of reasoning about them is usually pretty straightforward.

Part of what makes this age-old example of an argument a wonderful philosophical chestnut is that it is pretty obviously a valid argument. There is no way that its premises could be true and its conclusion false. If Aristotle really is a man, and if it really is true that if he is a man then he is mortal, then there is no way for him not to be mortal. The truth of the premises guarantees that of the conclusion. If you think back to what we said about the meaning of conditionals in the previous section, it should not be at all surprising that this argument is valid. After all, the conditional that is the second premise in the argument simply says that Aristotle's being a human is sufficient for his being mortal. And the first premise simply states that that sufficient condition for his being mortal does in fact obtain. If his being a human is enough to make him mortal, and if he is human, then how could he not be mortal? So the argument is valid.

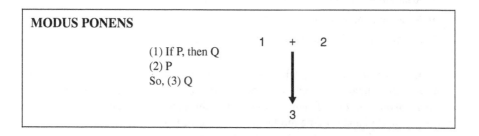

MODUS PONENS

(1) If P, then Q
(2) P
So, (3) Q

1   +   2

3

This form of reasoning about necessary and sufficient conditions is called **modus ponens,** or affirming the antecedent. **Any argument of that form is valid.** The validity of modus ponens turns on the fact that if a conditional is true then the antecedent is sufficient for the consequent.

Another valid form of reasoning about necessary and sufficient conditions turns on the fact that if a conditional is true, then the truth of the consequent is necessary for that of the antecedent. Here is an example.

If Jones were a bachelor, then he would be unmarried.

Jones is not unmarried.

So, Jones is not a bachelor.

This form of reasoning is called **modus tollens,** or denying the consequent. It is always valid, too, just like modus ponens. If it is true that being unmarried is necessary for being a bachelor, which is what the conditional premise asserts, and if it is true that Jones is married, which is what the other premise asserts, then it has to be true that Jones is not a bachelor. This form of reasoning is valid just because if a conditional is true, then the consequent must be true if the antecedent is true.

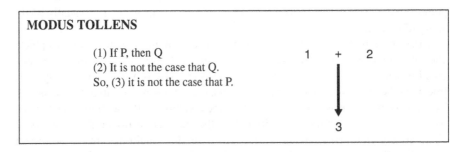

MODUS TOLLENS

(1) If P, then Q
(2) It is not the case that Q.
So, (3) it is not the case that P.

The two forms of reasoning we have looked at so far involve claims about necessary and sufficient conditions as premises, but we can also reason to conclusions about necessary and sufficient conditions. Here is a valid form of this kind of reasoning.

If Aristotle is human, then Aristotle is mortal.

If Aristotle is mortal, then Aristotle is not God.

So, if Aristotle is human, then Aristotle is not God.

In this form of reasoning, which we can call **Pure Conditional Reasoning** (we can call it that since all the premises and the conclusion are conditionals), we reason along from one pair of sufficient conditions to a third one. If being human is sufficient for being mortal, and if being mortal is sufficient for not being God, then it has to be true that being human is sufficient for not being God. So this form of reasoning is valid too.

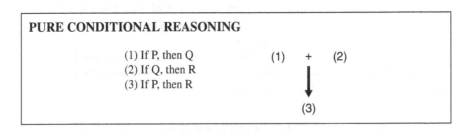

PURE CONDITIONAL REASONING

(1) If P, then Q
(2) If Q, then R
(3) If P, then R

We have seen three valid forms of reasoning about necessary and sufficient conditions. There are, of course, mixed cases that are valid too.

If we raise taxes to pay for the new bridge, then the public will turn against the construction. If the public turns against the project, then it will surely fail. But we cannot let it fail. So we should not raise taxes to pay for it.

This bit of reasoning combines pure conditional reasoning and modus tollens. We could put the reasoning symbolically as follows:

If P, then Q

If Q, then R

But it is not the case that R

So, it is not the case that P.

This example of mixed reasoning using both modus tollens and a pure conditional is valid.

5.11   INVALID FORMS OF REASONING ABOUT NECESSARY AND SUFFICIENT CONDITIONS

We have identified three forms of reasoning about necessary and sufficient conditions that are always valid. Modus ponens, modus tollens, and pure conditional reasoning are always valid. In this section we will look at two forms of reasoning about necessary and sufficient conditions that may appear to be valid, but are not always valid. And when they are valid this has nothing to do with the conditional premise. The appearance of validity comes from confusing a necessary condition for a sufficient one or a sufficient one for a necessary one.

Consider this example.

If Jones has diabetes, then he should not be eating that cake and ice cream. But he does not have diabetes, so he can eat some of it.

On its face, this bit of reasoning, which we can call **denying the antecedent,** can seem very persuasive. If you look through letters to the editor or listen to friends talk, you will probably find lots of examples of it. But this reasoning is not always valid.

Denying an antecedent confuses a sufficient condition for a necessary one.

To see this, think about it in terms of necessary and sufficient conditions. The first premise says that having diabetes is a sufficient reason for avoiding eating sweet desserts. Suppose that is true. But that premise does not say that having diabetes is necessary for avoiding sweet desserts. It does not say that only people with diabetes should avoid desserts. Indeed, we know that there are lots of other good reasons for sometimes avoiding sweet desserts. Maybe Jones is on a strict diet. That would be a good reason. Maybe Jones is lactose intolerant, and so should avoid ice cream. Maybe Jones' wife is avoiding sweets and by eating them himself he would weaken her resolve, which he does not want to do. There are lots of reasons to avoid that kind of dessert, and some of them but not others might apply to Jones. So even if the premises are true, even if he does not have diabetes, the conclusion of this bit of reasoning might still be false. In other words, arguments of this form are not guaranteed to be valid in the way that arguments of the form of modus ponens are guaranteed to be valid. This mistake comes from taking a sufficient condition to be a necessary one.

I said that denying an antecedent is not always valid. Some cases of it are valid. Here is one example.

If Peter is single, then he is a bachelor. Peter is not single. So, Peter is not a bachelor.

This argument denies the antecedent. But if its premises were true, then its conclusion would have to be true too. That is, if it were true that being single was sufficient for being a bachelor and that Peter was not single, then it would have to be true that Peter was not a bachelor. But notice that the conditional premise is not really needed in this argument. For if we leave it off, the argument remains valid.

Peter is not single. So, Peter is not a bachelor.

The conditional premise is actually not doing any work in this argument. For being *not single* is sufficient for being *not a bachelor*. This example illustrates a general point: when an argument that denies the antecedent is valid, this is because the antecedent of the conditional is **necessary** for the truth of the consequent. That is why, if the antecedent were false, then the consequent would have to be false too. But if that is the rationale behind the argument, then it would be much better to make it explicit as follows:

Peter is a bachelor only if he is single. Peter is not single. So, Peter is not a bachelor.

This argument is modus tollens, which is valid. And it captures the idea that lay behind, but only in a confusing way, the valid case of denying the antecedent. All of this is just another way of saying that arguments that deny the antecedent confuse sufficient and necessary conditions.

Here is an example of another form of reasoning about necessary and sufficient conditions that is not guaranteed to be valid, but whose surface appearance of validity comes from confusing a necessary condition for a sufficient one.

Susan feels sick most mornings, which is exactly how she would feel if she were pregnant. So, I think she is going to have a baby.

Let us first analyze this into premises and conclusion. The presence of the conclusion indicator "so" tells us that the final sentence is the conclusion. The first complete sentence—Susan feels sick most mornings—is one premise. The other premise is stated in a complex way. But it can be reformulated as follows:

If Susan were pregnant, then she would feel sick most mornings.

Now we can see that the reasoning has the following form:

If P, then Q
Q
So, P.

This form of reasoning is called **affirming the consequent**. But it is not always valid. The first premise—the conditional one—says that Q is a necessary condition for P. That means that for P to occur or be true, Q has to occur or be true too. But we know that a necessary condition does not have to be a sufficient one. So, even if Q is the case, the fact that it is necessary for P does not show that P also obtains.

Affirming a consequent confuses a necessary condition for a sufficient one.

This reasoning seems persuasive only if we confuse a necessary condition for a sufficient one. Suppose that it is true that if Susan is pregnant then she will feel sick in the morning. And suppose that she does feel sick in the morning. Couldn't it just be a coincidence that she is sick? Maybe she is suffering from some other condition that makes her sick in the morning. Even if feeling sick in the morning is necessary for being pregnant, it need not be sufficient. So this reasoning is not valid either.

DENYING THE ANTECEDENT AND AFFIRMING HE CONSEQUENT

Denying the antecedent	Affirming the consequent
If P, then Q	If P, then Q
Not P	Q
So, not Q	So, P

I said that Affirming the Consequent is not always valid, but just as with Denying the Antecedent, some cases of it are valid. Here is one example.

If X is a square, then X has four equal sides and four internal right angles. X has four equal sides and four internal right angles. So, X is a square.

This argument Affirms the Consequent. But it is valid. If its premises were true, then its conclusion would have to be true too. But here too, notice that the conditional premise is not really needed in this argument. For if we leave it off, the argument remains valid.

X has four equal sides and four internal right angles. So, X is a square.

The conditional premise is actually not doing any work in this argument. For having four equal sides and four internal right angles is sufficient for being a square. This example illustrates a general point: when an argument that Affirms the Consequent is valid, this is because the consequent of the conditional is **sufficient** for the truth of the antecedent. That is why, if the consequent were true, then the antecedent would have to be true too. But if that is the rationale behind the argument, then it would be much better to make it explicit as follows:

> If X has four equal sides and four internal right angles, then X is a square. X has four equal sides and four internal right angles. So, X is a square.

This argument is modus ponens, which is valid. And it captures the idea that lay behind, but only in a confusing way, the valid case of Affirming the Consequent. All of this is just another way of saying that arguments that Affirm the Consequent confuse necessary and sufficient conditions.

We have identified some valid forms of reasoning about necessary and sufficient conditions. We use modus ponens when we know that a condition that is sufficient for something is true. We use modus tollens when we know that a condition that is necessary for something is absent. We use pure conditional to trace links between a series of sufficient conditions. So long as we can keep clearly in mind the difference between a necessary and a sufficient condition and the way we use our words to state and formulate those kinds of conditions—our reasoning about them—we can avoid the mistakes and make sure that our conditional reasoning involves premises that support the conclusions we draw.

As we know, for an argument to be sound it needs to be valid and have true premises. A sound argument is perfect. An argument that has a false conditional is thus not a good argument, because it is not sound, even if it is valid. So it is always a mistake to reason with a false conditional. But we have a special name for this mistake when it is extreme enough. We call it a **Slippery Slope** mistake. Here is an example.

> We should not let the county go ahead with plans to close the mental hospital. For, if the hospital closes, then all of its inpatients will be let out on the streets. And if that happens, then the crime rate will rise sharply. If the crime rate rises sharply, then everyone will move out to the suburbs, and the cities will die. This would be unacceptable. We have to keep the mental patients in the hospital.

The author of this argument makes claims about the effects of closing the county mental hospital. There is, he is suggesting, a cascade of negative effects that would follow, creating a kind of slippery slope, and the effects would be so negative that avoiding them justifies keeping the hospital running. Suppose that those conditional claims are false. Suppose that either those effects would not follow (because, perhaps, the patients would be transferred to another hospital, or the impact on crime of their release would be negligible) or that the author has no good reason to believe that they would follow. In that case, the author would be committing the slippery slope fallacy, by reasoning with a false conditional.

> ## CRITICAL THINKING MISTAKES: SLIPPERY SLOPE
>
> It is a mistake to reason with a false conditional. It is a mistake because the argument is not sound. This kind of mistake sometimes occurs in assessing policies or proposed actions, when someone argues that adopting the policy will lead to bad (or good) consequences, and either the causal claim is not justified or else the claim that the consequences are bad (or good) is not justified.

This example involved arguing that very negative things would be caused by some event, but the same mistake could involve arguing without sufficient justification that very positive things would happen.

> We should all stop driving our cars to work. If we did this, the pollution in our skies would drop by 80%, the rivers would become clean once again, and fewer children would be killed in car crashes.

In the absence of a very good reason to think that these positives would be the effect of a ban on driving, this author commits the fallacy of slippery slope.

5.12 MAKING NECESSARY AND SUFFICIENT CONDITIONS EXPLICIT

All of the examples we have looked at so far have conditional sentences that make explicit the author's assumptions about necessary and sufficient conditions. But we know that there are other ways to make claims about such conditions. It is helpful when analyzing such an argument to rewrite the claim in conditional form. Here is an example

> To get a good job, Jones will need to go to University. But he will not get accepted in any University. So he is not going to get a good job.

The conclusion of this argument is that Jones will not get a good job. None of the premises is formulated as a conditional sentence, but the first sentence does make a claim about a necessary condition. It claims that going to University is necessary for Jones to get a good job. We could formulate it in a conditional in either of the following ways.

> Jones will get a good job only if he goes to University.

> If Jones gets a good job, then he will have gone to University.

Now that we have rewritten that premise, we can rewrite the entire argument as follows:

> Jones will get a good job only if he goes to University. But he will not go to University, so he will not get a good job.

Now we can more easily see that this argument has the form of modus tollens, and so is valid. Depending on whether the premises are true, this might be a good argument for the conclusion. As this example illustrates, it can be helpful in assessing reasoning about necessary and sufficient conditions if we can rewrite the relevant claims in the form of conditionals.

Here is another example.

The restaurant does not deserve five stars. The food was too greasy.

Here, the author does not make any claim at all, at least not explicitly, about necessary or sufficient conditions. But it is plausible to think that the author is assuming that the fact that the restaurant's food is so greasy disqualifies it from deserving five stars. In other words, the author is assuming that not having greasy food is necessary for deserving five stars. We can formulate this assumption as follows:

A restaurant deserves five stars only if its food is not greasy.

We could also formulate it as follows:

If a restaurant's food is greasy, then it does not deserve five stars.

Now we can see that the author's reasoning, with the missing premise added, can be formulated in the following way.

If a restaurant's food is greasy, then it does not deserve five stars. That restaurant's food is greasy. So, it does not deserve five stars.

Again, now we can see that the reasoning is valid. Whether the argument is ultimately good depends on whether the two premises—the one about what is required to deserve five stars, and the other about the food's greasiness—are true (or at least acceptable).

EXERCISE 3

A. Comprehension Questions
    a. What is modus ponens?
    b. Using the concepts of a necessary and a sufficient condition, explain:
        (i) Why modus ponens is valid. Give two examples.
        (ii) Why modus tollens is valid. Give two examples.
        (iii) Why denying the antecedent is not valid. Give two examples.
        (iv) Why affirming the consequent is not valid. Give two examples.

B. Look back at the arguments in the last set of exercises. Assess them for validity.

C. Look at the letters to the editor and find five letters that involve reasoning about necessary and sufficient conditions. Rewrite the reasoning into arguments involving conditionals and assess them for validity.

5.13 WHEN ARE CLAIMS ABOUT NECESSARY AND SUFFICIENT CONDITIONS ACCEPTABLE?

We have been considering when reasoning about necessary and sufficient conditions is valid. As we know, we want more from our reasoning than just for the premises to support the conclusion; we want our premises to acceptable. In the case of reasoning about necessary and sufficient conditions, this means that we want our claims about these conditions to be acceptable. We know, in a general way, what it is for a conditional sentence to be true: it is true just in case the truth of the antecedent really is sufficient for the truth of the consequent; or, put the other way around, a conditional is true just in case the truth of the consequent really is necessary for the truth of the antecedent.

> A counterexample to a conditional is an example that shows that the antecedent is not sufficient for the consequent.

The **Counterexample Strategy** can help us to decide whether a conditional is acceptable or true. A counterexample to a claim is an example that shows that claim to be false. If we can imagine or conceive of a way that the antecedent might be true and the consequent false (or if we know for a fact that the antecedent is true and the consequent false), then we will know that the conditional itself is false. Imagining or conceiving of such a way is a matter of thinking of some alternative possibilities, ones where the world is the way the antecedent claims it is but not the way the consequent claims it to be. It is a bit like creating a little story of the world.

Consider the following example.

If Jones is a bachelor, then Jones is happy.

PRACTICAL STRATEGY: LOOK FOR COUNTEREXAMPLES

An important step in assessing the acceptability of conditionals is looking for counterexamples. A counterexample is a case, either real or fictional, that shows that the conditional is false. A counterexample would be a case where the antecedent is true but the consequent is not (showing that the antecedent is not sufficient for the consequent).

If you think that a conditional is false, then you should be ready to present a counterexample to it.

We might know that this is false because we know that Jones is a miserable bachelor who longs to marry Susan, who has spurned him more than once. In this case, we know both that the antecedent is true and that the consequent is false—this is enough to know that the conditional is false. But what if we do not know any of this? Suppose that we do not even know Jones very well. We can still assess the truth of the conditional by trying to imagine or conceive of the antecedent being true and the consequent false. In effect, this involves imagining or conceiving of an alternative possibility, a kind of story of the world where Jones is a bachelor but he is unhappy. Doing this requires the same skills and strategies we discussed when we studied reasoning about alternatives. If we can come up with such a story, if we can identify a possibility where the antecedent is true and the consequent is false, then we will have shown that the conditional is not acceptable. In this case, it is not that hard to do—after all, we all know lots of miserable bachelors. In other cases, it can be quite difficult to come up with such a counterexample. In what follows, we will look in some detail at two kinds of necessary and sufficient conditions—those that derive from definitions and those that involve causal relations—and we will study some strategies for deciding whether they are acceptable.

CRITICAL THINKING MISTAKES: APPEAL TO IGNORANCE

It is a mistake to believe something just because you do not have evidence that it is false. This is a mistake because a bit of investigation might show that it is false, and thinking critically requires looking for evidence when one can. One form of this mistake is to believe that a conditional is true just because you do not know of any counterexample to it. Critical thinkers should look for counterexamples before believing conditionals.

But just one reminder: finding a counterexample to a claim proves that the claim is false; failing to find one does not prove that it is true. Suppose that we are unable to think of a counterexample to some conditional. This would not by itself prove that the conditional is true. Thinking that it would is a case of **appeal to ignorance**, which as we saw in our discussion of reasoning with alternatives is a mistake. The fact that we cannot think of a counterexample to a conditional is not a good reason to think it is true, just as our inability to think of a third alternative is not a good reason to think that a disjunction is true. Maybe our imaginations are just too limited.

5.14   REASONING WITH DEFINITIONS AND STANDARDS

We sometimes reason about necessary or sufficient conditions that derive from **definitions**. These include ordinary dictionary definitions but also such things as standards for evaluation, systems for classification and categorization, legal definitions and the clauses and stipulations in contracts and agreements, standards for medical and other kinds of treatment, and rules for games and ordinary practices. Here are some examples, starting with one we have already seen.

A person is a bachelor only if he is unmarried.

A geometrical figure is a triangle if and only if the sum of its internal angles is 180 degrees.

A restaurant deserves five stars only if the service is exceptional.

If the fever persists for more than 24 hours, then call the doctor.

If a player is on first, second and third bases, then the bases are loaded.

If your filing status is Single, and at the end of 2006 you are under 65, then file an income tax return if your gross income was at least $8450, unless you are being claimed as a dependent on someone else's tax return.

As these examples illustrate, there is quite a range of different kinds of claims in this group, and assessing the acceptability of a conditional depends on what kind of claim it is. The acceptability of claims about rules and conventions requires looking at what the relevant rulebooks or contracts say. Appealing to a dictionary might settle whether some definition is acceptable. For technical terms in science or the law, appeal to experts might be needed. But even though different procedures are needed for deciding whether one kind of conditional or another is true or acceptable, when we reason with them we can follow the same strategies we have been discussing until now. Modus ponens, modus tollens, and the pure conditional are valid forms of reasoning for every kind of conditional.

Claims about what our words mean or what certain standards should be are simply claims about necessary and sufficient conditions. In Chapter 2 we discussed definitions, and we learned how to assess them. We learned that it is helpful to use the SEEC definitional method to clarify what we mean by our words and claims. When we reason using definitions and standards, or when we analyze and evaluate someone else's reasoning of this kind, we can use that SEEC method to clarify the definitions and standards. We saw that to assess whether a definition is acceptable we can use the counterexample method. Now we can see that these same methods can be used to clarify, analyze, and assess reasoning using definitions and standards.

To equivocate is to use a word to mean different things without realizing it.

Reasoning about necessary and sufficient conditions that derive from definitions and standards runs the risk of **Equivocation**. This happens when a word has several different meanings. Using a word that has different meanings is fine, so long as we are aware of this fact. If we are paying careful attention to the fact that the word has these different meanings, then we will not confuse ourselves or our audience. But there are two kinds of cases where it is a mistake to equivocate. First, it is a mistake to equivocate in one's reasoning if one's words must mean one thing for the premises to be acceptable but another for them to support the conclusion. Here is an example.

Only man is a rational animal.

Susan is not a man.

So, Susan is not a rational animal.

The argument is valid only if the word "man" means the same thing in both premises. But the premises are acceptable only if it means something different. For the first premise to be true, it has to mean something like "human"; for the second premise to be true it has to mean "male human." This **equivocation** makes this into a bad argument.

CRITICAL THINKING MISTAKES: EQUIVOCATING

To equivocate is to use words in different senses without realizing it. One form of this mistake occurs in arguments. It is a mistake if a word must mean one thing for the premises to be true and another for the argument to be valid. This is a mistake because then the argument cannot be sound.

Equivocation can also occur during discussions or in debates, and can make what are really disagreements over definitions and standards look like disagreements over the facts. Two movie reviewers who watch the very same film might disagree over its quality as a thriller. It might be that one knows something more than the other about the film, and that their disagreement derives from this difference. But it might instead be that they simply have different standards or ideas about what it means for a movie to be a "good thriller." Perhaps, one thinks that the espionage film noir *The Thirty-Nine Steps*, with its dark scenes and shady characters, is the standard against which to assess and compare thrillers, while the other thinks that *Vertigo*, with Jimmy Stewart hanging from the top of the tower, sets the standard. If that is the case, and if they do not realize that they have different standards in mind, then they are really talking past one another when they argue about whether a certain film is a good thriller or not. They mean different things, or have different standards in mind. There is nothing wrong with that, and it can become itself a topic of discussion, with one side trying to persuade the other to adopt its standard. But it would be a mistake not to recognize that the discussion involves an **equivocation** about standards.

CRITICAL THINKING MISTAKES: EQUIVOCATING IN A DEBATE

To equivocate is to use words in different senses without realizing it. One form of this mistake occurs during debates or conversations. It is a mistake for participants in a discussion not to recognize that they mean different things by the key words and phrases they use. This is a mistake because it will be very hard to agree on the truth if we mean different things by our words. This can be recognized and avoided by a careful use of the SEEC method.

The risk of equivocation is also high in discussions over values and morality. Debates over the morality of abortion, for instance, sometimes involve disagreements about how to balance off the rights of the unborn with those of the pregnant woman and the father. Sometimes, the debate turns on complex medical and physiological facts that are not well known by either side. But sometimes, debates over abortion seem to turn on hidden disagreements over what is to count as a person. Is a 3-month-old fetus a person? In part this is a physiological question, since the physiological features of a 3-month-old fetus are relevant. But it does not seem like a question that can be settled through appeal to physiology alone. Even if we settled all of the physiological facts, we could imagine sincere and reflective people continuing to disagree over whether a 3-month-old fetus "counts" as a person. This would be a case where the debate turns on a difference over definitions or standards, which is fine, so long as all sides recognize this for what it is.

What can be done to make a progress when a discussion or debate turns on a difference over standards or definitions? It is important, first of all, to make the difference as clear as possible, and here the definitional method discussed in Chapter 2 can be useful. Formulating a clear statement of the definition or standard might, of itself, move the discussion along, as the two sides come to better understand what the other has in mind. Examples and contrasts can be useful too, though they can also sometimes be just as controversial as the original disagreement. But the goal should be to find as much common ground as possible. If the different sides in the discussion can get clear on where they agree—on the physiological issues, for instance, and on some clear examples of persons and of what makes them persons—then they can move on to discuss the controversial cases. It might be, though, that in the end the discussion turns on competing visions of what is valuable, all sides agreeing on the nature of something but disagreeing about its relative value. Such disagreements are among the hardest of all to settle.

PRACTICAL STRATEGY: LOOK FOR COMMON GROUND

It is important in a discussion to find common ground, so that areas of disagreement can be clearly identified and resolved. Two kinds of common ground are important. First, one should find common **factual** ground: it is important in a disagreement to find what all sides agree on, in order to help them focus on their actual disagreements. But it is just as important to find common **linguistic** ground: it is important that all sides agree on how to use their words to say what the facts are or might be. To avoid the risk of equivocation in a discussion or debate, use the SEEC definitional method from Chapter 2 to construct and evaluate definitions of the key words.

The SEEC definition method can also help us to avoid the **Strawman** mistake. In a discussion, it is very important to be as accurate as we can in representing another person's position or proposal. Just as we want them to take our views seriously and not to distort or trivialize them, we too have an obligation to try as hard as we can to correctly and fairly formulate their position or proposal. When we fail to do this, when we distort or trivialize or otherwise misrepresent another person's view, we have made the Strawman mistake, so named because it is usually easier to take apart (in the sense of criticize) a Strawman than a real man. Sometimes this mistake in unintentional. People's views are often pretty complex, especially on important topics, and this means that it will be tricky to find a neat concise way to state them accurately. Just think of how complex are your own views on, say, abortion, the desirability of a universal health care system, or of the justice of rising student tuitions. It would be hard for you to find a neat concise way to put your views. You want others to take as much care in formulating your views, as you would take in formulating them. You want them to use something like the SEEC definitional method in stating your views, before they raise objections or criticism or state their own position. But sometimes, in debates and discussions, people deliberately distort their opponent's views, in order to gain a dialectical upper hand. This is always rude and boorish. But, even this makes it terrible at least from a critical thinking point of view, distorting another person's view is always counterproductive. For by distorting or trivializing it we lose the opportunity to see whether there is any truth in it, and truth is after all one of the key goals of critical thinking.

CRITICAL THINKING MISTAKES: STRAWMAN

It is a mistake to distort or misrepresent another person's beliefs or their reasons. It is a mistake because it is very rude and it prevents you and the other person from getting to the truth together. While everyone has a duty to make her beliefs and reasons clear, we also have a duty to represent each other's beliefs and reasons as clearly and charitably as we can.

5.15   NECESSARY AND SUFFICIENT CAUSAL CONDITIONS

One of the most important kinds of reasoning about necessary and sufficient conditions is reasoning about causes. If we want to know what caused little Joan's fever, what makes unemployment rise and fall, why some restaurant chains succeed and others fail, or why some hard-boiled eggs have dark coloring around the yolks and others do not, we need to reason about necessary and sufficient **causal conditions**. In the rest of this chapter we will study this kind of reasoning.

A causal condition is a condition that is necessary or sufficient to produce or bring about some event or phenomena.

Does everything have a cause? Is it always true that when something happens, it was caused to happen by something else? Some physicists and some philosophers think the answer is No. According to those physicists, sometimes a physical event will take place and nothing will have caused it to take place. It will have happened randomly, in the sense that nothing in what came before it caused it to happen. And some philosophers have argued that when people act freely nothing causes their action. Their action will not exactly be random in the sense of having no explanation—since it is something the person did on purpose—but it will be random in the sense that nothing in what came before it caused it to happen. These physical and philosophical views are deep and difficult to understand. They are usually discussed in advanced courses. Thankfully, we will not need to think about them here. We are going to focus on things that do have a cause. Reasoning about the causes of an event is reasoning about necessary and sufficient conditions.

We have many ways to say that one thing caused another. Here are some examples.

Salmonella causes illness.

Smoking leads to lung cancer.

Water helps to make grass grow.

Wine stains teeth.

Alcohol impairs judgment.

Teasing your sister will make her angry.

Inflation produces unemployment.

If you take Motrin, then your fever will subside.

We do not always use the word "cause" when we are saying that one thing caused another. We can instead use causal verbs, like "makes," "produces," "leads to," "brings about." These verbs are more or less synonyms for "cause." We can also say that one thing caused another using a verb that stands for a specific kind of causation. So, for example, "stains" and "impairs" are verbs that stand for specific kinds of causation. To stain something is to cause it to have a stain. And, we can even formulate claims about causal conditions using conditionals, as the example about Motrin illustrates.

As the examples show, we use the word "cause" and the other causal verbs in a somewhat confusing way to talk about both necessary and sufficient causal conditions. The following state sufficient causal conditions.

Drowning causes death.

Wine stains teeth.

Drowning is not the only way to die. There are lots of ways to make something die, but drowning will do. Drowning is a sufficient causal condition for death, but (unfortunately, since drowning is easily avoided) not a necessary one. Likewise, wine is one way to stain teeth, but it is not the only way to stain them. Coffee and tea will also stain teeth. So these sentences are naturally understood as saying that something is a sufficient cause, not a necessary one.

By contrast, the following identifies a causal condition that is necessary but not sufficient.

Watering makes lawns grow.

Salmonella causes illness.

Watering is not all that a lawn needs to grow. Sunshine and the proper nutrients are also needed. But without water, the lawn will die. The presence of water is thus a necessary, but not a sufficient, causal condition for lawn growth. Likewise, salmonella is not enough all on its own to make a person sick; there usually has to be other factors involved as well. But Salmonella is a necessary part of a sufficient cause.

A condition can be necessary for something to happen without being sufficient. And a condition can be sufficient for something to happen without being necessary. (And a condition can be a necessary part of a condition that is sufficient but not necessary for something to happen!)

These examples show that we cannot always tell, just by the occurrence of the word "cause," whether it is a sufficient or a necessary causal condition that is being identified. Still, it is usually pretty easy to tell which kind of cause a person has in mind when they make a causal claim. We can avoid this ambiguity altogether if instead of using the word "cause" we use conditionals.

If a thing drowns, then it will die.

A lawn will grow only if it has water.

Once we formulate these claims about causal conditions using conditionals, then there is no ambiguity. The first one only states that drowning is sufficient for death, not that it is necessary, and the second one only states that water is necessary for lawn growth, not that it is sufficient.

THINKING CRITICALLY IN HISTORY

Sometimes, we can discover the causes of an event by thinking about what would have happened if things had been different. This is reasoning involves the use of contrary-to-fact (or "counterfactual") conditionals, like:

If Hitler had not invaded Poland, World War II would not have happened.

If humans had not emigrated from Africa thousands of years ago, there would not be humans now in North America.

If inflation had not spiked, the recession would have been less severe.

I would be living in France today, if only I had won that lottery.

In using a counterfactual conditional, one asserts (or at least, assumes) that the event specified in the antecedent did not occur, and one asserts that if it had occurred, the consequent would have been true too.

As the examples suggest, reasoning about counterfactuals is extremely common in the study of history. Thinking about how things might have turned out had the past been different in certain ways is one method historians use to discover the actual causes of actual events. (It is also very common in science.) Of course, knowing whether a counterfactual conditional is true can be just as difficult as knowing whether an indicative conditional is true.

5.16   REASONING WITH CAUSAL CLAIMS

Reasoning with causal claims is just reasoning about necessary or sufficient conditions of a certain kind, and the valid forms of reasoning we discussed can be used when we reason about causal relations. The following are thus valid.

Taking Motrin will lower Joan's fever, and Joan just took some Motrin; so her fever will lower.

If inflation is rising, then unemployment is rising too. But unemployment is not rising, so inflation is not rising, either.

If the cake batter was stirred too long, then the gluten will have transformed. If the gluten transformed, then the cake will be dry. But the cake is not dry, so the batter was not stirred too long.

To reduce teen pregnancy rates, people need to change their incentives. People's incentives can be changed only by spending more on targeted education. So, to reduce teen pregnancy, spend more on target education.

The forms of reasoning that are valid for reasoning about necessary and sufficient conditions are the same whether we reason about causal conditions or about conditions that derive from definitions and stipulations.

5.17   DISCOVERING CAUSAL CONDITIONS

As always, we want our reasoning not just to be valid, we also want our premises to be true. In the case of reasoning about causal conditions, this means that we want our causal claims to be true. Finding out what causes what is usually extremely difficult. But we will look at some methods that help.

Just think of how long scientists and doctors have been trying to identify the causes of cancer. We have made a huge amount of progress, and we have been able to identify the causes of certain kinds of cancers, but a lot of expensive and sophisticated research remains to be done. But while the research and investigations needed to decide whether a causal claim is true are often time consuming and difficult, the methods involved in figuring out what causes what are, at least in the abstract, pretty straightforward, especially if we keep in mind the difference between a necessary and a sufficient condition. What makes it rare to find conclusive proof of the causes of an event is not that we lack a clear understanding of how to go about finding the proof—at least in the abstract. Rather, what makes it difficult is that we usually lack the evidence that our methods tell us that we need to find.

> The causes of an event are always in the past.

One thing we know is that the causes of an event must have happened before that event. Causes are always in the past. But it would be a mistake to conclude that just because one thing happened before another, the first thing caused the other. This mistake is called the **Post Hoc Fallacy**. While it is true that the causes always precede the effect, this is just a necessary condition for a causal link, not a sufficient one. Indeed, as our examples have illustrated, much more evidence is needed than merely the temporal order of two events before one can draw any conclusions about the causal relations between them.

This mistake is a very common one. One often hears politicians championing the virtues of their tax-cut plans by noting that unemployment fell, government revenues rose, and the general level of happiness soared to an all-time level, right after their favored tax cuts went into effect. Such claims should always be taken with a grain of salt. The historical order of those events is quite simply insufficient evidence on which to base such a claim. (Moreover, those politicians are not trustworthy witnesses: they are probably not properly trained or informed in the economics of tax cuts and they are probably biased.) Of course, as always, they might be right: a true belief might be based on inadequate or unacceptable evidence. But if this is the sole basis for their belief, then that belief is unjustified.

CRITICAL THINKING MISTAKES: POST HOC

It is a mistake to conclude that one thing caused another just because the one thing happened first. This is a mistake because while causes do precede their effects, this is just a necessary condition for a causal link not a sufficient one.

5.17.1 Discovering a Necessary Causal Condition

Knowing that something is a necessary causal condition of some event can be very useful. Imagine that we could find a condition that is necessary for some terrible disease. That is, suppose that we had identified something that was needed for a person to develop leukemia. If we could remove that condition, then we could prevent leukemia. That would be a wonderful thing. So identifying necessary causal conditions can be quite useful.

To tell whether something is a necessary causal condition for some effect, all we need to do is to see whether it was present every time the effect is present. The idea is that everything necessary for the event must have been present whenever the event is present. So, to find an event's necessary causal conditions, what we need to do is to look for the common factor. John Stuart Mill (1806–1873) called this the **Method of Agreement**. It is a method for identifying an event's necessary causal conditions. Here is an example.

> After eating lunch at the same restaurant, five individuals became ill with hepatitis. What caused the illness? Inspectors from the Health Department did a survey and found that some of the individuals had eaten potatoes, and that others had eaten mushrooms, but that all had eaten tomatoes in their salad.

> To identify a necessary causal condition for some effect, look for what all cases of the effect have in common (the common factors).

The fact that some of those who got sick did not eat potatoes is evidence that eating potatoes was not a necessary condition for all the cases of the illness. It could not be necessary for all the cases if it was missing in some of them. Likewise, the fact that some of those who got sick did not eat mushrooms shows that eating mushrooms was not a necessary condition for all the cases of the illness. The Method of Agreement works well to show that something is NOT a necessary condition. The researchers also found a factor that was common to all the cases: the eating of the tomatoes. The fact that tomatoes were eaten in **all the cases** where the illness was present is some evidence that eating the tomatoes was a necessary cause of the illness.

We have to be very careful here. The fact that all of those who got sick ate tomatoes is not **conclusive** evidence that eating the tomatoes was a necessary causal condition. The fact that they all ate the tomatoes might still have been a coincidence. There are at least three reasons for this.

Other Necessary Conditions. The method of agreement yields conclusive evidence of a necessary causal condition only if we have identified all the common factors. But it is difficult to do this, and even difficult to know for sure that we have. Perhaps, those who got sick also shared a drink of beer, and it was the beer that was infected, and so just a coincidence that they all ate tomatoes. Because there are usually so many different factors present in any series of cases, we can rarely be certain that every single common factor has been identified.

Different Necessary Cause for Each Effect. The method of agreement yields conclusive evidence of a necessary causal condition only if the effects being studied have the same cause. Perhaps the potatoes and the liver were infected, and not the tomatoes, and that some of the sick people ate only the potatoes and others ate only the liver, and it was just a coincidence that they all ate the tomatoes. It is hard to know whether all of the cases had the same cause without knowing what each of their causes was. But that is precisely what we are trying to find out.

Overlooked Cases of the Effect without the Condition. The method of agreement yields conclusive evidence of a necessary causal condition only if all the cases of effect have been investigated. Maybe, someone who got sick did not report it, and was not included in the study, and perhaps that person did not have the tomatoes. This would show that eating the tomatoes was not a necessary cause at all.

The more certain one is that one has found all the similarities among the effects, that one has ruled out possible multiple causes, and that one has studied all cases of the effect, the more certain one can be in one's conclusion about the effect's necessary causal conditions.

One final word of caution is in order. The sort of evidence the health inspectors collected cannot show that eating tomatoes was also a **sufficient** cause. It might have been sufficient. But the sort of evidence the health inspectors collected will not show this. Even if the health inspectors had studied every single case of the illness, and even if they had found that in every case the sick person had eaten tomatoes, this would not show that eating tomatoes caused the illness all alone. To show that eating tomatoes was sufficient, they would have to study every single case of someone eating the tomatoes—they did not do that. So, the most that this evidence could show is that the tomatoes were a **necessary** part of the story. It does not show that they are the whole story. Let us look at this in more detail.

5.17.2   Discovering a Sufficient Causal Condition

Knowing that something is a sufficient causal condition is often very valuable. Imagine that we could identify a combination of exercise and diet that would be sufficient to prevent obesity, or a treatment that would make cavities disappear (or a study trick that would guarantee any student an A+). That would be wonderful. So knowing that something is a sufficient cause of some effect can be quite useful.

To tell whether something is a sufficient causal condition for some effect, all that we need to do is to see whether the effect follows every time that thing is present. The idea is that if something is sufficient for an effect, then it is enough to guarantee that effect. John Stuart Mill called this the **Method of Difference**. It is a method for identifying a sufficient causal condition.

> To identify a sufficient causal condition for some effect, look for a condition that is always followed by that effect.

Here is an example.

Simon wanted to find a way to remove wine stains from his tablecloth. He poured salt onto some of the stains and let it sit for a while before washing the tablecloth. He also poured sugar onto some of them. He found that the stains he had salted disappeared while the stains he had not salted and that he had sugared were still there.

The fact that the stains Simon had sugared were still there shows that sugaring is not sufficient to remove the stain in the wash. If it were sufficient, then those sugared stains would have disappeared in the wash. That is decisive. The Method of Difference works well to show that something is not a sufficient condition. Simon also found that pouring salt onto a wine stain seemed to make a difference. It seemed to make the stain disappear in the wash. This is some evidence that salting a wine stain is sufficient to make it disappear in a wash.

Here again, though, we must be very careful. The evidence Simon collected is not conclusive. It might just have been a coincidence that the stains that disappeared had all been salted. There are at least three reasons for this.

Other Sufficient Conditions. The evidence would be conclusive only if the salting were the only thing that could have made the difference. Maybe the salt that Simon used contained traces of a mineral that makes the stains disappear in the wash, and it was just a coincidence that the stains had been salted. Or maybe all the stains that disappeared in the wash were on a part of the tablecloth made of a special fabric designed to make wine stains easily removed in the wash, and it was just a coincidence that Simon salted them. Because there are usually so many possible sufficient causes, we can rarely be certain that every difference has been identified.

Different Sufficient Cause for Each Effect. The method of difference yields conclusive evidence of a sufficient causal condition only if the effects being studied have the same cause. Perhaps, some of the stains were removed because they had been mixed with milk which made them disappear in the wash, and others because they were still wet when they were washed, and that it was just a coincidence that they had all been salted. It is hard to know whether all of the cases had the same cause without knowing what each of their causes was. But that is precisely what we are trying to find out.

Overlooked Cases of the Condition not Followed by the Effect. The method of difference yields conclusive evidence of a sufficient causal condition only if all the cases of that condition have been studied. Maybe Simon forgot that he had also salted one of the stains that was not removed in the wash. In that case, salting the stains would not be sufficient to remove them in the wash.

One last caution is in order. The evidence Simon collected would only show that salting a wine stain is **sufficient** to make it disappear in a wash. It could not show that it is also necessary. Maybe, there are other ways to produce that same effect. Perhaps, soaking the stain in certain alcohols would also make the stain disappear in the wash. To show that it is necessary he would have to show that salting was used in every case of the effect. But he did not show that.

5.17.3 Discovering Necessary and Sufficient Causal Conditions

The following example illustrates how to combine both methods to identify conditions that are individually necessary and jointly sufficient.

Eight inhabitants of a town contract a rare form of the plague. A doctor is flown to the town with a serum she thinks might be a cure. Only four of the inhabitants accept the serum, the other four insist on using home remedies. But all eight had been treated with home remedies before the doctor arrived. Eventually, the four who received the serum recovered, while the other four died. What caused the recovery? The doctor noticed that among those who survived, no single home remedy was given to all; and that each home remedy had been given to at least one of those who did not survive.

This evidence indicates that the serum is necessary for the cure, since it was present every time the cure was present. The evidence also indicates that the home remedies were not sufficient for the cure, since each of them was taken by someone who was not cured. Finally, the evidence indicates that the serum was sufficient for the cure, since every time it was used the patient recovered. So the evidence indicates that taking the serum is both necessary and sufficient for the cure. As before, though, this evidence is not conclusive, for all the reasons we have noted.

5.17.4 Concomitant Variation

When phenomena vary together—what we call **concomitant variation**—then this is some reason to think that there is a causal link involved. But we have to be very careful about drawing causal conclusions from concomitant variation.

If the rise in interest rates is always accompanied by a rise in unemployment, then this is an evidence that a causal process is responsible for the correlation. If a lowering of a lake's water temperature is correlated with an increase in a frog population, and that population decreases when the temperatures rise, then this too is some reason to think there is a causal link involved. Likewise, if changes in one phenomenon can happen without any changes in another phenomenon, then this is some reason to think the two phenomena are causally independent or isolated from one another. If changes in the blood sugar level of white mice occur without any change in the rate of spread of their cancer cells, then this is some reason to think there is no causal link between the two. If the amount of mineral residue is the same even when there are changes in the amount of soap used in a restaurant dishwasher, then this is some reason to think that the soap is not causally relevant to the mineral deposits.

But the mere existence of concomitant variation among phenomena does not tell us much about the causal link. It might be that changes in one of the phenomena are causing the changes in the other. Or, it might be that changes in the observed phenomena are being produced by changes in some underlying phenomena.

5.17.5 Experimenting and Simulating

One of the main difficulties we face when trying to figure out what causes what is that our evidence is often very limited. We can use experiments and simulations to help overcome this difficulty.

We saw this difficulty in the cases we have already discussed. The health inspectors were not able to discover everything the sick people had in common. They simply have too many things in common. This made it difficult for the inspectors to know for sure that eating the tomatoes had caused the illness. Likewise, Simon was not able to study every last case of salted wine stains. So it was difficult for him to know for sure that salting makes the stain disappear in the wash. These limits to the evidence we have make it very difficult to know for sure what causes what.

Experimentation can help. As we saw, the methods of agreement and difference usually do not provide conclusive evidence because there are usually too many commonalities to know for sure which ones are causally relevant and which are merely coincidental. Only in very special and rare cases can we get conclusive evidence of an event's cause. This limitation is especially troublesome when, as in the examples we discussed, only a very small number of very similar cases are studied. For the smaller the number of cases studied, and the less diversity there is among them, the larger the number of commonalities, both of those things present and of those things absent. What we need is a way to generate a greater number and variety of cases to study. This is where experimentation comes in handy. When we set up an experiment, we can create as many cases to study as we can afford, with as much variety among them as can we imagine and create.

Suppose you want to figure out what causes some phenomena, P. The first thing you need to do is to make a list of possible causes. You then have to design an experiment that will show, for each possible cause, whether it is necessary or sufficient. It is very important that only one possible cause be tested at a time. That is, you need to vary only that one condition; you must **control** for variations in the other conditions. If your initial hypotheses is right, and if your experimental controls are effective, then you will gain additional evidence of a cause. If not, then you have to reconsider either the hypotheses or the experimental design.

Suppose, the researchers in the restaurant case wanted to set up an experiment to test their hypothesis that eating the tomatoes caused the illness. Suppose, in particular, that they want to rule out the possibility of multiple causes. (Notice the way that this would involve reasoning about alternatives.) They want to test their hypothesis against the possibility that some of the people got sick from oysters and the others from shrimp. The researchers might take samples of all of the other foods and drinks that those who got sick had eaten and feed them to laboratory mice and see whether any of them get sick. If none do, then that is some reason to think that eating the tomatoes was indeed a necessary part of the cause of the original illness.

To see whether eating the tomatoes was also a sufficient cause, they might try feeding just the tomatoes to a group of mice, and see whether any of them get sick. If they do, then that is some reason to think that the tomatoes alone were the cause. If the mice fed the tomatoes do not get sick, the researchers might try combining tomatoes with other common elements to see whether some combination of the foods produced the illness. By creating more cases to study, and by making them as varied as possible, the researchers can gain additional evidence. The very same methods of looking for commonalities either present or absent are then used to draw conclusions from the newly gathered evidence. Experimentation can help us to discover the causes of things by providing new cases to study with the old methods.

DECIDING WHAT TO DO: COMPARING CONSEQUENCES

A crucial step in deciding what to do is identifying the likely consequences of various courses of action. This involves reasoning about causal conditions, about what would happen if one adopted each of the candidates under consideration. The negative effects of a course of action are that action's potential **costs**, while the positive effects are its potential **benefits**. Knowing the likely costs and benefits of a proposal usually requires knowing a lot about the case at hand. The methods we have studied in the text can help you figure this out.

In addition to considering the direct costs and benefits of a proposal, it is also important to consider the indirect costs, including the costs associated with lost opportunities. Adopting one course of action over another will impact what opportunities are available at a later date. (Buying a stereo now means not buying a government bond tomorrow.) In effect, in adopting a course of action, one would be giving up the benefits of those opportunities. They would be "lost opportunities." Any benefit from lost opportunities should be counted as an indirect cost—an "opportunity cost"—in assessing the overall effect of a course of action.

Researchers can sometimes use **simulations** when it is not possible or practical to produce actual cases for study. Researchers studying extreme weather events, such as hurricanes and tsunamis, cannot just to go into their lab and produce hurricanes and tsunamis to study. But they can create computer models that simulate weather conditions and run them to see how different factors affect the resulting weather patterns. Economists create models of financial markets and study how changes in one element in the market can change other elements. The military runs virtual "war games" to see how different tactics affect the battlefield. This kind of experimentation relies on the use of models, and the value of the evidence they provide of causal conditions depends on whether these models are accurate representations of the phenomena they are trying to study. In Chapter 6, we will look in more detail at the use of models in reasoning.

EXERCISE 4

A. Comprehension Questions
  a. What is the difference between a necessary and a sufficient condition?
  b. Give five examples of a necessary causal condition for an effect that are not sufficient conditions for it, and five examples of a sufficient causal condition for some effect that are not necessary for it.
  c. Could something be a necessary part of a sufficient causal condition for some effect without being a necessary casual condition for that effect? If so, give an example.
  d. Why is experimentation not a new method?

B. Which method of reasoning about causal conditions is being used in the following cases? Using the concepts we have been discussing, describe five factors that make the evidence less than conclusive. Be as specific as you can.
  a. Mary noticed that all the cookies that had been kept in the plastic bags were dry and those kept in the freezer or in a cookie jar had stayed fresh. She concluded that keeping cookies in a plastic bag makes them stale.
  b. The city noticed that many of the parking meters were broken, and found that all of the broken ones had been tampered with by having bubble gum

inserted into their coin slots. The city concluded that the gum was causing the problem.

c. Doctors at the county hospital noticed that many of their patients returned after a few days complaining about a skin rash. They did a quick survey of those complaining of the rash, and found that all of them had used the hand soap dispenser outside the entrance doors. The doctors concluded that something in the hand soap was causing the reaction.

d. The local radio station noticed that during the hours when they played only classical music their listenership went down, and that it went up again when they switched to bluegrass music. They decided to become an all bluegrass station in order to maximize listeners.

e. Voting just does not make a difference to what the government does. In every democracy, it is still big business interests that decide government policy. And in nondemocratic countries, it is still big business interests that decide what the government does. So voting makes no difference!

f. The drug company Pharmastock did a study of its new antiobesity drug. It found that those who took the drug regularly lost more every week than those who took a placebo (i.e., a tiny sugar pill). It kept a careful watch to make sure that nothing else was different between the two groups. Pharmastock reported to its shareholders that its new drug was a huge success.

g. Susan planted six rows of corn in her garden. She planted cone flowers alongside the first two rows, and miniature rose bushes along the next two, and then nothing at all along the last two. The plants all grew very well, but during the harvest she noticed that the ears of corn on the last two rows had all been eaten by bugs, but that the rest were fine. She decided that planting the flowers prevented bug infestations.

C. What conclusions about the necessary or sufficient causes could be drawn from the following evidence? Using the concepts we have been discussing, explain why your answer is right, but also why those conclusions are not conclusive.

a. Doctors at Harvard who studied 2000 nurses for 25 years found that those who had high cholesterol came from different ethnic backgrounds, and different economic classes.

b. Studies on tadpoles found the following. If the tadpoles were spawned in pond water that averaged more than 75 degrees F, the tadpole population had a larger percentage of mutations and if the water was on average below 65 degree F there were no mutations at all. However, if the temperature varied from a high of 75 degrees F to a low of 65 degrees F then there were also no mutations.

c. Four groups of pregnant mothers were studied. The first group was given a shake that was high in protein but low in iron every breakfast. The second group was given a shake low in protein but high in iron. The third group was given a shake high in both protein and iron. The final group was given a shake that contained no iron or protein. After three weeks, the women in the third group had more stable blood sugar throughout the day than the women in other three groups.

d. Partners at a local marketing firm did a study at 20 local shoe stores. The firm found the following: stores that played music with a slow beat had the worst sales of all the stores, even worse than those that played no music at all. Those that played music with a fast beat had the best sales, and among those, the ones that played it loudest had the best sales. The researchers found no other commonalities among the different groups of stores.

D. Describe an experiment to test the following causal claims. Using the concepts we have been discussing, explain how the test is designed to answer the question.

a. Adding speed bumps to residential city streets reduces the number of accidents.

b. Adding mustard to a salad dressing makes the oil and vinegar stay blended longer.

c. The more a runner stretches before her long runs, the fewer injuries she gets.

d. High temperatures make ladybug populations decline.

e. Kneading bread dough for more than 10 minutes reduces the number of air holes in the finished loaf.

E. The following chart reports information collected by health inspectors after four people were sickened in a restaurant. Answer the following questions.

a. Was eating tomatoes a sufficient causal condition for becoming ill?

b. Was eating oysters a necessary causal condition for becoming ill?

c. What do we know for a fact about the causal relevance of potatoes and peanuts?

Person	Did they get Sick?	Did they eat tomatoes?	Did they eat potatoes?	Did they eat oysters?	Did they eat peanuts?
Benjamin	Yes	Yes	No	No	Yes
Samantha	Yes	Yes	Yes	No	No
Joel	No	Yes	Yes	Yes	Yes
Susan	No	No	No	Yes	No

F. Complete the following chart so that it shows the following:

a. Staying up late night before a quiz is neither sufficient nor necessary for getting an A grade.

b. Studying using flash cards is necessary but not sufficient for getting an A.

c. Copying from another student's test is not sufficient for getting an A.

d. Eating a healthy breakfast is not necessary for getting an A.

Person	Did they get an A?	Did they stay up late?	Did they use flash cards?	Did they copy?	Did they eat healthy breakfast?
David					
Jane					
Emily					
Miranda					

5.18   CRITICAL THINKING IN PRACTICE

5.18.1   Critical Thinking Mistakes

False Alternative. It is a mistake to reason with a false disjunction. It is a mistake because an argument with a false premise is not sound. Moreover, in the case of Denying a Disjunct, if the disjunction is false, then the conclusion will be false too.

Affirming a Disjunct. It is a mistake to conclude that one disjunct is true just because the other one is false. This is a mistake because it involves a missing premise. Affirming a disjunct is valid *only if the disjunction is an exclusive disjunction*. But if one knows that the disjunction is exclusive, then one should add this piece of information as an additional premise in one's reasoning.

Denying the Antecedent. It is a mistake to reason as follows: If P, then Q; it is not the case that P; so, it is not the case that Q. It is a mistake because this form of reasoning is not always valid. To think that it is valid is to confuse a sufficient condition for a necessary one.

Affirming the Consequent. It is a mistake to reason as follows: If P, then Q; it is the case that Q, so it is the case that P. It is a mistake because this form of reasoning is not always valid. To think that it is valid is to confuse a necessary condition for a sufficient one.

Red Herring. It is a mistake to raise irrelevant matters when criticizing someone's beliefs or reasons. This is a mistake because it is rude and because it makes it harder to find the truth together. One form of this mistake is to criticize a disjunction in someone's argument by raising possibilities that are ridiculous or that have already been ruled out.

Appeal to Ignorance. It is a mistake to believe something just because you do not have evidence that it is false. This is a mistake because a bit of investigation might show that it is false, and thinking critically requires looking for evidence when one can. One form of this mistake is to believe that a disjunction is true just because you do not know of any other possibilities. Thinking critically about alternatives requires making sure that we have done what we can to make our disjunctions exhaustive. Another form of this mistake is to believe that a conditional is true just because one is not aware of any counterexample to it. Critical thinkers should look for counterexamples before believing conditionals.

Strawman. It is a mistake to distort or misrepresent another person's views or reasons. It is a mistake because it is rude and also because it makes it harder to find the truth together.

Equivocation. To equivocate is to use words in different senses without realizing it. This is a mistake because it is hard to know if an assertion is true if we are not clear about what it means.

One form of this mistake occurs during debates or conversations. It is a mistake for participants in a discussion not to recognize that they mean different things by the key words and phrases they use. This is a mistake because it will be very hard to agree on the truth if we mean different things by our words. This can be recognized and avoided by a careful use of the SEEC method.

Another form of this mistake occurs in arguments. It is a mistake if a word must mean one thing for the premises to be true and another for the argument to be valid. This is a mistake because then the argument cannot be sound.

False Conditional (Slippery Slope) Fallacy. It is a mistake to reason with an extremely false causal conditional. It is a mistake because the argument is not sound.

Post Hoc Fallacy. It is a mistake to conclude that one event caused another solely on the grounds that the first preceded the other. While it is true that a cause always precedes its effect, this is not a sufficient condition for causation.

5.18.2   Critical Thinking Strategies

Counterexample Strategy. A counterexample to a claim is an example that shows that that claim is false. To be effective, the example has to be one that everyone in the discussion can accept; otherwise it will simply beg the question. Finding a counterexample proves that the claim is false; failing to find one, though, does not prove that the claim is true.

Method of Agreement. To tell if some condition is necessary for an effect, see whether it was present every time the effect was present. If it was absent when the effect was present, then that condition is not necessary for the effect. The method relies on the idea that everything necessary for the occurrence of some effect will be present whenever the effect is present.

Method of Difference. To tell if some condition is sufficient for an effect, see whether the effect follows every time that condition is present. If the effect does not follow when the condition is present, then that condition is not sufficient for the effect. This method relies on the idea that anything sufficient for an effect will be followed by that effect.

Method of Concomitant Variation. If two phenomena vary together, then this is some evidence of a causal relation between them. But by itself, this does not reveal much about the link. Variations in one might cause variations in the other, or those variations might have a shared an underlying cause.

Experimentation and Simulation. Knowing for sure whether some condition is a necessary or sufficient cause of some effect requires ruling out a lot of alternative possible causes. Doing this requires accumulating more evidence. New evidence can be generated by producing real (through experimentation) or fictional (through simulation) cases of the phenomena in question. In both cases, it is best to try to vary one possible cause at a time. This is called "controlling."

6

REASONING BY ANALOGY

In Chapter 5, we studied reasoning about alternatives and about necessary and sufficient conditions. We saw that any argument of the form of **modus ponens, modus tollens,** or **denying a disjunct** is a valid argument. In this chapter, we will study **reasoning by analogy**. Reasoning by analogy involves drawing conclusions about some particular thing or about a certain kind of thing by comparing it to something else that is like it in relevant ways.

Reasoning by analogy is very common and very powerful. It is basic to a good deal of our ordinary, common sense reasoning about what to believe and what to do. But it is also basic to a good deal of the reasoning in the natural and social sciences. We will first study reasoning by analogy in the abstract and then look at some particular applications of it. But let us start with some examples, to get a sense of just how varied and common this kind of reasoning is.

6.1 REASONING BY PERFECT ANALOGY

Here are some examples of reasoning by analogy.

1. John is just like his brother Peter, and Peter is a really generous guy, so I think that John must be generous too.
2. The war in Iraq is just like the war in Vietnam. We lost in Vietnam because we left too early. So, we should not leave Iraq until the war is won.

A Practical Guide to Critical Thinking: Deciding What to Do and Believe, Second Edition. David A. Hunter.
© 2014 John Wiley & Sons, Inc. Published 2014 by John Wiley & Sons, Inc.

3. When you do chemistry, you have to be really careful and precise in your measurements and timing. And baking bread is just like doing chemistry. So it is important to be careful and precise when baking bread too.

4. Eighty percentage of those we surveyed believe that we should build a new bridge across the river instead of a tunnel. Clearly, the majority of the city prefers the bridge idea.

5. According to the computer models, the storm will continue to track north for another 2 hours, and then move east into the direction of the city. So, the city is probably going to get a big rainstorm in about 2 hours.

6. The map says the buried treasure should be right here. Start digging!

The first three arguments pretty clearly involve reasoning by analogy. Each has a premise that compares two things. In the first argument, John is compared to his brother; in the second argument, the war in Iraq is compared to the war in Vietnam; in the third argument, baking bread is compared to doing chemistry. And in all three arguments, a conclusion about one of those two things is supposed to follow from this comparison or analogy together with an additional claim about the other thing. The reason to think that John is generous is that he is (according to the arguer, anyway) just like his brother Peter and Peter is generous. In the second argument, the (supposed) fact that the war in Iraq is just like the war in Vietnam, together with the (supposed) fact that the war in Vietnam was lost because US troops left too early is supposed to show or prove that the United States will lose the war in Iraq if it leaves too early. In the third case, the reason to be careful in measuring when baking bread is that (according to the argument, anyway) baking bread is just like doing chemistry and doing chemistry requires careful measurement.

Before we consider the remaining three examples, let us use these three clear cases to identify the abstract form of reasoning by analogy. It is this:

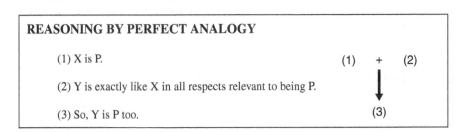

REASONING BY PERFECT ANALOGY

(1) X is P.

(2) Y is exactly like X in all respects relevant to being P.

(3) So, Y is P too.

(1)   +   (2)

↓

(3)

Some terminology will help. Let us call the premise that states the analogy or comparison, the **analogical premise**. Let us call the two things that are being compared, the **analogues**. Finally, let us call the property claimed to be true of the conclusion's subject, the **relevant property**. Notice that the analogical premise is somewhat special. It says that the analogues are exactly alike in all respects relevant to being P. That is why I call it Reasoning by **Perfect** Analogy. This will be very important in what follows.

6.2   IS REASONING BY PERFECT ANALOGY VALID?

We know that there are two very different questions to ask when evaluating an argument: are its premises true, and do they support the conclusion? We also know that these questions are independent of one another. Whether an argument's premises provide logical support for the conclusion has nothing to do with whether they are in fact true. Rather, it is a matter of whether the conclusion would have to be true *if the premises themselves were* true. But this is a difficult distinction to keep in mind, and it is easy to mistake uncertainty about the truth of an argument's premises for uncertainty about the argument's validity. The more we can do to keep these different kinds of uncertainty distinguished, the better we will be as critical thinkers. None of this is new; we have been making this point over and over in this book.

But it is of special relevance in this chapter, since it is often difficult—even for the best critical thinkers—to know whether the problem with a particular instance of Reasoning by Perfect Analogy is that the premises are unacceptable or whether they are insufficient (or both!). In this section we will make a start at learning how to draw this distinction. We will turn in a moment to when an analogical premise is acceptable. Let us first consider whether Reasoning by Perfect analogy is valid.

Let us recast our first example as follows:

1. Peter is generous.
2. John is exactly like Peter in all respects relevant to being generous.
3. So, John is generous.

And let us use the test for validity we discussed in Chapter 3. Suppose (just for the sake of the argument) that the two premises were true. That is, suppose that Peter is a generous person. And suppose that John really is exactly like Peter in all respects that are relevant to being generous. Could it nonetheless still be that John is not generous after all? Could it be that John is a tightwad, always refusing to leave a tip in a restaurant, say, or never offering to buy anyone a coffee or a cookie? How could it be? If John really is such a tightwad, then either he is not really just like Peter *in all respects relevant to being generous*, or else Peter himself is not really generous. In other words, if John is not generous, then either Peter is not generous or else there is some *relevant* difference between Peter and John that explains why one is generous and the other is not. At least one of those premises would surely have to be false if the conclusion was false. We might not know which was false, of course. But if we knew for a fact that John was a stingy guy, then we would surely know that either he is not like his brother, or else his brother is stingy too. All of this shows, I think, that if the argument's premises were true, then its conclusion would have to be true too. And this just means that Reasoning by Perfect Analogy is valid.

It might have already occurred to you that in reaching the conclusion that this form of reasoning is valid, we relied pretty heavily on one central part of the analogical claim. I even put it in italics: *in all relevant respects*. The analogical premise says that John is exactly like Peter in *all respects relevant to being generous*. What does this mean? What does it mean for them to be exactly alike in all relevant respects? Relevant to what? In this case, to generosity, of course.

Which respects are relevant in a case of reasoning by perfect analogy will depend on the **relevant property**. It might be that John is just as tall as Peter, or just as good at drawing. But these similarities are not relevant to generosity. Whether one is generous has nothing much to do with one's height or one's artistic abilities. But the fact that John is just as empathetic as Peter, and just as kind as Peter, and has the same keen sense of duty and justice as Peter, are similarities that are relevant to generosity. Whether a person is generous does depend on how well she can see things from another person's point of view (and so on how empathetic she is) and how keenly aware she is of her moral and social obligations. No doubt there are other elements that are also relevant to generosity. In claiming that John is just like Peter *in all relevant respects*, the analogical premise means that the two are alike in all the ways that are relevant to whether a person is generous or not. If Peter is very empathetic, and if being empathetic is relevant to generosity, then, that premise says, John is just as empathetic as Peter, and so on.

Now that we know the intended meaning of the phrase "in all relevant respects," the validity of reasoning by analogy should seem not very surprising. If X is P, and if X and Y really are exactly alike in all respects that are relevant to whether something is P, then Y would have to be P too. There is no way around that. If Y is not P, then either X is not really P either, or else there is some relevant difference between X and Y that explains why X is P but Y is not. Again, this is just another way of showing that Reasoning by Perfect Analogy is valid.

Notice that in this form of reasoning, the **relevant property** mentioned in the conclusion is also mentioned in the premise about the other analogue. This is crucial to this form's validity. In the following argument, this is not the case.

> Peter is very generous, and John is just like him in all the relevant respects, so John is a nice guy too.

The relevant property in this argument is being a nice guy. Being generous is not the same as being a nice guy. Probably, being nice requires being generous, but perhaps someone who is not generally very nice might still be generous—their one redeeming feature.

6.3   WHEN IS AN ANALOGICAL CLAIM TRUE OR ACCEPTABLE?

As we have now seen time and again, the fact that an argument is valid does not mean that its conclusion is true, nor does it mean that we yet have good reason to believe its conclusion. Whether an argument is good also depends on whether the argument's premises are true or acceptable. In the case of an argument by analogy, this comes to the question of whether the analogical premise is true or acceptable. In this section, we will study how to tell whether an analogical premise is true.

> To decide whether an analogical premise is true, we need to decide what the relevant respects are and whether the analogues are exactly alike with respect to them.

Deciding whether an analogical premise is true is difficult for two related reasons. An analogical premise asserts that the analogues are exactly alike in all relevant respects. The first difficulty is that any two things in the universe are alike in lots and lots of ways. (There may even be an infinite number of similarities between any two things!) Likewise, there are lots of ways in which any two things are different, perhaps even an infinite number of them. So, deciding whether some analogical premise is true is not simply a matter of deciding whether the analogues are alike: we already know that they are.

Crucially, of course, the analogical premise is that the analogues are alike in all *relevant* respects, and this is what introduces the second and greatest difficulty in deciding whether the analogical claim is true. For it is not always easy to know what the relevant respects are, let alone whether the analogues are alike in them. Take our example of John and his brother. In deciding whether it is true that they are alike in all respects relevant to generosity, we face two questions:

1. What respects are relevant to generosity?
2. Are John and Peter alike in such respects?

Or consider our second example, the one in which the war in Iraq is compared to the war in Vietnam.

1. What respects are relevant to losing or winning a war?
2. Are the wars in Iraq and Vietnam relevant in those respects?

Let us call the first kind of question the **relevance question**—since it asks what respects are relevant, and let us call the second kind of question the **comparison question**—since it asks whether the analogues are comparable in those respects.

Summary: In assessing whether an analogical claim is true, two questions need to be asked:

Relevance Question: What are the relevant respects?
Comparison Question: Are the analogues alike in the relevant respects?

The relevance question is often very difficult to answer. In some ways, answering a relevance question is like trying to decide whether a claim about necessary and sufficient conditions is true. As we saw in chapter 5, deciding whether a conditional is true can require knowing a lot of factual information about the subject matter of the conditional. We cannot know, just by thinking about it, whether a plant will die, if it is deprived of nitrogen. We need to do studies and experiments to find out whether nitrogen is necessary for plants to live. The same is true in the case of the relevancy question and so in reasoning by analogy. Knowing what factors are relevant to winning a war or to being generous may require knowing a lot about wars and generosity, and this is not knowledge one can acquire just by thinking about it. We need to do studies about wars and about human behavior in order to know what factors are relevant to winning a war or to being a generous person. This makes it difficult to evaluate the truth of analogical claims.

Comparison questions are also difficult to answer. Even if we did know what respects were relevant, it might still be difficult to know whether the analogues are exactly alike in those respects. Suppose we learn that being empathetic is relevant to being generous. How can we tell whether John is empathetic? And how can we tell whether he is *just* as empathetic as his brother Peter? How can we measure empathy? Suppose that lacking public support at home is relevant to whether a war is winnable. What is the best way to figure out whether the public really does support the war in Iraq? And how could we figure out whether the public support for that war is just like the public support for the war in Vietnam? This question can be just as difficult as the relevancy question.

An argument by analogy that has a false analogical premise commits the mistake we call **False Analogy**. As we have been seeing, it can be difficult to know for sure whether an analogical claim is true. It is the responsibility of the person advancing the argument to show that the analogical claim is true or acceptable. But if we are assessing an argument by analogy, we should not accuse it of committing the mistake of a false analogy unless we can back up that accusation. More specifically, we should not accuse an argument of False Analogy, unless we can point out some relevant difference between the analogues.

CRITICAL-THINKING MISTAKES: FALSE ANALOGY

It is a mistake when reasoning by perfect analogy for the analogical premise to be false. This is a mistake because an argument with a false premise is not sound. Recall that any two things are alike in a huge number of respects. An analogical claim is true only if the analogues are **exactly alike** in all of the respects that are **relevant** to the relevant property. Knowing what those respects are can be difficult, and can sometimes require a lot of investigation. Knowing whether the analogues really are alike in those respects can also be difficult.

If you are **constructing** an argument by perfect analogy to support some claim, then you need to make sure that the analogical premise is true.

If you are **evaluating** an argument by perfect analogy, and you believe that the analogical claim is not true, then you should be ready to identify some relevant respect in which the analogues are not alike.

We have been considering when an analogical claim is true or acceptable. Knowing whether one is true can be difficult, we have seen, both because it can be difficult to know which respects are the relevant ones and because it can be difficult to know whether the analogues really are alike in those respects. Often, this uncertainty is expressed by adding a word like "probably" into the conclusion, as in the following example.

> The model of the airplane was able to withstand strong cross forces, and the model is quite accurate, so the plane will probably be able to withstand those forces too.

It is always a good thing to be honest about how certain we are about the truth of an argument's premises. Using words like "probably" to make clear our level of certainty is a good thing. But none of this uncertainty about the truth of our premises would show that the argument is not **valid**. Uncertainty about the truth of an argument's premises is not uncertainty about whether the truth of the premises would be sufficient for the truth of the conclusion. Since it is relatively easy to construct a valid argument, we should never be uncertain about the validity of our arguments. We can be certain that an argument is valid, even if we are not certain whether its premises are true. This is such an important point that it is almost impossible to repeat it too often.

CRITICAL THINKING AND THE LAW

Reasoning by analogy plays a crucial role in legal theory in at least two places.

- *Similar cases should be treated similarly*. Crimes that are similar in relevant ways ought, all things considered, to be punished in the same way, and ones that are dissimilar in relevant ways ought, all things considered, to incur different punishments. In the absence of a relevant difference, it would be unfair to sentence one tax evader to jail but another to probation. Likewise, it would be wrong to punish a jaywalker as severely as a mass murderer. Of course, the difficulty is in deciding which respects are the relevant ones.
- *Filling legal gaps*. No matter how carefully laws are written, there are bound to be unforeseen cases. Judges (and prosecutors and legislators) have to decide how to treat unforeseen cases. Often, the similarities between the unforeseen and the intended cases play an important role. Again, the difficulty is in deciding which similarities are the relevant ones. Given that the US Constitution says nothing about the right to own submachine guns, is the ownership of such weapons more like the ownership of tanks or more like the ownership of muskets?

EXERCISE 1

A. Comprehension Questions
  a. What are analogues? Use the SEEC method from chapter 2 to develop your answer.
  b. What is the form of an argument by analogy?
  c. Using the concepts of a necessary and sufficient condition, explain why an argument by analogy that fits the form is valid.

    d. Under what conditions is it logically acceptable for the property mentioned in the conclusion of an argument by analogy not to be the same as the property mentioned in the premises?

    e. When is an analogical claim true or acceptable? Use the SEEC method from chapter 2 to develop your answer.

    f. What is the mistake of a false analogy and why is it a mistake? Use an example.

    g. Are the premises in an argument by analogy dependent? Use an example.

B. We have seen that analogues might be alike in respects that are relevant to one feature, but not alike in respects relevant to another feature. For each pair, find one feature with respect to which they are alike in all relevant respects and one feature with respect to which they are unalike in some relevant respect.

    a. A hockey game; a game of chess

    b. A garden; an economy

    c. A human; a mouse

    d. A car; the solar system

    e. A watch; the universe

    f. A toy train; a real train

    g. An electron; a planet

    h. Beef; tofu

    i. Loneliness; love

    j. Juliette; the Sun

C. Rewrite the following arguments to put them in the form of reasoning by perfect analogy. Insert a missing analogical premise if one is needed.

    a. Love is like a garden and if you do not tend a garden every day the flowers will die. Love needs tending too.

    b. I will not like that movie. It is just like that other one we saw last week, and I hated it.

    c. Cinnamon is just like mace, and the mace tasted good in the cake, so the cake too will taste good with cinnamon.

    d. The stock market is behaving just like it did 2 years ago, and back then we had a very deep recession, so another recession is on the way.

    e. Crime rates are about to drop. That is what happened in Europe when the economy boomed, and our economy is booming too.

    f. The samples taken from the patient's wound were infected, so the wound is now badly infected.

    g. The Sun has risen every day for nearly 6 billion years. Tomorrow will be no different. So, the Sun will rise tomorrow too.

    h. We repeated the tests 300 times and got the same results, so alcohol does kill germs on skin.

    i. Demolishing vacant buildings is like pulling out weeds. It increases the value of the surrounding buildings.

D. Look in the letters to the editor in a newspaper or magazine. Find three letters in which the author argues by analogy. Identify the analogues, and assess whether the analogical premise is acceptable.

6.4   REASONING USING REPRESENTATIONAL ANALOGY

Let us return to the arguments we started with. The first three are obviously arguments by analogy, since each of them has an analogical premise. But what about the other three examples?

1. Eighty percentage of those we surveyed believe that we should build a new bridge across the river instead of digging a tunnel. Clearly, the majority of the city prefers the bridge idea.
2. According to the computer models, the storm will continue to track north for another 2 hours, and then move east into the direction of the city. The city is probably going to get a big rainstorm in about 2 hours.
3. The map says the buried treasure should be right here. Start digging!

These arguments do not have an analogical claim as an explicit premise. The first one has a premise about a survey of public opinion; the second one has a premise about a computer model of a storm; the third one involves a claim about a map. Still, in each case, a comparison of one thing with another—the surveyed group to the general population; the computer model of the storm to the real one; the map to the island—is an essential premise in the reasoning. This is so even though the comparison is not explicitly stated. The presence of this comparison is what makes them all cases of reasoning by analogy. They are just like the case of John and Peter, only the comparison is not explicit.

Sometimes when we reason by analogy, we compare something to a model or representation of it.

Still, there is an important difference between these three cases and the ones with which we began. In the first three cases, the analogues are things of the same general kind: John and Peter are both humans; the wars in Iraq and Vietnam are both wars; and baking bread and doing chemistry are both activities that require measurement. But in the case of these last two arguments, the analogues are things of very different kinds: a computer model of a storm is not a storm, and a map is not an island. It might sound odd to suppose that a map could be in relevant respects just like a desert island, or that a computer simulation could be in relevant respects just like a real hurricane. But in these cases, the comparison rests on the claim that one of the analogues is an **accurate representation** of the other. Let us consider this idea in more detail.

The map is assumed to be a pictorial representation (i.e., a kind of picture) of the island and the computer simulation is assumed to be a representational model of the real storm. The reasoning relies on this assumed representational relation between the analogues. If the map is an accurate representation of the island, then one can rely on it when deciding where to dig for the treasure. If the computer model is an accurate representation of the real storm, then one can rely on it when predicting how the storm will move.

The very same is true of the argument involving the survey: the group of people surveyed is assumed to be **representative** of the entire population. If it is, then one can rely on what we know about it to draw conclusions about the entire group. Reasoning that draws a conclusion about something on the basis of a representation of it still counts as reasoning by analogy, and what we have said so far about reasoning by analogy applies to it as well. Let us look at each kind in turn.

6.5   REASONING WITH SAMPLES

Reasoning with samples involves drawing a conclusion about something on the basis of a claim about a sample of it. This kind of reasoning is extremely common and very powerful. We can use what we have been studying about analyzing and evaluate reasoning by perfect analogy to help us analyze and evaluate reasoning with samples.

Let us start with a few samples of reasoning using samples.

To decide whether her soup needs more salt, a chef might taste a spoonful of it. The spoonful is a sample of the soup.

To decide whether her patient has strep throat, the doctor might collect a sample of the infection on a long Q-tip.

A diabetic tests a drop of his own blood to see whether his blood sugar is high. To find out what Americans think about the risks of global warming, pollsters might ask a randomly chosen sample of 2500 Americans.

A movie's producers invite a sample audience to watch a preview before deciding whether to make additional changes to it.

All of these cases involve reasoning using samples. In this section, we will study when reasoning using samples is logically good.

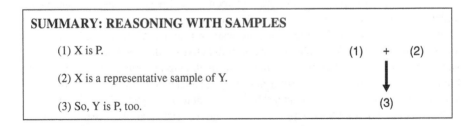

SUMMARY: REASONING WITH SAMPLES

(1) X is P.

(2) X is a representative sample of Y.

(3) So, Y is P, too.

$$(1) \quad + \quad (2)$$
$$\downarrow$$
$$(3)$$

The premise stating that X is a representative sample of Y, which is the **analogical premise**. Let us call X the **sample group** and Y the **target group**. And as before, P is the relevant property. Just as with reasoning by analogy, an argument of this form is valid: if its premises are true, then so is its conclusion. If Y is not P, but X is, then it must be that X is not really a representative sample of X. There must be some relevant difference between X and Y to explain why X is P but Y is not.

Sometimes, reasoning with samples involves a claim about some percentage or portion of the sample and target groups. Here is an example.

> A survey of students at University College found that 85% of them believe that tuition is too high. The sample group was representative of students across North America. So 85% of students believe that tuition is too high.

Let us look at how to analyze and evaluate these kinds of arguments.

The first premise includes the word "85%." Let us call that a **quantifier**. A quantifier is simply a word that specifies an amount or quantity. There are many different kinds of quantifiers in English. We can identify a quantity in numerical terms, either as a fraction (e.g., one half, or $1/2$) or as a percentage (e.g., 88%, or 25%). But we can also identify a quantity in non-numerical terms (e.g., most, almost all, a lot, a little.)

When reasoning with samples involves quantifiers, the quantifier should be thought of as part of the relevant property. The first premise is asserting that 85% of the sample group believes that tuition is too high. So we should analyze the first premise as follows:

Sample Group: the students at University College who were surveyed.

Relevant Property: 85% believe that tuition is too high.

The first premise asserts that the sample group has that property and then the conclusion of the argument is that the target has it too. The reasoning relies on the analogical premise that the sample is representative of the target. So, this reasoning is just the same as before, only with a relevant property that specifies a quantity.

Here is another example.

> Fifty percentage of seniors surveyed claimed to have been in a car accident last year. The seniors in the survey were representatives of seniors generally. It follows, then, that the vast majority of seniors are dangerous drivers.

There are two things to notice here. First, 55% is a majority; but it is not a *vast* majority. So the claim made about the sample does not support the claim made about the target group, even if the sample is representative of the target. Second, the claim made about the sample group is not the same as the claim made about the target group. We saw in the previous section that the argument might not be valid if the claim made about the two analogues is not the same. In this case, the claim made about the sample group does not support the claim made about the target group, even if the sample is representative of the target: being in a car accident is not the same as being a dangerous driver, and indeed being in a car accident is not sufficient for being a dangerous driver. This argument is thus invalid on two counts.

EXERCISE: REASONING ABOUT ALL AND SOME

We sometimes reason about what is true of all or some members of a group. Here are two examples.

All dogs are mammals, and all mammals have hearts, so all dogs have hearts.

All dogs are friendly, and all friendly things are cute, so all dogs are cute.

These arguments are both valid. In fact, all arguments of those forms are valid. (Remember, that does not mean that their premises are true!)

But here are two examples of invalid arguments about groups:

All cops love donuts; some people who love donuts love coffee; so some cops love coffee.

Some cats are friendly, so some cats are not friendly.

These are not valid arguments. Can you explain why?

Find two more forms of argument using "all" and "some" that are valid and two that are invalid.

6.6   WHEN ARE SAMPLES REPRESENTATIVE?

In assessing reasoning using samples, we need to know whether the sample group is representative of the target group. The basic idea is clear enough: the sample group is representative of the target group just in case the two are exactly alike in all relevant respects. But while this is clear, it provides little practical guidance in deciding whether some sample group is in fact representative of the target group. We will not always be able to tell. But there are some things to look for.

A sample may be representative of a target for one relevant property but not for another.

Whether a sample is representative of a target depends on the relevant property. A sample can be representative of a target with respect to one property but not another. For instance, suppose the sample consisted of 250 university students, and that the target consisted of all Canadians. That sample might be representative of the target when it comes to some topics but not for others. For instance, if we wanted to find out whether most Canadians have two arms, our sample might be representative. That is, we might be able to conclude on the basis of studying that sample that most Canadians do have two arms. But suppose we wanted to find out whether most Canadians have part time jobs. Then our sample group may not be representative at all.

To be representative of the target, a sample must be the right size.

Let us start with an example that will help us bring out the main points. Suppose that a chef is planning to taste his soup in order to decide whether he should add more salt. How many spoonfuls should he taste before he has sampled enough to know whether the soup needs more salt? This is a question about **sample size**: a sample is representative of the target only if the sample is large enough.

Just how big a sample has to be depends on how **homogeneous** the target group is with respect to the relevant property. Suppose that the soup in question is a simple clear chicken broth that we know has been well stirred. In that case, the soup is very homogeneous in terms of salt. That is, it is reasonable to expect in this case that the salt level in one part of the soup would be the very same as the salt level in any other parts of the soup. If so, then the chef would not need to collect a large sample—maybe even just one or two teaspoonfuls would be enough.

The size depends on how homogeneous the target is with respect to the relevant property. The more homogeneous, the smaller the sample can be.

Let us consider a different example. Suppose that a biologist wanted to measure the arsenic levels in a local lake, and that the lake had several rivers feeding into it, and that some of them had lumber mills on their shores. In this case, the biologist probably would have to collect lots of samples, since it is likely that the chemical composition of the lake water is not very homogeneous from one part of the lake to another. The risk, of course, is that if the biologist took only one sample, it might turn out that that sample was not at all representative of most of the lake's water. The biologist might end up falsely concluding that the arsenic levels are fine in the lake as a whole. This shows that the required sample size depends on the uniformity of the target group with respect to the relevant property: the more uniform it is, the smaller the sample has to be.

A sample of something is **random** just in case every part of it has the same chance of being in the sample.

The biologist example can also help us to see a second important point. Once she has decided to collect lots of water samples, how does she decide *where* to collect them? Obviously, collecting 100 samples from the very same spot would be a mistake. For if one sample of water at that spot is not representative of the water in the lake, then 100 samples from it would not be representative either. This shows that while sample size is essential to its being representative, it is not by itself sufficient. Clearly, the biologist needs to collect water samples from as varied a set of locations as possible. She needs to collect water from the mouths of the various rivers, some from the very middle of the lake, and so on. One way to ensure that her samples are representative of the lake water in general is to **randomly** select 100 sites in the lake from which to draw samples. (Let us assume that 100 samples would be enough. It might not be, but let us continue with this assumption, for the sake of the argument.) The idea of a random sample is a technical one: a selection of jellybeans out of a jar is a random selection just in case the chances of any one jellybean being selected are the same as the chances of any other bean's being selected.

A sample is more likely to be representative if it is both random and large enough.

However, just because a sample is randomly selected, it does not follow that the sample is representative. To be representative, a sample also has to be of the right size. A single, randomly selected sample of the lake water will not be representative of the lake's water, if the lake's water is not homogenous from one location to another. Likewise, asking one randomly selected American for their views on global warming could not possibly be enough to draw a conclusion about what Americans in general think about global warming. Remember, to be representative, the sample has to be just like the target in all relevant respects. If 10% of the target are working-class people, and if being working class is relevant to one's opinion on global warming, then 10% of the sample should be working class too. If 15% of the lake's water feeds in from one river, then 15% of the sample should be from that river too. The only way to make sure that the sample is like the target in the relevant respects is to make sure that the sample is large enough. That is why a sample has to be large enough in order for it to be representative.

HISTORY OF LOGIC: INDUCTIVE VERSUS DEDUCTIVE REASONING

A sharp distinction used to be drawn between two kinds of theoretical reasoning: deductive and inductive. But it is not clear what the distinction was supposed to be or why it mattered.

Sometimes the distinction was drawn as follows: deductive reasoning is from general to particular, whereas inductive reasoning is from particular to general. But modus ponens and denying a disjunct are often considered classic examples of deductive reasoning, and there is nothing especially general in them.

Sometimes the distinction was drawn as follows: deductive reasoning is valid, whereas inductive reasoning is not. But as we have seen, denying the antecedent is not always valid, even though it is often considered deductive reasoning. And reasoning by analogy can be valid too, even though it is usually considered to be inductive reasoning.

Sometimes the distinction was drawn as follows: deductive reasoning yields certainty, whereas inductive reasoning yields only probability. But this confuses the validity of an argument with the acceptability of its premises. Consider the following valid argument.

> Either the maid did it or the butler did it. The maid did not do it, so the butler did it.

If Sherlock Holmes is only 85% confident that the first premise is true, then he should only be at most 85% confident that the conclusion is true. But like modus ponens, denying a disjunct is often considered a classic deductive argument.

A better approach, it seems to me, than to distinguish two kinds of theoretical reasoning is to stay focused on the two questions we have been studying throughout this book:

> Is the argument valid?
>
> Are its premises true?

Since any (good) argument can be transformed into a valid one, these questions should be enough.

Self-selected samples should be treated as non-representative.

Sometimes, a sample group will be **self-selected**. A sample is self-selected just in case something is in the sample only if it decided to be in the sample. This is common with "instant" surveys on Internet sites, when anyone visiting the site is asked to answer a series of questions. The sample will be self-selected because the only people who answered the survey are people who decided to participate. They selected themselves, as opposed to having been selected by the surveyors. Sometimes magazines have a questionnaire for their readers to complete and mail-in. The questionnaires that are mailed in will constitute a self-selected sample because the readers themselves chose whether to fill it in. Student evaluations of their classes will involve self-selected samples if the students can decide on their own whether to complete the survey. A self-selected sample is thus not a random sample. Still, a self-selected sample *might* be representative, but there is no guarantee that it is. It would just be a lucky accident that it is. For this reason, a self-selected sample group should be treated as non-representative, unless there is independent reason to think otherwise.

SUMMARY: REPRESENTATIVE SAMPLES

1. To be representative, a sample has to be the right size.
2. Needed sample size depends on how homogeneous the target group is with respect to the relevant property. The more homogeneous it is, the smaller the sample size has to be; the less homogeneous, the bigger it needs to be.

> 3. Randomly selected samples of adequate size are more likely to be representative.
> 4. Self-selected samples should be treated as non-representative.

Of course, we might not know whether a sample is representative or not. As we have already seen, it is not always easy to know what the relevant respects are. And even when we do know this, it is not always easy to know just how big a sample has to be. And even if we do know all of this, it is still not always easy to tell whether a sample really was randomly selected. Polling companies usually include a statement of the margin of error of their poll, something like: "this poll is accurate to plus or minus 3 points, 24 times out of 25." This margin of error is meant to measure just how certain the pollsters are about whether the sample really is representative. There is an entire mathematical science devoted to calculating this margin of error, and we do not need to discuss that here.

CRITICAL THINKING IN RELIGIOUS STUDIES

A 2008 survey by the Pew Research Center reportedly found that 21% of self-proclaimed atheists in the United States believe in the existence of a God or Universal Spirit, and that one third of these are fully certain of the existence of such a being. This is a surprising discovery, since being an atheist means **not** believing in the existence of a God or supernatural being. Something obviously went wrong in the survey. We can represent the reasoning as follows:

1. Twenty-one percentage of the sampled atheists believe in the existence of God.
2. The sample is representative of American atheists.
3. So, 21% of American atheists believe in the existence of God.

The argument is valid, so because the conclusion has got to be false, at least one of the premises must be false.

Perhaps premise 1 was false. That is, maybe the survey was not a reliable measure of the opinions of those who took it. Maybe it used a question that was ambiguous, biased, loaded or otherwise bad. Or maybe the people who declared themselves atheists did not really understand the meaning of the word "atheist" or do not fully understand their own religious beliefs. Or perhaps they were somehow biased, and not being sincere either in claiming to be atheists or in reporting their religious beliefs their answers. Any of these possibilities might explain how premise 1 might be false.

Perhaps premise 2 is false. That is, perhaps the sample was not representative of American atheists. This would be so if the sample were too small. Maybe it was not a random sample. Since the survey asked the respondents to self-identify as atheists, this means that there was room for subject error and so for self-selection to have an effect.

Whatever the explanation, something went wrong in the survey, and using the critical thinking tools we have learned, we are able to describe what kind of error it might have been.

All of this means that, as critical thinkers, we need to be cautious before we accept the analogical premise of an argument by analogy that involves sampling. But being a critical thinker also means knowing what questions to ask, even if we cannot always find the answers.

1. Is the sample large enough? How homogeneous is the target in the relevant respects?
2. Was the sample randomly selected?

If we know what questions to ask, and if we have the needed vocabulary, then we are ready to think reflectively about reasoning with samples.

CRITICAL THINKING MISTAKES: HASTY GENERALIZATION

It is a mistake to rely on an unrepresentative sample when reasoning using samples. This is a mistake because the analogical premise is false, and an argument with a false premise is not sound. This mistake is a special case of the mistake of a false analogy.

The mistake is called a "hasty generalization" because the argument's conclusion is a general claim about the target and it is hasty because not enough care was taken to ensure that the sample was representative.

If you are constructing an argument using samples, then you have an obligation to ensure that the sample is representative.

If you believe that a sample is not representative, then you have an obligation to explain why.

6.7   REASONING WITH MODELS AND MAPS

We have been studying how to reason using analogies, and have looked at the case of reasoning with samples. Reasoning by analogy is also very useful in cases where the phenomenon we are investigating is very complex, or very large, and it is easier to reason about the phenomenon by reasoning about a model or map of it.

You may remember from grade school reasoning about the solar system by studying a model of it, with the planets and some of their moons, all orbiting the Sun. Biologists and geneticists do tests on animals in order to find out how various treatments would work on humans. Meteorologists and economists use computer models of storms or financial markets in order to understand and predict real storms and markets. We all use maps to find our way in a strange city. All of these are examples of reasoning about one thing by thinking about something that is a model or map of it. Evaluating this kind of reasoning is just the same as evaluating reasoning by analogy.

Let us use an example to bring out the key points. Suppose that an economist wants to predict what would happen to housing prices in a certain region if interest rates were to rise and the level of unemployment was to fall. The economist's model is dynamic in the sense that she can affect it by changing the interest and unemployment rate. In designing the model, the economist used what she knows about housing markets and about the relations between them and interest and unemployment rates. She knows that some features of the market are irrelevant—such as the color of the house—and that others are relevant—such as the age or size of the house.

Once her computer model is up and running, she can use it to predict how changes in real interest rates might affect the regional housing market. She could input a rise in interest rates of one-fourth of a percentage point and then see how the computer model of the regional housing economy is affected. She might see lower sales or a difference in the average sale price. If the model is sophisticated enough, she might be able to see different changes in different parts of the regional market. The better the model represents the real market, the more reliable her predictions will be. In other words, the more the computer model is like the real model in all the relevant respects, the more reliable her predictions will be.

In designing her computer model, the economist will ignore features of the real situation that she believes are not relevant. We already mentioned that she might ignore the colors of the houses in the region, since it is unlikely that a house's color makes much of a difference to housing prices. As we have already seen, it is not always easy to tell what features are relevant to a given property and which ones are not. Our economist might discover that something that she thought was irrelevant is in fact quite relevant. If her model's predictions are always wrong, then one possibility is that her model is not a very good representation of the real market because it ignores something that is actually quite relevant. Indeed, this is one way that we can figure out what features of a situation are relevant and which are not. In other words, the process of trial and error involved in trying to construct a genuinely representative model of some phenomena can itself teach us about a good deal about the nature of that phenomenon.

When we reason using models and maps, we often make idealizations to simplify our reasoning.

In designing her model of the regional housing market, the economist might deliberately ignore something that she knows is relevant, but only in very minor ways. Suppose that the number of windows in a house makes only a very insignificant difference to its sale price, and suppose that it would take a long time to collect and include window information in the model. She might decide to go ahead with the model anyway, leaving out the information about the number of windows. Her model would then be an **idealization**, pretending that the housing market is simpler than it really is. Strictly speaking, this means that her model is not an accurate representation of the real market. And it follows from this that it is not a perfectly reliable source of information on the real market. Still, this sort of idealization is acceptable, so long as one keeps track of it. So long as she keeps in mind that the model's predictions are based on an idealization, and so long as she is right about how insignificant those idealizations are, she should be able to rely on it to provide fairly accurate predictions.

EXERCISE 2

A. Comprehension Questions

a. What makes reasoning using samples a kind of reasoning by analogy? Use examples to develop your answer.

b. What is a representative sample? Use the SEEC definition method from chapter 2 in developing your answer.

c. Is a large sample guaranteed to be representative? Explain using examples.

d. Is a randomly collected sample guaranteed to be representative? Explain using an example.

e. Could a sample be representative even when it is not randomly collected? Explain using an example.

f. What is it for a target group to be homogeneous? Use the SEEC definition method to develop your answer.

g. What is a self-selected sample and why do they tend not to be representative?

h. Suppose that Jones and Henry are both collecting a sample of Americans for a survey. Suppose that Jones' sample is randomly collected and that Henry's is self-selected. Is it possible that the two samples contain the very same members? Explain.

i. What is a hasty generalization, and what makes it a critical thinking mistake?

B. In assessing whether a sample is large enough, we need to know how homogeneous the target group is with respect to the relevant property. To your knowledge, are the following target groups very, somewhat, or not at all homogeneous with respect to the following properties?

a. Males in your courses; study habits

b. Males in your course; political opinions

c. Males in your course; anatomy

d. Mice; anatomy

e. Roses; genetic makeup

f. Soft drinks; sugar content

g. Cars; safety features

h. Cars; reliability records

C. For the following groups, identify three properties with respect to which they are homogeneous and three with respect to which they are not.

    a. Maple trees

    b. Planets

    c. Sweaters

    d. Cars

    e. Humans

    f. Shoes

    g. TV shows

D. For the following pairs of samples and targets, identify one property with respect to which the sample is representative of the target, and one property with respect to which it is not.

    a. Ten people waiting for a bus; users of the city's public transit system

    b. Ten people waiting for a bus; residents of the city

    c. About 1500 Americans responding to an online survey; Americans in general

    d. Three mice; all mice

    e. Three mice; humans

    f. Five randomly selected cars; all cars

    g. Five randomly selected cars; manufactured products

    h. US companies; worldwide companies

    i. Three glasses of water taken at 8-hour intervals in your kitchen; the water in your pipes

---

CHAPTER SUMMARY

Reasoning by analogy is reasoning about one thing by comparing it to another that is just like it in relevant respects. This reasoning can be valid, but it is usually not easy to tell what the relevant features are or to tell whether the analogues really are similar in all of those respects. Reasoning using samples and models are examples of reasoning by analogy.

6.7.1   Critical Thinking Mistakes

False Analogy. It is a mistake for an argument by analogy to include a false analogical premise. This is a mistake because the false premise means that the argument is not sound. An analogical premise claims that the analogues are alike in all relevant respects. There are two ways to be mistaken in making an analogical claim. One might be mistaken about which respects are the relevant ones, or one might be mistaken about whether the analogues are alike in those respects. You should accuse an argument of committing a false analogy, only if you can identify a relevant difference.

Hasty Generalization. It is a mistake to draw a conclusion about a target group based on an unrepresentative sample. This is a mistake because since a premise is false the argument is not sound. This mistake is a form of the False Analogy.

6.7.2   From Theory to Practice: Applying What We Have Learned

6.7.2.1   Thinking Critically in Your Own Life   We have been emphasizing that we can and should think critically in every aspect of our lives. This includes in our thinking about our own life, about what we learned from life, about what kind of person we might want to be. In Chapter 1, you identified some features that you think are essential to being a morally good person and you were asked to give some reasons for thinking that they are in fact essential. In Chapter 2, you worked to construct definitions of them using the SEEC definition method. Now that we have discussed what it is for reasons to be good ones—they must be acceptable and sufficient—try to construct an argument in a paragraph or two giving your reasons in such a way that it is clear that they are both acceptable and sufficient. You could use reasoning by alternatives, or about necessary and sufficient conditions, or by analogy. Ensure that the arguments that you construct are valid. Once you have constructed your arguments, identify the main weak points in them.

6.7.2.2   Thinking Critically in the Classroom   This exercise is designed to help you identify the different forms of reasoning that you have to rely on in studying or engaging in your chosen discipline. We have studied several forms of reasoning: reasoning about alternatives, reasoning about necessary and sufficient conditions (including both reasoning about definitions and reasoning about causal conditions), and reasoning with analogies (including the use of samples and models.)

  (i) Look through one of the textbooks for your discipline, and find two examples of each of the kinds of reasoning we have studied in chapters 5 and 6.
  (ii) Write out the reasoning in the form of an argument, making sure that it is valid, and assess the acceptability of the premises.

6.7.2.3   Thinking Critically at Work   This exercise is designed to help you think critically about the kinds of reasoning you or the organization you work for rely on for success. In Chapter 1, you compiled a list of tasks that you regularly perform at work that require critical thinking. Look over that list, and identify those tasks that require you to reason about alternatives, or about necessary and sufficient conditions (including reasoning about definitions or about causal conditions), and those that require you to reason using analogies (including samples and models.)

7

CRITICAL THINKING IN ACTION

Critical thinking is reasonable and reflective thinking aimed at deciding what to believe and what to do. In Chapter 1, we saw that part of what makes critical thinking reasonable thinking is that it requires that we have reasons for our beliefs. More specifically, we saw that thinking critically requires having epistemic reasons: reasons for thinking that our belief is true, or for accepting some claim that we are considering. In Chapter 2, we studied the ways that concepts and terms help to frame our investigations and our problems and we identified some practical strategies for clarifying and defining concepts and claims. Chapter 3 focused on what it is for reasons to provide **sufficient** support for a belief, and in Chapter 4 we studied what it is for our reasons themselves to be **acceptable** and, more specifically, when we are justified in trusting the information we receive from observation, testimony, and measurement. In Chapters 5 and 6 we looked at several very common and very powerful **forms of reasoning**—reasoning about alternatives, reasoning about necessary and sufficient conditions, and reasoning with analogies. This final chapter is about pulling together the ideas, concepts, tips, and tricks we have learned into some practical strategies for helping us put critical thinking to work.

The aim of this chapter is to identify some general practical strategies that can help us to think critically at home, in our studies, and in the workplace. The approaches are the same whether we are thinking about our own lives, about the discipline we are studying or engaging in, or about our tasks and responsibilities at work. Since you are probably reading this book in a college or university course, we will study how to apply the approaches in our studies. And since your discipline is likely not the same

A Practical Guide to Critical Thinking: Deciding What to Do and Believe, Second Edition. David A. Hunter.
© 2014 John Wiley & Sons, Inc. Published 2014 by John Wiley & Sons, Inc.

as most of the people in your class, we will explore how these approaches can be applied across the curriculum. The point is not that what it is to think critically varies from one discipline to another; it does not. But disciplines do differ in the concepts they employ, in the sources of evidence they rely on, and in the kinds of reasoning that predominate. Remember that critical thinking is **reflective** thinking, and part of what this means is that thinking critically requires reflecting on the concepts one is thinking with, on kinds of evidence one is relying on, and on the kinds of reasoning one is employing. One goal of this chapter is to provide you with some tools to help you be as reflective as you can.

7.1 THINKING CRITICALLY ABOUT A DISCIPLINE

There are three things involved in mastering a discipline. First, you need to master its **key concepts**. What are the key ideas, concepts, and terms that experts in the discipline use to state their claims, to formulate their hypotheses, and to analyze their evidence and data? Second, you need to master its **sources of evidence**. How do experts collect the data and information they need to answer their questions and to solve their problems? Finally, you need to master the discipline's primary **modes of reasoning**. How do experts in the discipline draw conclusions from the information they collect? In this section, we will look at these three tasks in turn.

7.1.1 Identifying a Discipline's Key Concepts

In Chapter 2, we saw how key concepts are used to frame both problems and potential solutions. Part of what distinguishes one discipline from another are the concepts that experts in the discipline use to think about a phenomena. As we saw, different disciplines might study the very same phenomena from different points of view or perspectives, approaching they very same facts or puzzles with different conceptual resources, methods, and explanatory models. Indeed, this is part of why it can be so fascinating to study what experts in different fields have to say about some phenomena.

Consider the study of human sexuality. Sociologists and psychologists have a lot to say about it. But so do biologists and novelists. Even philosophers have tried their hand at making sense of it. To some extent, these researchers are interested in different aspects or elements of human sexuality. A psychologist might be more interested in exploring the central place that sexuality plays in our own self-conceptions, while a biologist might be more interested in the anatomical facts about how it works. But they might both be interested in the complex and subtle ways that sexuality interacts with social and group relations. The question: "Why do so many humans mate for life" will be understood and approached in very different ways in different disciplines.

Thinking about a phenomenon from the perspective of a given discipline requires using that discipline's **key terms and concepts**. Thinking about human sexuality from a psychological perspective requires thinking about it using the terms, concepts, and ideas that are not the ones that a biologist or a sociologist would use. Or, to change the example, the sport of football could be studied from many different perspectives. The sorts of questions and descriptions that a sociologist might give of a football game—perhaps focusing on the complex relations between individual players and the team, or between the fans and the team—would be very different from the kinds of questions and descriptions a sports physiologist would give, focusing on the anatomical features of players in different positions and the importance of different muscle groups. If, however, one wanted to think of it from a football-fan's point of view, one would have to use the concepts from the football rulebook. Different disciplines approach the very same phenomenon using different concepts and questions. Mastering a discipline requires knowing what its key terms and concepts are.

Identifying a discipline's key concepts is not usually a very difficult task. An introductory textbook in the field will usually include a glossary of key terms. The textbook's author will include in that glossary the words and concepts that she thinks one has to be familiar with to understand and engage in that discipline. Consider the key concepts and ideas in critical thinking. If we had to make a list of all of the technical terms we have been using in this book, we might produce the following list: epistemic reasons, nihilism, realism and skepticism, validity, argument, premise and conclusion, subargument, independent premise, truth, acceptable reasons, sufficient reasons, observation, testimony, reliable, measurement, accuracy and precision, necessary and sufficient conditions, exclusive disjunction, modus ponens, modus tollens, analogues. If one could master the meanings of each of these words (especially the word "validity"!), then one would be well on the way to mastering the study of critical thinking itself. (This, however, would not be the same thing as being a strong critical thinker. I might be an expert on football, but a terrible football player!)

7.1.2 Clarifying a Discipline's Key Concepts

Of course, mastering a discipline's key terms requires more than just being able to make a list of them. One has to know how to use them properly and for this it helps to be able to say or explain what they mean. In Chapter 2, we studied a method for constructing and evaluating definitions. We can use that method to define a discipline's key terms. Here is an example from the study of critical thinking.

> An argument is valid just in case if its premises were true, then its conclusion would have to be true too. In other words, it is not possible for the premises of a valid argument to be true and yet for its conclusion to be false. There is no way that its conclusion could somehow turn out to be false if its premises are in fact true. The premises provide conclusive evidence for the conclusion. For example, the following is a valid argument: All men are mortal; Socrates is a man, so he is mortal too. Here is an example of an invalid one: All mortals are men; Socrates is a man, so he is mortal too. The first one is valid because if its premises were true, then it would have to be true that Socrates was mortal too. But the second argument is not valid: maybe Socrates is a mortal cat! A valid argument is not the same as an argument that has true premises or that has a true conclusion. Whether an argument is valid is a matter of whether the conclusion would *have* to be true, *if the premises were true too*. An argument that is both valid and has true premises is called a sound argument. It is important not to confuse validity with soundness.

In this explanation of the meaning of the word "valid" the first sentence contains the initial slogan-like version of the definition. It is useful to have a short and simple-to-remember statement of the meaning. The next three sentences provide a longer expansion or elaboration of the slogan, putting the idea in other, equivalent terms. Then there are a few examples. Examples may not be useful or convenient for some sorts of definitions. Then the text provides some contrasting concepts or terms. Since the goal of providing a definition is to help to avoid confusions, it is very useful to contrast the concept being defined with nearby concepts, ones that someone might easily mistake or confuse with the one being defined. This SEEC method is not the only possible way to provide a definition. But it is extremely handy, and as we saw in Chapter 2, it can be used to explain what is meant by a statement or claim as we all to explain the meaning of some concept or term.

Let me repeat something from Chapter 2. The definition of validity I just gave provides necessary and sufficient conditions: it states what all and only valid arguments have in common, and it does this in a way that provides a rule to tell for any argument whether it is valid or not. But it is not always possible to provide such a precise definition, and sometimes it is not even very desirable. The key terms that define a discipline are usually not so precise that they can be given a definition in terms of conditions that are necessary and sufficient. In practice, this allows room for flexibility. It allows researchers to formulate hypotheses, raise questions, consider objections, and state alternatives that might not be possible if each and every word had a precise definition.

SUMMARY: IDENTIFYING AND DEFINING A DISCIPLINE'S KEY CONCEPTS

Mastering a discipline requires mastering its key concepts. These can usually be found in introductory textbooks. But knowing what they are is not enough. One has to be able to use them to think about the phenomena, and for this it is useful to use the SEEC definitional method discussed in Chapter 2.

EXERCISE 1

A. Visit the library and find an introductory textbook on human sexuality from psychology, sociology, evolutionary biology, and chemistry. Compare and contrast the textbooks' key words.

B. For your own discipline: identify the 10 most important concepts and terms. Using the SEEC method, compose a definition of each one.

7.2   IDENTIFYING A DISCIPLINE'S SOURCES OF EVIDENCE

We have been discussing the way that mastering a discipline requires mastering its key concepts. But mastering a discipline also requires understanding what kinds of evidence it relies on, and this is usually a matter of knowing what kind of sources it uses. In Chapter 4 we explored three kinds of sources: observation, testimony, and measurement. To some extent, every discipline relies on all three sources of evidence. Indeed, it is hard to imagine any serious branch of science—pure mathematics and philosophy aside—that do not depend on observation, testimony, and measurement. As we know, part of what makes critical thinking reflective thinking is that it involves making explicit the sources of evidence that we are relying on as we go about deciding what to believe or what to do. Let us consider a couple of examples.

Suppose that a criminologist wanted to find the most cost-efficient form of incarceration. What sorts of information would he need? He might visit several institutions, doing direct observation of the conditions at each one. He might interview managers and government officials, seeking their views on management practices and on the budgets and financial conditions of their institutions. He might develop a questionnaire to learn about the inmate's attitudes. In other words, he would rely on evidence from direct observation (the on-site visits), testimony (the interviews), and measurement (the survey). This study, in other words, might well require relying on evidence from all of the kinds of sources of evidence that we have studied in this book.

Sometimes, a discipline will rely on a source of evidence that is unique to it. This is the case in the brain sciences, where researchers use highly sophisticated brain imaging techniques. While the basic technology that produces these images is used in other disciplines too, it has been developed specifically for use in studying the brain. It provides information that simply cannot be collected in any other way. Indeed, until fairly recently, scientists studying the human brain had very little information to go on, since our access to living active brains was extremely limited. But now with the invention of brain imaging techniques, we are able to collect an enormous amount of information about how the human brain changes and grows, about its structure and functional organization, and about how various diseases and accidents can affect it. The development of brain imaging technology provided a new source of evidence and information, one that helped the scientific study of the brain make greater progress than it had for hundreds of years.

CRITICAL-THINKING MISTAKES: APPEAL TO IGNORANCE

It is a mistake to believe something just because you have no evidence that it is false. This is a mistake because a bit of investigation might show that it is false, and thinking critically requires looking for evidence when one can. One form of this mistake is to discount or ignore potential costs or benefits of a proposal just because you do not know how to measure or compare them. It is important for critical thinkers to do what they can to discover these costs and benefits.

EXERCISE 2

A. What sources of evidence do the following disciplines rely on? Be as specific as you can.

    a. History

    b. Nutrition

    c. Political science

    d. Early childhood education

    e. Social work

    f. Architecture

    g. Restaurant reviewing

B. What kinds of evidence might be needed to do the following studies? Be as specific as you can.

    a. To compare the effectiveness of relaxation over medicine for treating ordinary headache pain.

    b. To identify the impact on commuting of adding a stop sign at a busy intersection.

    c. To discover whether there is a greatest prime number.

    d. To understand the influence of popular music on fashion styles.

    e. To complete a review of a new Broadway show.

    f. To learn the effect that taking a critical thinking course has on a student's subsequent university education.

    g. To find which of three paint varieties is most mildew resistant.

    h. To learn the effects of substituting baking soda for baking powder in a cookie recipe.

    i. To learn the impact that stay-at-home fathers have on their children's socialization.

7.3   IDENTIFYING A DISCIPLINE'S FORMS OF REASONING

Finally, mastering a discipline requires mastering the kinds of reasoning that experts in it rely on. In this book, we have studied three main forms of reasoning: reasoning about alternatives; reasoning about necessary and sufficient conditions (including causal conditions); and reasoning with analogies (including sampling and modeling). As with the sources of evidence, most disciplines use all of these modes of reasoning to some extent or another.

Consider again our criminologist trying to identify the most cost-effective prison system. What kinds of reasoning will he engage in once he has collected his information and data? He might reason about alternatives, for he might have started with several candidates for being the most-efficient system, and is hoping that his data and evidence will help him narrow down the list to one or a small number of equally efficient systems. He might reason about necessary and sufficient conditions too, since he would need to begin with some definition or criterion of "most efficient." Indeed, he might combine these two forms of reasoning, ruling out certain candidates by showing that they lack features that are necessary for satisfying that definition or criteria. Since the researcher is interested in comparing and contrasting different prison systems, there will have to be some reasoning by analogy as well. This study will thus employ all of the forms of reasoning we have discussed in this book.

We have been discussing how the researcher might use these three forms of reasoning to draw conclusions from the evidence of data he has collected. But these forms of reasoning are often employed at other stages in an investigation as well. We have already noted that the researcher will likely begin with some sort of conception of what it is for a prison to be cost-efficient. Developing and checking this conception will likely involve reasoning about necessary and sufficient conditions, and may involve using the counterexample method to help identify just what makes a prison system efficient. Indeed, it is likely that the conception might change and improve as the researcher begins to collect the data: it is only in very unusual cases that the definitions are crystal clear at the beginning of an investigation. Designing the questionnaire to uncover inmate opinions also requires reasoning: one has to decide what questions to ask and ensure that they are well formed, that they are not leading, and that they are not biased. Identifying a sample group requires thinking about the prison population in general in order to ensure that the sample is representative.

Reasoning about alternatives, about necessary and sufficient conditions, and about analogues can thus occur at many different stages in an investigation. It might occur at the very beginning as the researcher works to formulate and clarify her hypotheses. It might be involved as she decides on what sources of evidence to use and on what methods of measurement to employ. It will guide her as she makes those measurements, and collects the data. And it will be her guide as she draws conclusions from the evidence she has collected. Indeed, this kind of reasoning is pervasive as we try to decide what to believe.

7.4   CRITICAL-THINKING QUESTIONS

So far in this chapter, we have been studying the three things one needs to learn in order to master a discipline. One must learn the discipline's **key concepts**, its **sources of evidence**, and its **modes of reasoning**. Knowing what kinds of questions to ask is of great value in thinking critically. Throughout this book, we have looked, sometimes in great detail, at different elements of critical thinking. But the kinds of questions we have learned to ask can helpfully be categorized intro three kinds: questions about meaning, questions about truth, and questions about value.

One can ask questions about **meaning**.

(i) What is the claim being defended, or the course of action being proposed?
(ii) What are the claim's key words and what do they mean?

(iii) Can we provide examples to illustrate them and can we identify some contrasting concepts?

(iv) What is the framework within which this claim or proposal is being raised?

 (v) What are some alternative or contrasting frameworks?

One can ask questions about **truth**.

 (i) Some questions about truth are about the **acceptability** of premises. What are the sources of the information in the premises? Are those sources reliable? What objections to the truth of those premises are there, and how are they to be addressed?

(ii) Some questions about truth are about the **sufficiency** of premises. What forms of reasoning are in use? Would those premises constitute a valid argument for the conclusion? What conclusions could be validly drawn from those premises?

(iii) Some questions about truth are about **alternatives**. What other views on this subject are there? What are the strongest reasons in their favor? What are the strongest objections to them?

One can ask questions about **value**.

 (i) Why is it important to perform this study?

 (ii) What is the context that makes this study important or interesting?

(iii) Would the answers to these questions impact or influence studies in other disciplines?

(iv) How does this conclusion fit into the author's broader argument?

PRACTICAL TIP: THE RULE OF THREES

An important skill in thinking critically is being able to imagine alternatives and to identify contrasting concepts. It is a useful rule to try to find at least three alternatives or contrasting concepts. Often, finding the first two will be relatively easy—it is finding the next one or two that proves enlightening.

Critical thinking is aimed at deciding what to believe or do. We think critically whenever we try to decide what some evidence shows about some question or phenomena, whenever we assess or evaluate what someone else believes or is arguing, and whenever we try to present our own reasons for believing something. Keeping these three kinds of questions in mind can help us to organize our thinking. As we read or listen to someone develop their reasons for believing something, we should be asking these three kinds of questions. As we plan our own investigation we should keep in mind the importance of defining the key concepts and problems clearly, of ensuring that our sources are reliable and trustworthy, and of keeping an eye on the big picture.

7.5   THINKING CRITICALLY IN YOUR OWN DECISION MAKING

Sometime during your university career, you will be expected to write an essay or report in which you present and defend a point of view. Indeed, it is quite likely that you already do this on a regular basis. And it is inevitable that once you start a career you will be expected to present suggestions and recommendations. What we have learned in this book can help you think about how to structure your essay or report.

7.5.1   Clarify Your Views

The single most important thing is to be as clear as you possibly can about what your claim or proposal is. If your reader is not clear what exactly you are claiming or what course of action you are recommending, then there is little chance that you will persuade them, and some chance that any agreement will be based on a misunderstanding. If your claim or proposal is formulated using technical or specialized concepts, make sure that you carefully and clearly define them. We have seen, in Chapter 2, that the SEEC definitional method can be used to state a claim or proposal clearly. In many cases, the most important thing is to prevent possible misunderstandings by explicitly noting views or proposals that you are not recommending but that you suspect others might confuse with the one you are recommending. Doing this is also a useful way for you to make sure that you are clear in your own mind about what your views are.

Usually, the claim or proposal that you are advancing will be part of a much larger investigation or project, and it is often very helpful to make explicit what this larger context is and how your piece fits into it. This will help your audience to locate your claim or proposal in a larger picture, and will help to make its importance and value clear.

7.5.2   Make Your Reasons Explicit

It is very important not to confuse your view or proposal with your **reasons** for accepting that claim or proposal. A statement of a view or of a possible course of action might take an entire paragraph, especially if you are using something like the SEEC method. Stating the reasons for your view might take as long. Sometimes, it might be helpful to formulate your reasons in the form of an argument, and then spend a paragraph clarifying each premise and the conclusion. There are different ways to organize your reasons, but none will succeed if the reader is not able to easily tell the difference between your reasons and your view.

There are many reasons for keeping a sharp line between one's views and one's reasons. First, someone might agree with your view or proposal but for different reasons. They might agree with you that building a bridge is the best option, but not for the same reasons as yours. Perhaps you think it is the most cost-effective option and they think it is the option that will do most to resolve traffic congestion. Second, someone who resists your view might in fact accept your reasons, and might not have realized that they support your view. By laying out the reasons clearly, and showing that they do in fact support your view, you could bring them around to your side. Third, someone might be able to offer additional (or even better) reasons in support of your view.

7.5.3 Show that Your Reasons are Acceptable and Sufficient

No matter what your view is or what your reasons are for it, there are bound to be objections, and it is important to be as honest as you can be about what they are and about how to respond to them. But as we know, there are really only two kinds of objections. Someone might object that your reasons are not **sufficient** to support your claim or proposal, or they might object that your reasons are not **acceptable** (or both!). The fact that people will raise objections to your view or to your reasons is actually a good thing, since the goal of critical thinking is to get at the truth. Objections are simply a healthy way of making sure that your reasons are sufficient and acceptable.

The best defense, they say, is a strong offense. One way to go on the offensive is to make it as clear as you can in your essay or report that your reasons are sufficient and acceptable. We have seen several forms of reasoning that are guaranteed to be valid (and so sufficient) and it would be good for you to try to present your reasoning in a valid form. Doing this is relatively easy if your reasoning is about necessary and sufficient conditions or about alternatives. But it is more complicated if you are reasoning about causal relations or using analogies. But the strategies identified in Chapters 5 and 6 can be helpful.

Objections to the acceptability of your reasons are more serious, and more difficult to defend against. It is good to be as clear as you can about the source of your reasons. If you are relying on observation, say so and do what you can to show that your observations were collected in optimal conditions. If you are relying on testimony, explain why the witness is appropriate, competent, and unbiased. If you are relying on measurements, say something about the accuracy and reliability of the measuring device. If you are reasoning about alternatives, make it clear that your disjunction is acceptable by showing that it is exhaustive. If you are reasoning about necessary and sufficient conditions, discuss whether the conditional states a definition or a causal relation and do what you can to show why it is acceptable. Considering and responding to possible counterexamples is a useful strategy for this. If you are reasoning using analogies, discuss what the relevant respects are and the reasons for thinking that the analogues are alike in those respects.

We have learned enough in this book to know that these tasks can be difficult. The most important thing, though, is to be as honest as you can be about just how acceptable you think the reasons or pieces of evidence are. If you suspect that there are difficulties with it, say so. Given our incomplete information, we are bound to have to make decisions about what to believe and do on the basis of evidence whose acceptability we are not able to prove beyond a shadow of a doubt. While admitting that you are sensitive to the question of acceptability may not make your argument any stronger; it will show you to be a strong critical thinker, and so increase the chances that others will be swayed to your side. And it will help your case if you can discuss these issues using the key critical-thinking concepts.

7.5.4   Identify and Respond to Alternatives

No matter how good your reasons are for your view or proposal, there are bound to be alternative views and proposals. Sometimes, people will hold the opposite view, and will have reasons that they think are sufficient and acceptable. Sometimes, though, people will hold a view that is close to your view but different in subtle ways, and will have reasons that they think are sufficient and acceptable. It is important to identify and respond to these alternatives. We have already seen that identifying them can be a useful thing to do as part of clarifying your own view and reasons.

Responding to alternatives involves doing two things. First, it is good to raise **direct objections** to the alternative itself. Direct objections are reasons to think that the claim is false or that the proposed course of action is not a good one or not as good as the one you are proposing. Second, it is good to raise objections to the reasons that have been or might be offered in support of that alternative. If the alternative you are considering is to build a tunnel rather than a bridge, then those who support the tunnel option will probably have reasons on their side, and it is good for you to identify what they are (making them as clear as you can so as to avoid the Strawman mistake) and then explain why you think they are either not sufficient or not acceptable. Perhaps you think they rely on evidence from a biased witness, or are based on measurements from an unreliable device. Whatever your objections might be, it is important to be as clear as you can about what they are. And for this, there is nothing better than using the key critical-thinking concepts to frame your objections.

SUMMARY: THINKING CRITICALLY IN YOUR OWN REASONING

In presenting your reasoning for some claim or proposal, it is important to:

- State your view clearly
- Separately state your reasons
- Defend your reasoning by discussing the acceptability and sufficiency of your reasons
- Consider alternatives and identify objections to them

7.6   THINKING CRITICALLY IN DISCUSSION

Thinking critically in a conversation involves knowing what kinds of questions to ask. But it also involves maintaining a kind of critical and emotional distance. And most crucially, it involves insisting on reasons.

7.6.1   Ask Open-Ended Clarification Questions

It is very important to ask for **clarification**. We are all familiar with the way that a disagreement that seemed at first to be quite substantive—about something very deep and important—can suddenly turn out to be a mere linguistic disagreement; a disagreement, not about the facts, but about how to state the facts. This is perhaps especially true in some of the most emotionally charged debates of our time. For this reason, it is important to make sure that you know exactly what people, you are in a discussion with, mean by their words. Of course, they have an obligation to be as clear as they can be, and to do whatever they can to avoid or prevent confusions and misunderstandings. But as a critical thinker, you have the same obligation. In a discussion, when you are the listener, you can fulfill this obligation by asking the right kinds of questions.

Questions that have a "yes" or "no" answer are usually not as informative as questions that require a long answer. This is especially true if an apparent disagreement rests on linguistic differences or misunderstanding. You want to do whatever you can to rule out this possibility and asking open-ended questions that require the speaker to restate her view in other ways, to elaborate or expand on her view, to offer examples of it, and to identify contrasting views is the way to do it. In other words, use the SEEC method to help develop open-ended questions. And you can ask these questions not just about her conclusion, but also about her reasons and premises.

7.6.2 Withhold Disagreement and Agreement

We all know what it feels like to explain our opinions and views to people who we know disagree with us. It puts additional pressure on us, pressure that is not really helpful if the goal is to get clear on the truth of the matter. For this reason, it is best to withhold disagreement until the speaker has had a full opportunity to explain, defend, and support her view. If she feels rushed into explaining it, she might leave out some crucial distinctions, and this might have the effect of weakening what might in fact be a fairly plausible position. Or she might skip over some of the premises or fail to mention a response to an objection. Your goal as a critical thinker in a discussion is to help the other people make a case for their views that is as clear, as strong, and as complete as possible.

It may be just as important to withhold agreement as to withhold disagreement. After all, you and the speaker might agree on the truth of the conclusion for very different reasons. Perhaps you would reject his reasons as either unacceptable or insufficient. Again, your goal is to help the speaker develop as clear, as strong, and as complete a case for his or her view as possible, and if you and the speaker reach an agreement too quickly, before all of the elements of his view have been laid out, your superficial agreement will end up hiding an underlying and perhaps very significant disagreement. It is, for this reason, just as important to question thoroughly people you agree with, as it is to question thoroughly people with whom you disagree.

7.6.3 Keep Emotional Distance

Being a critical thinker means that our beliefs should be based on epistemic reasons, and not on emotional or pragmatic ones. Basing one's beliefs on emotions rather than on epistemic reasons is a mistake, since how a claim or proposal makes one feel emotionally is not a reliable guide to whether the claim is true or the proposal is good. Emotions can also make it difficult to collect the evidence we need, or even from investigating further. Emotions get in the way when we identify too much with our own opinions and beliefs or with our own methods for collecting or evaluating evidence. If I become too emotionally attached to my beliefs and opinions, then I may react negatively when someone asks me for my reasons, or when they raise objections to my belief or when they state their own alternative beliefs. I might feel that they are criticizing me and not just my beliefs. The same is true if I am asked to defend my assessment of the evidence or my use of different methods for collecting evidence. If I come to identify too closely with these particular methods for assessing and collecting evidence, if I come to think of my value as a researcher as tied into their value, then I will react to criticisms of them as if they were criticisms of me and my judgment. This feeling of being under attack might make me feel defensive, and this can prevent me from thinking critically about the issue at hand. The same is true when I ask someone for his or her reasons. This sort of question is easily taken as aggressive or combative, even when the intention is simply to consider the issue from all sides as thoroughly as possible.

PRACTICAL TIP: DO NOT PERSONALIZE REASONS

Reasons and evidence do not belong to anyone; in this sense they are **universal**. And whether they are good has nothing to do with who accepts them; in this sense they are **objective**. To avoid personalizing reasons, replace the following:

  a. What evidence do you have?
  b. What are your reasons?
  c. Why do you believe that?

with the following impersonal ones:

  a′. What evidence is there?
  b′. What reasons are there to believe that?
  c′. Why should we believe that?

Knowing how to **distance** oneself from one's beliefs and opinions in order to think critically about them is not easy. It is one of the hardest things to achieve. But the best way to avoid this feeling is making sure that one's beliefs and opinions are based on enough of the right kind of evidence. Again: **think twice, decide once.** Another strategy is to avoid talking about "my reasons" or "your reasons" and to talk instead "the reasons" or "some reasons." This makes sense anyway, since reasons and evidence are not owned or possessed by anyone: they are universal and objective. Instead of asking "What are your reasons for believing that?" which can come across as confrontational, ask, "What reasons are there to believe that?" which makes the question sound less confrontational. Instead of asking, "What is your evidence?" you can ask, "What evidence is there for that?"

SUMMARY: THINKING CRITICALLY IN DISCUSSION

Since the goal of critical thinking is to get at the truth, it is helpful during a discussion to:

- *Ask open-ended clarification questions*, in order to allow everyone to fully state their views and reasons;
- *Withhold agreement and disagreement*, in order to find common ground and avoid merely linguistic disagreements;
- *Keep your emotional distance*, in order to enable a friendly and cooperative search for the truth.

7.7   FROM THEORY TO PRACTICE: APPLYING WHAT WE HAVE LEARNED

7.7.1   Thinking Critically in Your Own Life

Throughout this book, we have been emphasizing that we can and should think critically in every aspect of our lives. This includes in our thinking about our own life, about what we have learnt from life, about what kind of person we might want to be. In Chapter 1, you identified some features that you think are essential to being a morally good person and you were asked to give some reasons for thinking that they are in fact essential. In Chapter 2, you worked to construct definitions of them using the SEEC definition method. In Chapter 6, you constructed an argument in a paragraph or two giving your reasons. Now you are in a position to develop it into a full defense.

- Using the concepts that we have studied, discuss the sufficiency and acceptability of your reasons.
- Identify possible objections to your view, state them clearly and using the concepts that we have learned, respond to them.
- Identify some alternative views, state them clearly, present the very best reasons in support of them, and raise objections to them.

In writing it out, pretend that your audience is someone who has never taken this course or read this book.

APPENDIX A

CRITICAL THINKING MISTAKES

Critical thinking is reasonable and reflective thinking aimed at deciding what to believe and what to do. Throughout this book, we have identified mistakes that a good critical thinker should avoid. Some are mistakes that can arise in clarifying or defining a view. Others are mistakes that can arise as we collect or rely on evidence or reasons for a view. Still others arise when we try to draw conclusions for our evidence. And there are even mistakes that can arise as we assess other people's views or reasons. Knowing what they are will help us to avoid them in our own reasoning. But it will also help to make it clear just what the value is in being a critical thinker: thinking critically is valuable in part because it helps us to avoid some mistakes. This appendix lists all of the mistakes we have discussed.

Personalizing Reasons. It is a mistake to personalize reasons by treating them as if they belonged to someone. That is a mistake for two reasons. First, epistemic reasons are universal: if they are reasons for me to believe something, then they are equally reasons for anyone else to believe it. Second, epistemic reasons are objective: whether a piece of evidence is sufficient or acceptable is an objective matter. It has nothing to do with me or with anyone else. Personalizing reasons can obscure the fact that they are universal and objective. It can also allow emotion to get in the way of thinking critically, if one identifies too much with one's own reasons or if one rejects reasons just because someone else accepts them.

Appeal to Relativism. It is a mistake to just assume that truth is relative. This is a mistake because we always need to have good reasons for our beliefs, including our belief that relativism is the right attitude to take toward some subject matter.

A Practical Guide to Critical Thinking: Deciding What to Do and Believe, Second Edition. David A. Hunter.
© 2014 John Wiley & Sons, Inc. Published 2014 by John Wiley & Sons, Inc.

Relativism with respect to some subject matter is the view that the facts in that area are in some way dependent on our beliefs about them. Relativism might be the right attitude to take toward such topics as what is humorous or what is tasty. But for most topics, even religious and moral ones, it is best to assume that Realism is the appropriate attitude, unless one has powerful reasons not to. For most topics, in other words, it is wrong to assume that what is true for me might not be true for you, or that what is true for our community or culture might not be true for others. Truth is the same for everyone.

Sometimes, an appeal to Relativism will be used as an attempt to bring a discussion to an end. One person, perhaps tired of the debate or feeling that they are on the losing side, will say to the others: "Well, I'm entitled to my view and you are entitled to yours." This kind of response is fine if what is intended is that everyone is allowed to make up their own minds about what to believe or do. But if the point is that we can both be right even when we disagree, then this is a mistake that we should avoid, unless there is excellent reason to think otherwise.

Appeal to Emotion. It is a mistake to base our beliefs only on our emotions. This is a mistake because how a belief makes us feel is not an evidence that the belief is true, and a belief should be based on evidence that it is true. For a belief to be justified enough for knowledge it must be based on good epistemic reasons. Epistemic reasons are reasons to think that the belief is true. Emotional reasons are not epistemic ones. How a belief makes us feel has nothing to do with whether the belief is true. As we have already noted, critical thinking does not aim to eliminate emotion from our decision making. I doubt this would be worthwhile even if it was possible. Many of our beliefs are so fundamental to our deepest conceptions of ourselves, of our culture or our place in the Universe that the pain involved in abandoning them would be too great to bear. It is fine for our beliefs to have or even constitute these emotional supports, so long as they also have sufficient support from epistemic reasons. But it is a mistake to base our beliefs on nothing but emotional reasons. We also saw that it is a mistake to allow emotions to prevent us from collecting or assessing the evidence we need to make the decisions we must.

Privileging Confirming Evidence. It is a mistake to assume that evidence that confirms what we already believe is better than new evidence that conflicts with it. This is a mistake because what we already believe may be false, and if we were to consider the disconfirming evidence more carefully we would see this and change our minds. A critical thinker is always willing to reflect on whether his beliefs are based on sufficient and acceptable evidence.

Privileging Available Evidence. It is a mistake to assume that evidence that we currently have is better than evidence that we might collect. This is a mistake because if we were to collect more evidence, we might discover some that overrides or that undermines the evidence that we have. It might be that our current evidence is the best we can get, but we will not know this until we try to collect more. Crucially, even if we have excellent reason to rest content with the evidence we have, we should always keep an open mind that we might uncover new evidence that will override or undermine the evidence we now have.

Appeal to Tradition. It is a mistake to believe something just because that belief is traditional. This is a mistake because the fact that a belief has a long history is not evidence that it is true, and it is a mistake to believe something without evidence that it is true. Being a critical thinker does not mean abandoning all of our traditional beliefs. It just means that we need to have good reasons to continue holding them.

False Definition. It is a mistake for a definition to be too broad or too narrow, or both. This is a mistake because it means that the definition is false. A counterexample to a definition is an example that shows that the definition is too narrow or too broad. The SEEC method can help us to avoid this mistake by requiring us to look for counterexamples and contrasting concepts.

Equivocation. To equivocate is to use words in different senses without realizing it. This is a mistake because it is hard to know if an assertion is true, if we are not clear about what it means.

One form of this mistake occurs during debates or conversations. It is a mistake for participants in a discussion not to recognize that they mean different things by the key words and phrases they use. This is a mistake because it will be very hard to agree on the truth if we mean different things by our words. This can be recognized and avoided by a careful use of the SEEC method.

Another form of this mistake occurs in arguments. It is a mistake if a word must mean one thing for the premises to be true and another for the argument to be valid. This is a mistake because then the argument cannot be sound.

Straw Man. It is wrong to distort or misrepresent another person's beliefs or their reasons. It is a mistake because it is very rude and because it prevents you and the other person from getting to the truth together. While everyone has a duty to make her beliefs and reasons clear, we all have a duty to represent each other's beliefs and reasons as clearly and charitably as we can.

Post-Hoc. It is a mistake to conclude that one thing caused another just because the one thing happened first. This is a mistake because while causes do precede their effects, this is just a necessary condition for a causal link not a sufficient one.

Appeal to Ignorance. It is a mistake to believe something just because you have no evidence that it is false. This is a mistake because a bit of investigation might show that it is false, and thinking critically requires looking for evidence when one can.

One form of this mistake is to accept a piece of evidence just because one does not know of any overriding or undermining evidence. Critical thinkers should look for overriding and undermining evidence, before relying on some evidence.

Another form of this mistake is to discount or ignore potential costs or benefits of a proposal just because you do not know how to measure or compare them. It is important for critical thinkers to do what they can to discover these costs or benefits.

Another form of this mistake is to believe that a disjunction is true just because you do not know of any other possibilities. Thinking critically about alternatives requires making sure that we have done what we can to make our disjunctions exhaustive.

Another form of this mistake is to believe that a conditional is true just because you do not know of any counterexample to it. Critical thinkers should look for counterexamples before believing conditionals.

Unacceptable Testimony. It is a mistake to accept testimony from a witness if the topic is inappropriate, the witness is not properly trained, or not properly informed, or if the witness is biased. It is a mistake because such evidence is not acceptable. Testimony is appropriate only on topics for which there are recognized experts. An expert must be properly trained and properly informed. And a witness must not be motivated to lie about or exaggerate the facts.

Ad Hominem. It is a mistake to believe that a piece of testimony is false just because the witness is unreliable or biased. It is a mistake because it confuses undermining and overriding evidence. Testimony can be true even if it is from an unreliable or biased source.

This mistake is traditionally called "ad hominem" because it involves criticizing testimony by criticizing the witness (the "hominem"). But we need to be a bit careful here in identifying this mistake. For it is not always a mistake to conclude that a witness is unreliable or biased. There can be very good reason to believe this. But it is always a mistake to conclude that *a witness's testimony is false* just because they are unreliable or biased.

Bad Question. It is a mistake to ask a question that is ambiguous, contains charged or slanted words or that hides a controversial presupposition. It is a mistake because it makes it harder to know what the person answering the question really believes.

False Disjunction. It is a mistake to reason with a false disjunction. It is a mistake because an argument with a false premise is not sound. Moreover, in the case of reasoning by Denying a Disjunct, if the disjunction is false, then the conclusion will be false too.

Denying the Antecedent. It is a mistake to reason as follows: If P, then Q; it is not the case that P; so, it is not the case that Q. It is a mistake because this form of reasoning is not always valid. To think that it is valid is to confuse a sufficient condition for a necessary one.

Affirming the Consequent. It is a mistake to reason as follows: If P, then Q; it is the case that Q, so it is the case that P. It is a mistake because this form of reasoning is not always valid. To think that it is valid is to confuse a necessary condition for a sufficient one.

Affirming a Disjunct. It is a mistake to conclude that one disjunct is false just because the other one is true. This is a mistake because it involves a missing premise. Affirming a disjunct is valid *only if the disjunction is an exclusive disjunction.* But if one knows that the disjunction is exclusive, then one should add this piece of information as an additional premise in one's reasoning.

Red Herring. It is a mistake to raise irrelevant matters when criticizing someone's beliefs or reasons. This is a mistake because it is rude and because it makes it harder to find the truth together. One form of this mistake is to criticize a disjunction in someone's argument by raising possibilities that are ridiculous or that have already been ruled out.

Hasty Generalization. It is a mistake to rely on an unrepresentative sample when reasoning using samples. This is a mistake because the analogical premise is false, and an argument with a false premise is not sound. This mistake is a special case of the mistake of a false analogy. The mistake is called a "hasty generalization" because the argument's conclusion is a general claim about the target and it is hasty because not enough care was taken to ensure that the sample was representative.

False Analogy. It is a mistake when reasoning by perfect analogy for the analogical premise to be false. This is a mistake because an argument with a false premise is not sound. Recall that any two things are alike in a huge number of respects. An analogical claim is true only if the analogues are **exactly alike** in all of the respects that are **relevant** to the relevant property. Knowing what those respects are can be difficult, and can sometimes require a lot of investigation. Knowing whether the analogues really are alike in those respects can also be difficult.

Slippery Slope. It is a mistake to reason with an extremely false causal conditional. It is a mistake because an argument with a false premise is not sound.

APPENDIX B

CRITICAL THINKING STRATEGIES

Critical thinking is reasonable and reflective thinking aimed at deciding what to believe or what to do. It is reflective in part because it requires us to think about our reasons as reasons, and so to ask whether they are acceptable and sufficient. It is reasonable in part because it requires us to look for reasons for our decisions. Throughout this book we have identified strategies and tricks that can help us to be more reflective and reasonable in our thinking. Here are some of them, organized into different categories.

B.1 GENERAL PURPOSE CRITICAL THINKING STRATEGIES

The rule of Threes.   The rule of threes has such broad application that it is difficult to state simply. Here are some applications of it. Find three alternative courses of action when trying to decide what to do. Look for three objections to a view you are defending. Think about a problem from three different perspectives before trying to solve it. Look for three examples when trying to define a concept. Looking for three—or, even better, five!—will help you become more reflective in your thinking by forcing you to think "outside the box." Usually, finding one or two of the things you are looking for is relatively easy; trying to find more may force you to think harder, which is almost always good.

A Practical Guide to Critical Thinking: Deciding What to Do and Believe, Second Edition. David A. Hunter.
© 2014 John Wiley & Sons, Inc. Published 2014 by John Wiley & Sons, Inc.

Do Not Personalize Reasons.   Reasons and evidence do not belong to anyone; they are **universal**. And whether they are good has nothing to do with who accepts them; they are **objective**. To avoid personalizing reasons, replace the following:

a. What evidence do you have?
b. What are your reasons?
c. Why do you believe that?

with the following impersonal ones:

a'. What evidence is there?
b'. What reasons are there to believe that?
c'. Why should we believe that?

Think Twice; Decide Once.   To paraphrase the old carpenter's motto (measure twice and cut once), it is best to think twice and decide once. We know from psychological experiments that people are reluctant to change their minds. Once our opinions are set, it seems to take a lot of doing to revise them. For one thing, people tend to privilege evidence that confirms their already existing beliefs over evidence that conflicts with it. They assume that evidence that conflicts with what they already believe is probably not reliable. For another thing, people tend to prefer the evidence they have to evidence they would have to do something to get. To protect against these built-in obstacles to critical thinking, it is better to make sure that one has enough of the right kind of evidence before one makes a decision. It is better to think twice and decide once, than to have to go back and revise one's own decisions.

Withhold Disagreement and Agreement.   We all know what it feels like to explain our opinions and views to people we know disagree with us. It puts additional pressure on us, pressure that is not really helpful if the goal is to get clear on the truth of the matter. For this reason, it is best to withhold disagreement until the speaker has had a full opportunity to explain, defend, and support her view. If she feels rushed into explaining it, she might leave out some crucial distinctions, and this might have the effect of weakening what might in fact be a fairly plausible position. Or she might skip over some of the premises or fail to mention a response to an objection. Your goal as a critical thinker in a discussion is to help the other people make a case for their views that is as clear, as strong, and as complete as possible.

Keep Emotional Distance.   Being a critical thinker means that our beliefs should be based on epistemic reasons, and not on emotional or pragmatic ones. Basing one's beliefs on emotions rather than on epistemic reasons is a mistake, since how a claim or proposal makes one feel emotionally is not a reliable guide to whether the claim is true or the proposal is good. Emotions can also make it difficult to collect the evidence we need, or even from investigating further. Emotions get in the way when we identify too much with our own opinions and beliefs or with our own methods for collecting or evaluating evidence. If I become too emotionally attached to my beliefs and opinions, then I may react negatively when someone asks me for my reasons, or when they raise objections to my belief, or when they state their own alternative beliefs. I might feel that they are criticizing me and not just my beliefs. The same is true if I am asked to defend my assessment of the evidence or my use of different methods for collecting evidence. If I come to identify too closely with these particular methods for assessing and collecting evidence, if I come to think of my value as a researcher as tied into their value, then I will react to criticisms of them as if they were criticisms of me and my judgment. This feeling of being under attack might make me feel defensive, and this can prevent me from thinking critically about the issue at hand. The same is true when I ask someone for his or her reasons. This sort of question is easily taken as aggressive or combative, even when the intention is simply to consider the issue from all sides as thoroughly as possible.

Trust, But (Be Prepared to) Verify.   Most critical thinking theorists agree that it would be asking too much to require that before the evidence from some source can be accepted we must first know that the source is reliable. Instead, they recommend the following: evidence from some source is acceptable; unless one has reason to think the source is not reliable. Trusting our sources is a default right, as it were. But we should not let ourselves get carried away. For we know that some apparent sources are not reliable at all, and others even ones that are reliable can still yield mistaken evidence. To borrow Ronald Reagan's remark about the proper attitude to take to enemy superpowers: trust, but be prepared to verify.

B.2   STRATEGIES FOR BEING REFLECTIVE ABOUT MEANING

Testing for Conceptual Independence.   It is good to know how to test for conceptual independence. In Chapter 1, we considered Robert Ennis' definition of critical thinking as reasonable, reflective thinking aimed at deciding what to believe or what to. We also considered the standard philosophical definition of knowledge as justified, true belief. When an idea or concept is analyzed into several parts or elements, it is always a good idea to ask whether those parts or elements are conceptually independent of one another. To do this, simply ask yourself whether you can think of an example of something that has some of the elements but not others. For instance, we noticed that simple arithmetical calculations are a kind of thinking aimed at deciding what to believe but are not reflective because they do not require thinking about the method one uses. This example shows that being reflective thinking and being thinking that is aimed at deciding what to believe or do are conceptually independent. In one of the chapter's exercises, you discovered that in the case of knowledge, a belief's being true is conceptually independent of its being justified. Whenever a concept or problem has elements or parts, ask: how are those parts related to one another?

Look for Counterexamples.   Looking for counterexamples is an important step in constructing or evaluating a proposed definition or in assessing the truth of a conditional. A counterexample is a case that shows that the definition is either too broad (includes things that it should not) or too narrow (excludes things that it should include). The case could be an actual one, or it could simply be a fictional one. If you think that a proposed definition is too broad or too narrow, then you need to present a counterexample and argue that it shows that the proposed definition is mistaken. If, on the other hand, you respond to an alleged counterexample to your proposed definition, then you have to either show that it is not a genuine counterexample to the definition or else revise the definition to include or exclude examples of that kind.

SEEC Definition Method.   A definition should state the meaning as clearly as possible and in as short a sentence as possible. This statement can usually take the form of a **slogan**. A definition should **expand** on that statement by filling in some of the detail that inevitably will get left out of a succinct statement. Among other things, the elaboration might say something about how the different elements in the statement are related one to another. This should take no more than a few sentences. A definition should provide an **example** or two, depending on the complexity of what is being defined. The example could be from real life or it could be fictional, so long as it is clear and uncontroversial. Finally, a definition should identify some **contrasting** cases with which the thing being defined might easily be confused.

Ask open-ended Clarification Questions.   When discussing topics with other people, ask them open-ended questions, not questions that allow an "Yes" or "No" answer. This will reduce the risk that superficial agreement will mask interesting and deep differences. Instead of asking:

"Do you think that . . ."
"Do you agree that . . ."

Ask:

"Why do you think that . . . ."
"What do you mean by . . ."
"What reasons are there for thinking that . . ."

B.3   STRATEGIES FOR ANALYZING REASONS AND ARGUMENTS

Be Charitable.   When reconstructing someone's reasons, it is best to try to turn it into a valid argument. This may require adding a missing premise. The reason to reconstruct arguments so that they are valid is that this focuses the discussion on whether the premises (including the ones that you added) are true, as opposed to the question of whether the premises are sufficient. As we know, adding a premise can make any argument valid. But this alone will not make an argument a good one: its premises must be true or acceptable as well.

The Assertion Test.   The premises in an argument are always assertions. But it is not always easy to tell in a passage or text just what the assertions are. To tell whether some proposition is asserted in a sentence of some text, ask whether the sentence as a whole could be true even if that proposition were false.

If the answer is Yes, then that proposition is not asserted.
If the answer is No, then that proposition is asserted.

Identifying Dependent Reasons.   It is important when analyzing a piece of reasoning to know whether the premises are working together (i.e., dependently) or whether they provide independent reason to accept the conclusion. There are two very useful strategies for deciding when the premises in an argument are dependent.

One is the **Words Test**: If the conclusion of an argument contains important words that occur only in one premise and important words that occur only in another premise, then those premises are probably dependent.

Another is the **False Premise Test**: If a premise would provide some reason to accept the conclusion even if another premise were *false*, then those premises are independent. So, to test whether premises are dependent, suppose that one is false, and ask whether the other one would still provide some support for the conclusion. If it would, then the premises are independent. If not, then they are dependent.

Testing for Logical Strength.   To test the logical strength of an argument, suppose that the premises were true. Then ask: how likely is that the conclusion would be true too? The higher the likelihood, the more logical support the premises provide.

INDEX

A Practical Guide to Critical Thinking: Deciding What to Do and Believe, Second Edition. David A. Hunter.
© 2014 John Wiley & Sons, Inc. Published 2014 by John Wiley & Sons, Inc.